LINGUISTIC MORPHOLOGY
A STUDENTS GUIDE

Amani Lusekelo (Ph.D.)

E & D Vision Publishing
Dar es Salaam

E&D Vision Publishing Limited
P.O.Box 4460
Dar es Salaam
Email: *info@edvisionpublishing.co.tz*
Web: *www.edvisionpublishing.co.tz*

Amani Lusekelo (Ph.D.)
Department of Languages and Literature
Dar es Salaam University College of Education
(A Constituent of the University of Dar es Salaam)
P. O. Box 2329, Dar es Salaam, Tanzania
alusekelo@duce.ac.tz OR amanilusekelo@gmail.com

ISBN: 978-9987-735-25-9

Layout & Design: SANOL

Table of Contents

Preface

This book covers topics related to linguistic morphology, a course designated as core in most universities worldwide. At least all mechanisms of word-creations have been discussed in this volume. However, much effort is devoted to major word-building processes: affixation (derivation and inflection), reduplication, borrowing and compounding. In order to offer theoretical orientations to morphological data analyses, three theories have been incorporated at the end of the book: lexical morphology theory, templatic (autosegmental) theory and optimality theory. However, the theoretical part is limited in length and details because it is meant only to introduce these apparatus to students of linguistics. Thus, interested parties should consult other volumes which offer detailed descriptions and usage of the theories.

Basically this book derives illustrations from **English** and **Kiswahili** languages. Almost every topic covered herein is exemplified by these languages. **French** examples are only used in a few sections and for some topics, e.g. compounding, borrowing, gender etc. In providing examples to illustrate other sub-topics herein, a couple of other languages are also used, e.g. Tagalog, Mandarin Chinese, Hausa etc.

In this book, guiding questions are given at the end of each chapter. The intention is to allow students of linguistics to weigh their level of understanding of the substances offered in the discussion. It is advised that after completing reading each question, readers should attempt to answer these questions. In addition, I recommend specific resources for each topic at the end of each chapter. This organisation has been opted due to the behaviour demonstrated by students who do not read other sources traditionally suggested at the end of the books. I opted to offer the resources immediately after completion of discussion of each topic in question so as to assist readers getting other suggested sources right within the chapter they read. In several other cases, students opt to read only a chapter or a section of a chapter. Thus, suggested references should appear at their glance, and not at the end of the book, which they may not read in full.

There are, however, some significant resources which have been used throughout the book, e.g. Bauer (1983), Katamba (1993), Plag (2002), Booij (2005) etc. These are offered only in chapter 1 of the book.
Amani Lusekelo (Ph.D.)

Dar es Salaam, Tanzania, May 2014

Acknowledgement

This book is a result of long-term learning which took place over nine years. Thus, several people helped me advance points in materials offered herein. Firstly, my knowledge of linguistic morphology began with teachings and later discussions with my teacher of morphology, Dr. Abel Mreta and then advanced by linguists in African languages who introduced me to Bantuistics (Bantu linguistics), specifically Prof. Josephat Rugemalira and Prof. Henry Muzale at the University of Dar es Salaam. Connected to this, the discussions during L(anguages) o(f) T(anzania) [LOT] workshops and editorial retreats shaped, in a special manner, the way I view, among other topics, linguistic morphology.

Secondly, a number of other scholars have contributed to my way of thinking about various topics in linguistic morphology. Specifically, I would mention Professor David Massamba for his teachings on morphophonology at the University of Dar es Salaam. Later, between 2010 and 2012, I benefited much from discussions with the following Professors: Herman Batibo, Joyce Mathangwane, Stephen Lukusa and Andy Chebanne from University of Botswana.

Some of my students at Dar es Salaam University College of Education (DUCE) have commented on the entire manuscript. I would like to proudly mention three second year students, 2012/2013 academic year, for being helpful towards improving the book. First, I register much appreciation to Juma Ramadhani, with whom I spent two days revisiting the whole manuscript. Also, two other students, Ojijo George and Abayo Jonathani, reviewed the whole manuscript and provided me with a seven-page typed review report. The publishing house, E&D Vision Publishers, organized a thorough review of the manuscript and the input from the review is hereby recognized. These encounters helped me to re-think about and re-shape several parts of the manuscript. It is my great expectation that readers of the book will be guided well through the coursebook of linguistic morphology.

I would like to register my thanks for encouragement and advice from colleagues at DUCE. Many colleagues encouraged me to concentrate on the book and publish it. Here I will like to acknowledge benefits I benefited from discussions on Kiswahili morphology from Ms. Faraja Mwendamseke and comments from Mr. Emmanuel Ilonga. Mr. Rueben Ndimbo and Mr. Rodrick Ndomba encouraged me to work hard and publish the book.

This book is dedicated to my family, Happiness, Atupakisye, Tabitha, Lusekelo, Saita and Tuntufye who deserve 'unmeasurable' acknowledgement for great support, tolerance, indurence and above all love. Much of the writing was done at home, in the sitting room, where the family TV is stationed. You may imagine how disturbing the writing was to my family. I am grateful to them all.

Abbreviations and symbols

Adj	Adjective
ACC	Accusative case
AGR	Agreement
Adv	Adverb
CONJ	Conjunction
DAT	Dative case
DEF	Definiteness
FUT	Future tense marker
INF	Infinitive (*to*)
INFL (or I)	Inflection
N	Noun
Neg	Negation marker
Nom	Nominative case
OBJ	Objective case
PERF	Perfective aspect
PER	Person
POSS	Possessive
PP	Preposition phrase
PST	Past tense marker
PROG	Progressive aspect
SUBJ	Subjective case
V	Verb
1, 2, 3 etc.	Bantu noun classes
Ø	Empty or zero category
-	Morpheme boundary
1sg	First Person Singular
2pl	Second Person Plural
*XX	Ill-formed token

1 Introducing Linguistic Morphology

1.1 Introductory remarks

This book is an effort to introduce students of linguistics to various topics surrounding linguistic morphology. This chapter is envisaged to offer an introduction to the various terms used in morphology. The intention is to help students of linguistics to grasp the basic topics surrounding linguistic morphology, a course designed to be compulsory in most universities and colleges around the globe.

Morphology is a technical term in linguistics which entails identification, analysis and description of structure of words and other units of meaning in a language. Such units are like morphemes, affixes, parts of speech, lexicon and other elements. This is in line with Katamba (1993: 3) who defines morphology as 'the study of the internal structure of a word'. In Spencer (1991), we find that while words are generally accepted as being the smallest units of syntax, it is clear that in most languages, if not all, words can be related to other words by rules, i.e. grammatical rules. Also, it is a common knowledge in linguistics that words and morphemes are related.

This book is generally meant to introduce students to seven general topics in morphology. Also, it initiates students to engage themselves in theoretical analysis of morphological data. These topics are organised as follows:

(1)   i.   *Introduction to morphology*
         ii.   *Word-building processes*
         iii.   *Derivation*
         iv.   *Inflectional processes*
         v.   *Reduplication*
         vi.   *Lexical borrowing*
         vii.   *Compounding*
         viii. *Morphological theories*

The reasons to write this book emanates from the need to offer proper description of various topics in **linguistic morphology**. Also, it intends to supplement existing literature. As for Kiswahili, *A Sketch of Swahili Morphology* by Schadeberg (1992) is sketchy in coverage because it deals with affixation (derivation and inflectional) processes and focuses only on verbs, nouns and adjectives. Major topics such as reduplication and borrowing are least covered in that publication. This book, therefore, is geared to uncover as much as possible the details pertaining to the morphology of the language as such topics as derivation, reduplication, inflection, borrowing and compounding are covered in great depth. Rubanza (1996) offers the description of the Kiswahili morphology in his coursebook entitled *Mofolojia* 'morphology' and geared for the students of the Open University of Tanzania. Though that book is meant to be an introductory one, it has some shortfalls, e.g. division of affixational processes, to a lesser extent, needs rectification.

English morphology is described in depth in several available books for the past four decades (cf. Bauer 1983; Spencer 1991; Katamba 1993; Plag 1999; Minkova & Stockwell 2009, among many others). However, the theoretical part in sources such as Spencer (1991) and Katamba (1993), which focus on lexical morphology theory, would require some kind of an update. The current book offers the whole of Chapter 8 which covers other theories which are involved in analysing morphological data.

Based on topics covered in this book, the guide is appropriate for both undergraduate and postgraduate university levels of education. This is because the topics are ordered in a manner that a reader in undergraduate level could take the general chapters, such as this chapter (introduction to terms in morphology) and chapter two (word-building) while postgraduate readers could opt for the specific chapters with specific topics like chapter three on derivational processes, chapter five on borrowing etc. Also, some theoretical backgrounds are covered in the last chapter, chapter 8, for readers interested in introduction to the theory of morphology.

In addition it is plausible to say that the main focus of the book is more of an academic contribution to institutions of higher learning in East Africa in particular and beyond because the course linguistic morphology is offered in all universities which proffer degrees in languages and education. For instance, in Tanzania, several universities offer courses on linguistic morphology at both undergraduate and postgraduate levels.

The other motivation for preparing this kind of book surrounds the focal languages, namely English and Kiswahili (and at a lesser extent French). In the world, specific courses for the morphology of languages are offered. For example, the University of Dodoma and University of Dar es Salaam offer specific courses for morphology of French, Kiswahili and English. It is the case in Kenya where universities offer courses on Kiswahili morphology at and above a bachelor degree level. Thus, this book serves to cater for the need of the compiled informative and comprehensive data on the subject matter under discussion as well as proper arrangement of the topics surrounding the field of linguistic morphology.

This chapter is organised as follows. Section 1.2 introduces students to definitions of 'word' and 'morpheme'. To substantiate the definitions, specific examples for Kiswahili and English are provided. Section 1.3 offers the discussion surrounding the concepts 'lexeme' and 'word-forms' whereby English and Kiswahili are used as focal languages. The chapter moves to sections 1.4 and 1.5 where it presents the definitions of various terminologies related to morphemes and allomorph. A number of general sources are listed at the bottom of this chapter.

1.2   The notions word and morpheme

It is a common knowledge in linguistics that words and morphemes are related. Nonetheless, the conceptualization of the terms **word** and **morpheme** differs. One of the obvious differences is the fact that a morpheme may or may not stand alone but a word stands alone to provide sense. Another difference is that one or several morphemes may compose a word (Spencer 1991).

In any language such as English, Kiswahili or French, a **word** is a unit which is readily and easily recognized and identified by all sections of the population, say it be illiterates in the western perspective or the educated ones. It means that in any speech community, say it be in the western or eastern world or even down to sub-Sahara Africa, a word needs to be known by native speakers of a particular language. We would correctly presume that this is the reason most, if not all, books of morphology provide an analogue of the uneducated and rural persons who are able to dictate word-for-word in their languages. Such knowledge of individual expressions representing "identifiable" and "isolatable" entities in a language by any native speaker puts the word at a position that remains very essential in the linguistic studies.

In a volume edited by Dixon and Aikhenvald (2002: 5), it is said that the literature show that the definitions of the terminology **word** are horrifying in terms of their complexity and difficulty, while others are simple and appealing. All in all, the term word has received attention and its meaning is associated with the question of *identifiability* [being in a position to be isolated from the rest in the list and being marked as a typical entry in a lexicon of a given language] and *semanticity* [carrying meaning that is delineatable to it] of the entity called word in a given language. However, these two properties of the notion *word* spackle questions like: who has the authority to recognize an entity as a word in a language? Is it a linguist, a leader of the community, a native speaker, an elite, an elderly person, or a political leader? Another question would be: what is the minimum meaning that qualifies an entity to be called a word in a given language? Such questions (and many more to follow) will be addressed in the course of discussion in this book.

Perhaps we should start describing mankind as the sole source of the notion *word* in a language. It is assumed, and we would think correctly here, that the existence of the term *word* in the human minds is couched in the assumption that each language is made of words which in turn combine to make sentences which we use for communications. This is also couched in the other assumption that native speakers of a given language know that their language is made of words which can be repeated over and over, in the same sequence, when asked to do so. It might be true that specific speakers of English, French or Kiswahili are aware of the existence of words in their language with which they use to communicate.

Nevertheless, the definition of the notion word remains vague because even specialised authors of linguistic morphology (or any other field in linguistics) would fail, in some occasions, to distinguish between *word* and *morpheme, phonological word* from *orthographic word* or even *lexical word* and *grammatical word* (see also Dixon & Aikhenvald 2002; Bauer 2004).

The purpose of this instruction, therefore, is to present the detailed discussion about *word* or *words* which is the central concern of this branch of linguistics called morphology.

This is the reason that we begin defining *words* as opposed to *morphemes*.

Perhaps the best way to approach the topic is by introducing a definition from a book that deals with morphology terminologies. Bauer (2004), though she mentions of the difficulties faced by scholars in defining the term, she offers this definition, I quote:

> We can define a word as a constituent which is intermediate in structure between the morpheme and the syntactic phrase, and which has a certain psychological silence. .... The psychological silence can be seen in the fact that many languages have an expression meaning 'word'..... and that speakers of many languages can cite 'words'; of their language. .... (Bauer 2004: 108)

It is the assumption of this book that this kind of definition provides a syntactic approach to the notion word (as a constituent) and provides a semantic outlook (as a psychological unit) but still does not answer efficiently the two questions raised above and repeated here for expository purposes: who has the authority to recognize an entity as a word in a language and what is the minimum meaning that qualifies an entity to be called a word in a given language?

In trying to answer such questions, readers should notice that it is represented in most of the literature that, with regard to word, the idea is that each language is made of words but the recognition of the typical words in a language would surely be dependent upon the innate ability and traditional experience of the native speakers of such a language to pin down each word in the language in question (see Bauer 1983: 9; Katamba & Stonham 2006: 17). Thus, speakers of a give language are the working dictionary or rather, encyclopedia of that language because they carry with them all the list of words in the language.

Perhaps we should also recall that, in trying to make readers understand what is the essence of the notion *word*, most of the books on morphology tend to begin with a list of forms which seem to be some kind of *word forms* in a written configuration in certain languages. To achieve the same, in our case, let us use examples from Kiswahili (2) to illustrate the real meaning of the term *word* in the language from a point of view of native speakers.

In the course of discussion about these entries, two assumptions are considered: first, the written form is fits literate Kiswahili speakers and second, the illiterate group of people would receive the pronounced side for these words. This entails that a phonological unit similar to a word counts a lot in identifying words.

(2)			
hewani	*hwalo*	*hatarisha*	*hatiza*
rara	*reli*	*rosi*	*rarua*
nena	*ninoza*	*naam*	*namalo*
arama	*alama*	*atama*	*atima*
mawini	*mawizo*	*mawio*	*wiwo*

For academic purposes, from illustrations in (2) above, we would provide explanation for the entries in the four cells of the first row. Notice that the rest of the entries are offered to allow our readers (perhaps native speakers and non-native speakers) to practise.

In the set of four example word-like appearances in (2) above, we have the combinations of sounds (for spoken language) or alphabets (for written texts) which are typically used in the language. Looking at these tokens, they seem similar thus they might be typical Kiswahili words. However, based on the spelling and sounds, the native speakers of Kiswahili will easily identify the typical words in the language. One would accept that native speakers of Kiswahili will recognize that two forms, *hwalo* and *hatiza* are not Kiswahili words while the remaining two in the same row are typical *words* in the language. Although the spellings or sounds resemble Kiswahili words, e.g. *hwalo* resembles words like *bwalo* 'auditorium, hall' and *gwato* 'crutch, prop, support', the native speakers would never accept it as a Kiswahili word. The same applies to the form *hatiza*, which resembles words like *katiza* 'cross' and *batiza* 'baptize', yet Kiswahili speakers will naturally say that this form is not a word in their language.

We have known, so far, the idea that each language is made of *words* but the recognition of the typical *words* in a language would surely be dependent on the innate ability of the native speakers of such languages (Katamba & Stonham 2006: 17). At this point it would be important to use English examples in (3) below to illustrate further this point:

(3)   *stroll*
        strike
        stlody
        sprot

In the set of examples in (3) above, we have combination of sounds (for spoken language) or alphabets (for written texts) which are typically used in this language. Thus, the native speakers of the language in question will easily identify the typical *words* in the language. For example, the native speakers of English will recognise that *stroll* and *strike* are words in their language but *stlody* (Katamba & Stonham 2006: 17) and *sprot* are NOT words in the language. Although the spellings or sounds resemble English words, e.g. *sprot* resembles *sprat* 'small sea fish' and *sprout* 'grow, develop, produce', the native speakers would never accept *sprot* as an English word[1].

After the explanation above, we may agree that the term *word* is used to refer to an abstract idea which fits in a certain language only. In a dictionary, the entry for word may look like:

> *A word is a given sound or a combination of certain sounds or its representation in a form of writing or printing, which symbolises and communicates a certain sense (or in other words 'meaning') and may consist of a single morpheme or of a combination of morphemes.*

Given this definition, a *word*, therefore, should have at least the following qualities: (i) be a phonological unit (being represented either in sounds or written (or printed) form), (ii) carrying some semantic content embedded in itself (concrete and abstract communicative meaning), and (iii) being shared by members of the speech community in question.

---

1 Katamba (1993: 17) used a different term, i.e. *splody, to illustrate the notion word. It is assumed that there could be introductions of words which were initially not there in the language. In that case, however, the new words must be nativised first (see chapter 6 for details on nativisations of loanwords).

More importantly, linguists specialised in the structure of words realised that the native speakers of the languages recognize words in their languages because they have innate ability to do so (Bauer 1983; Katamba & Stonham 2006).

At this juncture, we should remember that the foregoing discussion does not rule out that some native speakers could not recognize the typical elements that comprise the words in their languages. For example, Spencer (1991: 1) suggests that all moderately speakers of English language would recognize that the word *antidisestablishmentarianism* is the longest English word; also it is composed of several elements, like *anti-, dis-, -ment, -rian* and *-ism* which are attached to the origin *word* establish, which functions as a **lexeme** (a terminology whose attention is paid in the subsequent section below). But these speakers may fail to provide the meaning of the word *antidisestablishmentarianism* or its particles. Therefore, this is one of the reasons that compelled morphologists to dedicate their work towards the analysis of the morphology of words in the world languages.

Thus, the discussion above brings us to another term that is needed to be described here in order to keep whatever is grasped for the notion word into a straight-line, i.e. **morpheme(s)**. But before we proceed to present the essence of morphemes, a summary of the criteria for identifying a word are worth capturing since they help to distinguish a *word* from a *morpheme*.

There is no body of literature which has well presented the criteria for defining a *word* other than Dixon and Aikhenvald (2002). The introduction chapter by Dixon and Aikhenvald (2002: 10-12) has offered several literatures they have cited. In the current book, I will summarize at least three main criteria they provided for identifying a *word*. Also, in the concluding remarks of the same volume, based on typological analysis of words, Mathews (2002: 272) has provided other criteria for defining the notion *word* which I will add to those in the introduction.

Therefore, five criteria towards proper identification of a *word* would be:

i.   Presence of at least a pause is a sufficient criterion to signal a word.
ii. A word must be a unit made of speech sounds for a particular meaning and for a particular grammatical purpose.
iii. A word must be a free form (and I will add here that independence is connected to the ability to convey some meaning).
iv. It is important to envisage a phrase as another way of identifying a word. Thus, a word would really be no more than a minimum phrase, from a syntactic point of view, with at least a conventionalised meaning.
v.   A word is characterized by a lexeme, on one hand, and inflections on the other hand. Thus, a word could be centred on a root or combinations of roots for compound words, from a grammatical point of view, and the ability to take, at least in some languages, the inflectional particles.

As far as these criteria are concerned, a pause could easily be a phonological one, like **stress patterns** in synthetic languages like English as exemplified by nouns: *ex'port* and *re'spect* which differ from verbs: *'export* and *'respect* due to stress patterns or **tone**

patterns which do work to mark word-divisions in languages like Mandarin Chinese and tonal Bantu languages such as Herero (Namibia/Botswana). Perhaps we should offer a tonal pause in Mandarin Chinese: *duitóu* 'correct' vs. *duitou* 'enemy' (Lin 2001: 88) and a tonal pause in Herero: *hora* 'be stiff' vs. *hóra* 'to remove hair' vs. *hórá* 'to ripen' (Möhlig & Kavari 2008: 41).

In Kiswahili, words, especially loanwords, differ due to stress patterns. Mohamed (2001: 12) said that in Kiswahili, stress occurs, as a rule, on the penultimate syllable (i.e. on the second last syllable). Words can be distinguished using stress in Kiswahili. The entries in (4a) below are isolated words because they are differentiated by stress patterns, hereunder marked by the diacritic. Another pause in Kiswahili is aspiration patterns. Massamba (1996: 5) has shown lexical differences due to aspiration in Kimtang'ata dialect of Kiswahili. For example, Kiswahili words in (4b) differ due to aspiration, hereunder marked by the superscript.

(4) a. *bara'bara* (N)   'road, highway'   *ba'rabara* (Adv)   'exactly'
         'ala (N)   'instrument, tool'   *a'la* (Adv)   'excl. of fear'
         wa'lakini (N)   'a defect'   *wala'kini* (Conj.) 'but'

     b. *paa* (V)   'rise, ascend'   *pʰaa* (N)   'gazelle'
         kaa (V)   'sit, stay'   *kʰaa* (N)   'crab'

At this point let us have a look at the term **morpheme**. Preliminarily, we may approach a *morpheme* from two angles. One angle being that a *morpheme* is the smallest component of a word, or other linguistic unit, that has semantic content or inherent features which give sense in a given language (Katamba & Stonham 2006). Therefore, this term is used as part of morphology. Some examples from English are provided in: *book-s, move-r-s* and *teach-ing-s*.

Thus, the hyphens function to mark the morphemes available in the lexemes in English words above. It should be noted that some morphemes like *-s, -er, -ing* etc. cannot stand alone rather they depend on the other morphemes like *book, move* and *teach*.

Another angle which we can look at *morpheme* is by saying that it is composed by phoneme(s), i.e. the smallest linguistically distinctive units of sound in spoken language and made of grapheme(s), i.e. the smallest units of written language (Spencer 1991).

Katamba and Stonham (2006: 24) definition of a *morpheme* which given below is worth to be mentioned here as it explicitly provides us with clear picture of what I have tried to explain above:

> The smallest difference in the shape of a word that correlates with the smallest difference in word or sentence meaning or in grammatical structure.

With experience of teaching linguistic morphology, most undergraduate students of linguistics are familiar with this basic meaning of the word morpheme. Bauer (2004: 70-72) defined it in three pages. I capture a section of the definition hereunder:

> Perhaps we can define a morpheme relatively uncontroversially as 'a set of **signs** whose members are synonymous and in complementary distribution', while adding to that definition (i) that s set may contain only one member, (ii)

that in most clear-cut instances, members of the set are clearly phonologically related to each other, and (iii) that the conditioning factor(s) for complementary distribution can be stated in phonological rather than in lexical terms. Thus the plural endings of *cows* /kaʊz/, *horses* /hɔːsɪz/ and *cats* /kæts/ clearly resemble each other (in sharing a sibilant fricative) and are conditioned by the last sound in the base, and clearly meet the definition..... [Emphasis Bauer's] (Bauer 2004: 71-72).

Given the morphological differences between languages, my observation is that definitions provided by scholars such as Bauer (2004) and Katamba and Stonham (2006), which seem to be simplistic, are indeed as complex as definitions in other references like Minkova and Stockwell (2009: 64-70).

For instance, it is hinted above, however, that agglutinative languages like Kiswahili would differ, to a great extent, from synthetic languages like English, whose words, as you can see, Bauer (2004) uses in his definition. Therefore, while I take this kind of explanation as a benchmark, the proper definition of the notion morpheme would rather be captured using Kiswahili words.

In the analysis of Kiswahili morphology, chapter three of the book on morphology by Kihore et al. (2003: 36-49) treats a morpheme with some good examples. I recommend my readers who are fluent in Kiswahili to refer to that book too. Generally they argue that:

(a) Words split into units e.g. *wa-tu* 'people'.
(b) Some words are free morphemes e.g. *hakimu* 'magistrate'.
(c) Some words and sounds are morphemes e.g. *oa* 'marry, to wed'.
(d) Morphemes create new words e.g. *oana* 'to wed each other'

Nonetheless, as a way of benefiting a discussion in this book, the word-like configurations below would help to make us grasp the essence of the notion morpheme here. It should be mentioned here that, my understanding of morpheme should not be erroneously equated to the way Mgullu (1999) presents the essence of the notion morph in Kiswahili. My position takes a different approach to the definition of morpheme, which is distinct from the way Mgullu's position.

This book goes on defining a *morpheme* with the Kiswahili words offered in (5) and English words in (6). Such words may be divided in a manner that a central word will be found and some other particles to the central words will be split out.

(5) *hewani*
     hatarisha
     vijidudu

(6) *undressing*
     impossible
     happiness

The first Kiswahili word *hewani* 'in the air' is divided into two morphemes, *hewa* 'air, atmosphere' and *-ni* 'a marker of location'. The following word could be split as follows:

hatari 'danger' and *-ish-* 'a section of a word which indicates causation' and *-a* 'the final default vowel'. Lastly, it is *vi-ji-dudu* 'germs, small insects' which has three sections as marked by the hyphen: *vi-* 'Bantu noun class 8', *-ji-* 'dimunitive prefix' and *-dudu* 'germ, thing'. These units of words which cannot be decomposed into further smaller units are called morphemes. Thus, the words *hatarisha* and *vijidudu* are made of three morphemes while *hewani* 'in the air' has two morphemes.

English language examples also reveal the same division of morphemes in words. The word *undressing* is made up of three morphemes, namely, the prefix *un-*, the base *dress* and the suffix *-ing*. The next word is made up of two morphemes: root *possible* and the prefix *im-*, while the word *happiness* can be divided into two morphemes as *happy-ness*. This is in line with Spencer (1991: 4-5) who states that the components like *anti-*, *dis-*, and *-ism* that make the longest word in English, *antidisestablishmentarianism*, are not words but morphemes which: (i) seem to constitute some sort of meaning, or at least function, to the word of which they are component, and (ii) cannot themselves be decomposed into smaller morphemes. Since morphemes are smallest carriers of meanings which exist in words in a language, they are very a significant section of morphology.

A proper definition does not end with indivisibility rather it transcends to what Minkova and Stockwell (2009: 65-69) talk about when mentioning the properties of a morpheme: a morpheme is a smallest unit associated with a meaning, e.g. *car*, *carrot*, *discard* etc. This is also exemplified by single morpheme verbs in Kiswahili, e.g. *l-a* 'eat', *f-a* 'die', *p-a* 'give', *j-a* 'come', *w-a* 'become' and *t-a* 'hit, lay eggs'. The first consonants represent morphemes in their own. However, a morpheme may also be made of two or more consonants and vowels. For example, the single morphemes listed here may not occur as morphemes but syllables in other Kiswahili words like *la-la* 'sleep', *faham-u* 'sense, know', *tatiz-a* 'confuse' and *m-gonjwa* 'sick person' (see also Mohamed 2001; Massamba 2004).

The other important point to take into consideration is the ability of a morpheme either to be independent, as Kiswahili words *meza* 'table' and *sasa* 'now' or dependent upon a free morpheme, as in sections *m-*, *ku-* and *-a* in Kiswahili words *m-zazi* 'parent' and *ku-tet-a* 'to whisper' (see Rubanza 1997; Mohamed 2001). As for English, we saw in (6) above that the word *undressing* is made of dependent morphemes, namely, the prefix *un-* and the suffix *-ing* and an independent base *dress*.

Furthermore, morphemes are recyclable units, i.e. it can be used again and again to form many words. This is just shown above where the morphemes are recycled in other words. For example, the Kiswahili words, we may also use the Kiswahili morpheme *go* to show that it is used in many words like *go-go* 'log', *go-ma* 'stop, strike', and *m-go-mba* 'banana tree'.

Morphemes must not be confused with syllables because a morpheme may be made of one or more syllables and, as units of pronunciation, syllables have nothing to do with meaning. We may also use the Kiswahili syllable *-go-* which has no meaning though it is used in many words like *go-go* 'log', *go-ma* 'stop, strike', and *m-go-mba* 'banana tree'. On its own, as a syllable, it is meaningless hence it is not a morpheme. But configurations like -ish- and -me- are morphemes because they have meanings in their own. The former shows causation as in *imb-ish-a* 'cause to sing' while the latter indicates past tense as in *a-me-fik-a* 's/he has arrived' (see also Mohamed 2001).

Lastly, one and the same morpheme may take phonetically different shapes. A good example is the causative formative in Kiswahili which appears as -ish- as in *imb-ish-a* 'cause to sing', surfaces as -esh- in words such as *chez-esh-a* 'make play', -z- as in *o-z-a* 'to wed', sometimes its manifestation is -ez- as in *wek-ez-a* 'install' as well as -y- as in *ogof-y-a* 'frighten' (see Chapter Three in this book and Lodhi 2002: 12-14 for further details).

1.3   The concepts lexeme and word-forms

Words are technically termed as **lexemes** in morphology. Katamba and Stonham (2006) appear to accept this stand. The term lexeme therefore would simply be translated as the form of the word which carries inherent semantic content. Put in other words, some linguists would suggest that the term **word** would be replaced by **lexeme**. Katamba (1993) appears to accept this position. Thus, we need to define these terms. In what follows, therefore, we struggle to distinguish the semantic contents of these terms as used in morphology.

However, there is more than terms word and lexeme. Spencer (1991) mentions that there are two senses of the term word and the distinction between these two senses of "word" is arguably the most important one in morphology. The first sense of "word", the one in which *dog* and *dogs* are "the same word", is called a lexeme. The second sense is called word form. We thus say that *dog* and *dogs* are different forms of the same lexeme.

Therefore, lexeme would be defined as the word with inherent semantic content while a word form would be the different realizations of the same lexeme. Perhaps the following examples will suffice to drive this point home.

(7)	**steal**	steals	stole	stolen	stealing steal
	buy	buys	bought	bought	buying buy
	wash	washes	washed	washed	washing wash
	book	books	book		
	house	houses	house		

In English examples above, the lexemes *steal*, *wash* and *buy* [verbs] have been given in their different realizations, namely the present-singular, past form, past-participle and well as the present-plural. Likewise, the nouns *book* and *books* and *house* and *houses* appear in singular-plural distinctions. These are the different "word-forms" in English. In short, the different word forms function to designate different grammatical roles hence it is also termed **grammatical word**.

However, such word structures pervasive in English nouns and verbs are rare in Kiswahili. Kiswahili allows less inflectional word-forms and more of derivational word-forms. Perhaps we should use examples in (8) below to substantiate this claim.

(8)	a.	-meza	'swallow'
	b.	amemeza	'she has swallowed'
	c.	walimeza	'they swallowed'
	d.	-mezesha	'cause to swallow'

In (8a) above we find that the verb *meza* 'swallow' in Kiswahili could not provide us with the typical word-forms attested in English. This happens because English is an inflectional language while Kiswahili is an agglutinating language (Spencer 1991: 38). Kiswahili provides the present-singular function by addition of the prefix *a-* as well as the tense marker *-me-* (8b). For present-plural, we have the prefix *wa-* as well as the tense marker *-li-*(8c). In the language, (8d) shows that the suffix *-esh-* is derivational hence seems to provide a new word altogether.

Data in other Bantu languages will set the proposal that the issue of word-forms seem to be functional in Inflectional languages only. The Kiswahili nouns have different ways of showing singular and plural and these are partly associated with the semantic change of the nouns (Contin-Morava 1994; Mohamed 2001). Perhaps examples in (9) below will illustrate this idea.

(9)
mtanzania	'Tanzanian'	*watanzania*	'Tanzanians'
mlango	'door'	*milango*	'doors'
sanduku	'suitcase'	*masanduku*	'suitcases'
kitanda	'bed'	*vitanda*	'beds'
nyanya	'tomato'	*nyanya*[2]	'tomatoes'

The agglutinating language Kiswahili has fewer word forms which are for singulars and plurals. This suggests that word forms differ from language to language.

Also, if we change the prefixes, the semantics of the Kiswahili nouns are bound to change too as in (10a) below. This suggests that the word-forms are available in plenty in inflectional languages and unavailable in agglutinating languages.

(10)   a.
ka*lango*	'small door'[3]
vi*lango*	'bad doors'
ki*sanduku*	'small suitcase'
ji*sanduku*	'huge suitcase'

The problem just mentioned above becomes tense when we bring in data from tonal languages. The differences between English and Kiswahili as regards the word-forms are stiffened by the words which differ in nothing but tone. Morphologists (see Bauer 1983; Spencer 1991; Katamba 1993; Booij 2005) appear to have overlooked this problem.

In tonal Bantu languages, words of the same segmental elements are plentiful but such words may differ in tone patterns. This is exemplified by the following words from Herero (spoken in Namibia) (Möhlig & Kavari 2008: 41). It is interesting to establish the deeper understanding of the notion word-forms from this kind of morphological pattern.

(10)   b.
hora	'be stiff'
hóra	'to remove hair'
hórá	'to ripen'

---

2 Notice that class 9/10 nouns in Kiswahili (as well as in other Bantu languages) use nasal consonants to mark both singularity and plurality, e.g. *mbwa* 'dog' vs. *mbwa* 'dogs'. Perhaps this will be similar to zero derivation as well.

3 For some examples above, it has been brought to my attention that alternative words and readings could be: *kalango* 'small door', *kilango* 'bad door', *lisanduku* 'huge suitcase' and *msanduku* 'huge suitcase'.

The segmental structure of these words seems to be made of consonants and vowels, i.e. C-V-C-V. The differences in semantic contents emanate from their difference tone patterns. The first word has the tone pattern L-L, the second has H-L and the last one has H-H. It would be well argued here that if we decide that word-forms functions to instantiate grammatical differences rather than lexical-semantic differences, and then tone differences do not result in word-forms.

Another challenge to the question of word-forms lies on the way grammatical notions like plural formation. It is known that vowel lengthening or doubling renders the proposal that there exists different word-forms null. Perhaps we should borrow examples from Storch (2004: 167, 174) for Dinka language of Southern Sudan (Nilotic language). In Nilotic languages, plural formation, which is one of the ways that lead to regular word-forms in inflectional languages like English, is formed through stressing, vowel affixation, vowel lengthening, tone alternation and other mechanisms like sound changes during articulation. The illustrative examples in (11) provide us with the alternatives for plural formation.

(11) (a) *tír*   'cricket'   *tíír*   'crickets'
      (b) *méy*   'root'   *meey*   'roots'
      (c) *awet* 'crane/winch'   *awéet* 'cranes/winches'
      (d) *wál*   'medicine'   *wal*   'medicines'

Studying the data in (11) above, we find that Dinka language allows plural formation by several alternatives. First, we find that vowel lengthening is employed, as in (11a), then vowel lengthening coupled with tone deletion as in (11b), the other mechanism involves the lengthening or doubling of vowel and insertion of the high tone as in awéet 'cranes/winches', and lastly via deleting the high tone as in wal 'medicines'. Storch (2004: 167) suggests that vowel lengthening is the most common way of plural formation in the language. Nonetheless, one would therefore wonder whether these are word-forms or two distinct lexemes.

Before we conclude on the differences between word and lexeme, it is better to recall that it was mentioned above that another term used here is **grammatical word** (also referred to a **morphosyntactic word** (Bauer 1983: 12)). The essence of this term is that a word as a lexeme may also realise particular grammatical features which manifest, in most cases, by change in the morphology of that word. This is the reason that propelled morphologists like Bauer (1983: 13) to posit that 'the notion of grammatical word is of more value in inflectional morphology than it is in word formation'.

Perhaps we should borrow an idea from another source. Katamba and Stonham (2006: 19) who define a grammatical word as a representation of a lexeme that is associated with certain morphosyntactic properties, i.e. partly morphological and partly syntactic properties. Such features are associated with the word categories, namely nouns, verbs, adjectives, adverbs etc. (see Radford 1997) or other syntactic features like number, gender, case, person, tense etc (see Bauer 1983; Katamba 1993). This is well illustrated in English words given in the sentence: *He **cuts** the bread on the table* where we identify lexical feature such as a verb and several grammatical features such as person (third person), number (singular) and tense/aspect (present tense). A difference example is *Jane has a **cut** on her finger* in that this one has a lexical feature as a noun (word category) and inflectional features such as number (singular) and accusative case (objective). Thus, the word *cut* demonstrates two grammatical-word-forms. It functions as a verb and shows the features person, number and tense. Also, it functions as a noun that has the feature number.

The notion *grammatical word* should be taken with caution in Kiswahili. This is because, as said earlier, for nouns and adjectives, the change in word morphology means the change in meaning hence formation of a new word. The words *mtu* 'person' used to substantiate this point (12). With regard to verbs, the situation is worse because word-forms seem not to occur without derivational ends. The word *lima* 'cultivate' is used to substantiate the second point (13).

(12)	*Word-form*	*Gloss*	*Features*
	mtu	'person'	noun, singular
	watu	'persons'	noun, plural
	utu	'humanity'	noun, abstract

(13)	*Word-form*	*Gloss*	*Features*
	lima	'cultivate'	verb, infinitive
	mkulima	'cultivator, farmer'	noun, singular
	atalima	's/he will cultivate'	verb, singular, future tense

The grammatical words for the category noun in Kiswahili differ somehow with the English ones. First, the Kiswahili nouns carry inflectional morphemes like the nominal prefixes *m-* and *wa-* while the English ones didn't change *cut* in the previous example. The same noun takes a derivational morpheme *u-*. Also, as stated earlier, the verb has several morphemes attached to it which brings about derivational senses as well as inflectional functions. The conclusion here is that the notion word-forms functions well in inflectional languages like English and works hardly well in agglutinative languages like Kiswahili.

1.4   Other important terminologies in morphology

Perhaps it should be noted that there are about five other technical terms which are very essential in the study of word structures. These terms include: affix, allomorph, root, base and stem. In the following sub-sections, they are presented in that order, with examples to illustrate their essences.

1.4.1 Affix

A widespread understanding is that an *affix* is a morpheme that is attached to a word stem to form a new word (Spencer 1991). Such affixes may be derivational, like English *-ness* and *pre-*, or inflectional, like English plural *-s* and past tense affix *-ed* (Katamba 1993) (see 14a). In Kiswahili, affixes also function to delineate several roles, e.g. derivational and inflectional purposes (see 14b).

(14) a. *happy*   *happiness*
          wash   *washed*
          pay   *prepay*
          school   *schools*

      b. *zaa*   'give birth'   *mzazi*   'parent'
          vua   'to fish'   *wavuvi*   'fishermen'
          uza   'sell'   *wauzaji*   'sellers'

I would like to re-iterate that in inflectional (e.g. English) as well as agglutinative (e.g. Swahili) languages, an affix is an essential unit of morphology. Therefore, in English examples in (14a) above, some affixes above are derivation, e.g. *ness*, while others are inflectional, e.g. *-s*. Likewise, Kiswahili, an agglutinative language, permits a number of affixes to occur around the nucleous. These elements do function to designate several linguistic purposes. This could be exemplified by the word *wauzaji* 'sellers' in (14b), which can be divided as *wa-uza-ji*. Here the element *wa-* represents the noun class that designates plurality, the affix *-uza-* 'sell' is the root (or basically stem). The other element is *-ji* which is derivational as it functions to extend the meaning of the root or stem.

Perhaps we should have a quick glance at the literature to see what is offered for the definition of this term. An inclusive definition of an affix is offered by Minkova and Stockwell (2009: 71):

> All morphemes which are not roots are affixes. Affixes carry little of the core meaning of a word. Mainly affixes have the effect of slightly modifying the meaning of the base – a base is either a root or a root plus an affix, or more than one root with or without affixes – to which more affixes can be attached.

It is generally assumed that affixation is the linguistic process speakers use to form different words by adding morphemes (affixes) at the beginning (prefixation), the middle (infixation) or the end (suffixation) of words. Such an approximation of the notion affixation process is very narrow because we have circumfixation or synaffixation (addition of affixes on both sides, i.e. before and after root, affixes with unitary function (Bauer 2004: 29)), interfixation which is related to empty morphs (Bauer 2004: 57), transfixation which seems to be related to infixation in Semitic languages etc.

Generally, as mentioned above, affixes are divided into several categories, depending either on their position in a word to which they are attached or depending on the meanings in them. Depending on their position with reference to the stem, we get *prefix* and *suffix* which are extremely common terms but *infix* and *circumfix* are less so, as they are not important in European languages, but significant in other languages like Arabic, thus these terms are uncommon in the works such as Bauer (1983) (which is for English) and Booij (2002) (which focuses on Dutch).

Some common examples, for each category of affixes, are provided below.

(15)

	Prefix:	*wa*-toto	'children'	*ki*-baya	'bad'	[Swahili]
	Suffix:	end-**esh**-a	'drive'	pelek-e-a	'send to'	
	Circumfix:	**a**sexual	**a**forementioned			[English]
	Infix:	kitab	'book'	katib	'secretary'	[Arabic]

Affixes may also be **bound** morphemes (dependent affixes), i.e. prefixes and suffixes that cannot stand alone or **free morphemes** (independent affixes), i.e. may be separable affixes which can carry sense on their own.

As shown above, **free morphemes** are also termed as free affixes which indeed function on their own. Such free morphemes/affixes include words like *lima* 'cultivate' and *nyumba* 'house'. In words like *lim-ish-a* 'cause to cultivate' and *nyumba-ni* 'at home'; such free affixes are combined with bound morphemes.

On the other hand, we have **bound affixes** or bound morphemes whose function rely solely on the words they are attached to, as for *-ish-* 'causative' and *-ni* 'locative'. Therefore, a morpheme is **free** if it can stand alone as in *vaa* 'wear', *mto* 'river' and *sasa* 'now' or **bound** if it is used exclusively alongside a free morpheme, e.g. a causative *-ish-* in *valisha* 'cause to wear' and a locative *-ni* as in *mtoni* 'at the river'. Though it will be discussed further in section 1.4.5, in the literature, for the different shapes of the causative in Kiswahili, it is indicated that its actual phonetic representation is the morph, with the different morphs (see Spencer 1991). This is shown by the different forms of the causative morpheme in Swahili: *-z-* as in *toza* 'cause to pay', *-esh-* as in *vesha* 'cause to wear', *-ish-* as in *lisha* 'make eat' etc. All these are representing the same morpheme being grouped as its allomorphs.

To capture the summary of the definition of the term affix, we should quote that affixes differ from roots in three ways: (i) affixes do not form words in themselves – they have to be added to a base, (ii) affixal meaning, in many instances, is not as clear and specific as is the meaning of roots, and in many of them are so opaque (not clear) that may be almost completely meaningless, and (iii) compared with to total number of roots, the number of affixes is relatively smaller (see Minkova & Stockwell 2009: 71-72).

1.4.2 Root

The meaning of the term **root** is well presented in Katamba (1993) who underscores that the root is an irreducible core of the word to which nothing whatsoever is attached. Here words like *jump* and *eat* are roots without any additions while the word *read* is either a root (for its infinitive form) or a base because it might have already been added with a past tense marker through voice.

Languages differ with regard to the status of their roots. Denning and Leben (1995) hint that in our native and nativised vocabulary, say in English, on the one hand, a **root** can usually appear as an independent word, for which reason they are called free morphs. Thus, the morphology of English permits free morphemes to be roots, as shown in (16):

(16)   *white, go, host, fair, fire*

Following Minkova and Stockwell (2009: 69), all the items in (16) can be extended by other affixes, as shown in (17):

(17)   *whit-ish, go-ing, host-ess,*   *un-fair, fire-s*

This makes it particularly easy to find the roots of words like *black-bird, re-fresh* and *book-ish-ness*. In Latin and Greek, on the other hand, roots most often do not occur as separate words rather they are bound morphs, i.e. they can only appear when tied to other components. For example, the root of concurrent is *curr* 'run' which is not an independent word in English or even in Latin.

The morphological structure of Kiswahili is quite interesting (and perhaps confusing to some students of linguistics). Hence the notion root in Kiswahili would be approached through syllabic structures of Kiswahili. First, Kiswahili has both verbal and nominal roots which surface as mono-consonants and some as di-vowels, as illustrated in (18a) and (18b) respectively. Some roots in Kiswahili are monosyllabic and have the structure C-V, as in (18c) and V-C as in (18d). A number of roots in Kiswahili are made of a structure C-V-C, the common structure across Bantu languages (Ashton 1944; Kihore et al. 2003). This is shown in (18e). The rest of the roots are polysyllabic, as in (18f).

However, all the data in (18) should be read with caution. Bantu languages like Kiswahili have word-structures (mainly for verbs) which, in most cases, do not end in consonants rather they have the default -a (TUKI 2001, 2004). To this effect, the default final vowel, appearing as -a, could not be ignored in case the meaning of the roots have to be deciphered. Notice also that some of the English glosses appear in infinitive form in order to distinguish verbs from nouns.

(18)   Roots in Kiswahili

a.	*l-*	'eat'
	f-	'die'
	w-	'become'
	p-	'give'
	t-	'hit, beat'
b.	*oa*	'marry'
	ua	'1. flower, 2. kill'
c.	*va-*	'wear'
	vu-	'undress'
	to-	'remove'
d.	*og-*	'to bath'
	ot-	'to grow'
	ib-	'to steal'
	ap-	'to swear'
e.	*som-*	'read'
	beb-	'carry'
	pak-	'smear'

f. *kumbuk-*   'remember'
    pasuk-   'split'
    zunguk-   'rotate'

At this point, it is necessary to underline that the root forms the centre of the word. Also, it is essential to notice that affixes may be isolated from roots. Here we should approach it by demarcating simple roots from complex words.

In the literature, it is found that even non-morphological works recognise the significance of a word, or to be precise, that of a **root** in their delivery of the information. Thus, roots and affixes may be isolated.

For instance, Simpson (1997) mentions that morphologically **simple words**, which contain only a single root morpheme, may be compared to morphologically **complex words** which contain at least one free morpheme and any number of bound morphemes. Simpson (1997) gives an example of the word like *desire* in English which may be defined as a root morpheme constituting a single word. This would be like the simple words like *cheza* 'play', *vaa* 'wear', *oa* 'marry' and *ua* 'kill' in Kiswahili which are typically simple words carrying independent meanings.

Simpson (1997) offers the word *desirable*, which by contrast, is complex, combining a root morpheme with the bound morpheme *-able*. Such words may be compared to words *chezea* 'play at', *vesha* 'make to wear' and *oana* 'to marry each other' in Kiswahili whereby each root carries a single affix.

Furthermore, Simpson (1997) gives more complex words like *undesirability* which comprises one root and three bound morphemes: *un-desire-able-ity*. It should be noted here that Kiswahili has the longest sentential-like words such as *walichezesheana* 'they caused to play for each other at'. Thus, readers should notice also how, in complex words of this sort, the spelling of the root may be altered to conform to bound morphemes around it. Thus, *desire* becomes *desir-*. Another example is the word beauty which becomes *beauti-* in the formation of beautiful (Ibid).

It is a common understanding that **complex words** typically consist of a **root** morpheme and one or more affixes. Here we would agree that the root, therefore, constitutes the core of the word and carries the major component of its meaning.

Roots typically belong to a lexical category, such as noun, verb, adjective, preposition etc. in languages with such categories. Unlike roots, affixes do not belong to a lexical category and are always bound morphemes. For example, the affix *-er* in English is a bound morpheme that combines with a verb such as teach, giving a noun with the meaning 'one who teaches'. Likewise, the prefix *wa-* in Kiswahili words, for instance, *wazazi* 'parents' is non-lexical.

1.4.3 Base

It is difficult to demarcate a base, root and in some cases a stem. A **base**, at one stage could be a root, in most cases, the two are used interchangeably to refer to the indivisible unit of a word to which nothing whatsoever is added or attached.

Katamba (1993) says a base is the root added with derivational affixes but minus the inflectional affixes. This is also accepted by Bauer (2003) and Booij (2005) who say a base is a root or stem minus inflections. Minkova and Stockwell (2009: 71) underscore that 'a base is either a root or a root plus an affix, or more than one root with or without affixes – to which more affixes can be added'. This is shown in examples such as *child* vs. *childish* vs. *childishly* vs. *childishness* in English (Ibid). Here the base is *childish* which already has an affix *-ish* and it can receive another affix *-ly* or *-ness*.

The precise definition of a **base** is offered by Bauer (2004: 21) who says 'a base of a word is the part of it to which any affix is added or upon which any morphological process acts'. This kind of definition, in my opinion, implies that what should be referred to as a base should be a content word.

Perhaps the best examples are verbs *cheza* 'play' and *zurura* 'wander, loiter' in Kiswahili. To these verbs, once an affix like *-ji* is attached to them, the m they lose the feature **rootness** and becomes **bases**, i.e. *-chezaji* 'player' and *-zururaji* 'wanderer, nomad'. These are bases because another affix, the plural noun class *wa-*, could also be added to them in order to make words like *wachezaji* 'players' and *wazururaji* 'wanderers, nomads'. Such changes set bases in the position of stems, which could be defined as in section 1.4.4 below.

1.4.4 Stem

In linguistics, a **stem** is a part of a word. The literature points towards the fact that the term is used with slightly different meanings. In one usage, a stem is a form to which affixes can be attached (see Bauer 1983; Booij 2005; Katamba & Stonham 2006). If we take English at this stage, therefore, in this usage, the word *friendships* contains the stem *friend*, to which the derivational suffix *-ship* is attached to form a new stem *friendship*, to which the inflectional suffix **-s** is attached. In a variant of this usage, the root of the word (in the example, friend) is not counted as a stem.

In a slightly different usage, which is adopted in the remainder of this book, a word has a single stem, namely the part of the word that is common to all its inflected variants (see Bauer 1983; Booij 2005; Katamba & Stonham 2006). Thus, in this usage, all derivational affixes are part of the stem. For example, the stem of friendships is friendship, to which the inflectional suffix -s is attached.

A stems may be a root, e.g. *kimbia* 'run', or it may be morphologically complex, as in compound words such as *mwanamichezo* 'player'. A stem may also be a word with derivational morpheme such as *chezeana* 'play for each other'.

1.4.5 Allomorphy

Two important points are described under this section, namely **allomorph** and **morph**. These terms are related to the way the various senses of the morphological units associated with morphemes are realized.

1.4.5.1   *Allomorph*

One of the tensions which should not interfere with the discussion in this section revolves around the terminology: **allomorph** vs. **allomorphy**. In the literature, the term allomorphy is used in Spencer (1991) and Minkova and Stockwell (2009) while Bauer (1983, 2004) and Katamba (1993) seem to like the term allomorph.

The notion **allomorph** (**allomorphy**) in the literature for Kiswahili seems to be given different lines of thinking. On one hand, there is a definition which is typically morphological, i.e. different manifestations of the same morpheme and on the other hand, some definitions assume a typical semantic stand point, i.e. the contents of the notion morph.

For example, Rubanza (1996: 22) associates allomorph with several representations of one morpheme. Thus, to him, the notion allomorph is associated with different manifestations of the same morpheme. He offers examples related to the different realisations of the nominal prefix for class 1 as *m-* in *mtu* 'person' and *mw-* in *mwalimu* 'teacher' (Ibid: 23). Probably to these examples we should add another allomorph of class 1 prefix as *mu-* in *muuguzi* 'nurse'. Other examples are related to the causative suffix which surfaces as *-ish-* in *pikisha* 'cause to cook' and *-esh-* in *semesha* 'make to talk' (Ibid: 25). To his examples, we will also include *-iz-* which manifests in Kiswahili verbs like *tuliza* 'cause to calm' and *-z-* which manifests in *liza* 'cause to cry'.

The line of thinking taken by scholars like Rubanza emanates from the traditional morphology indicated in the many works of morphology (Spencer 1991; Katamba 1993; Booij 2005). The idea is that there are different shapes of the regular forms in languages. The kind of inspiration is that one morpheme may be realised into several forms (Katamba & Stonham 2006). For example, Spencer (1991) mentions that some morphological rules are described as analogies between word forms: *dog* is to *dogs* as *cat* is to *cats*, and as *dish* is to *dishes*. In this case, the analogy applies both to the form of the words and to their meaning: in each pair, the first word means "one of X", while the second "two or more of X", and the difference is always the plural form *-s* affixed to the second word, signaling the key distinction between singular and plural entities. See the examples above.

We would argue that this school of thinking is typically engrossed in prototypical morphology which ignores fascinating issues surrounding semantics. Much of the literature of this kind borrows examples from English. For instance, as far as regular forms in (19) below are concerned, Spencer (1991) says that even cases considered "regular", with the final *-s*, are not so simple; the *-s* in *dogs* is not pronounced the same way as the *-s* in *cats*, and in a plural form like *dishes*. This is because an "extra" vowel appears before the *-s*. These cases, where the same distinction is affected by alternative forms of a "word", are called allomorphy. Thus, as presented in the data below, we get /s/, /z/ and /ɪz/ as realizations of the morph [s] or plural formation in English.

(19)	cat	cats	/kæts/
	hut	huts	/hʌts/
	dog	dogs	/dɔgz/

cow	cows	/kaʊz/
dish	dishes	/dɪʃɪz/
horse	horses	/hɔsɪz/

The data in (19) brings us to the next term related to allomorph, and which is controversial as well, i.e. morph.

1.4.5.2   Morph

The other school of thought takes the definition of allomorph as associated with the notion **morph** which is, according to us, the different senses of the same morpheme as represented in the different shapes of the same morph. However, with regard to its definition, the different schools of thought do exist.

On the one hand, we have eminent morphologists like Katamba (1993), Bauer (2003) and Booij (2005) who define a morph with relation to manifestation of one morpheme in different shapes. For example, Katamba (1993: 24-25) says that a morph is a physical form representing some morpheme in a language. It is a recurrent distinctive sound (phoneme) or sequence of sounds (phonemes). He offers examples of the different sounds representing the pas tense -ed in words like *painted*, *cleaned* and *park-ed* in English. In this line, in Kiswahili, scholars like Massamba (2004: 54) say a morph is a bodily representation of a word.

On the other hand, there are scholars who assume that a morph is not an abstract idea that represents the word rather it is the physical part. These scholars ascribe abstractness to morphemes. For example, Mgullu (1999) mentions that a morph is the central meaning whose senses could be realised into dissimilar shapes in the language. To him, the inherent semantic sense of the morph is central rather than the different shapes which realise it.

Our understanding is that a morph is the physical part represented by the central form like -ed for past tense in English or -ish- for the causative in Kiswahili. The different manifestations of the same morph, i.e. /ɪd/, /t/, and /d/ in English as well /ɪz/, /ez/, /z/, /ish/, and /esh/ in Kiswahili, refer to the physical realisation of the morph, i.e. phonological articulations and morphological representation via orthographic symbols. We would like to underscore here that this position differs strongly to that taken by Mgullu (1999) who seems to mislead readers[4]. The position taken in this book is to assume that a morph is the different physical (sound as well) manifestations of the morpheme (a term defined in section 1.2 above).

---

4 I will urge readers (who may read Kiswahili articles) to consult two important papers which offer details on the differences between, among others, morpheme and morph: Gambarage (2011) and Kihore (2011).

Major resources cited throughout the book:

The following references are recommended for the purpose of reading and understanding the whole topic of linguistic morphology. Readers are advised to revisit any of these general books of morphology. Moreover, these references are provided in this chapter so as to avoid repetitions because these resources are referred to now and then in this book.

Bauer, Laurie. 1983. *English Word-formation*. Cambridge: Cambridge University Press.

Bauer, Laurie. 2003. *Introducing Linguistic Morphology*. Second edition. Edinburgh: Edinburgh University Press.

Bauer, Laurie. 2004. *A Glossary of Morphology*. Edinburgh: Edinburgh University Press.

Booij, Geert. 2002. *The Morphology of Dutch*. Oxford: Oxford University Press.

Booij, Geert. 2005. *The Grammar of Words: An Introduction to Linguistic Morphology*. Oxford: Oxford University Press.

Katamba, Francis. 1993. *Morphology*. London: Macmillan.

Katamba, Francis & Stonham, John. 2006. *Morphology*. Second edition. New York: Palgrave Macmillan..

Kihore, Yared, David P.B Massamba & Y. Msanjila. 2003. *Sarufi Maumbo ya Kiswahili Sanifu (SAMAKISA): Sekondari na Vyuo*. Dar es Salaam: Institue of Kiswahili Research.

Newman, Paul. 2000. *The Hausa Language: An Encyclopedic Reference Grammar*. New Haven & London: Yale University Press.

Minkova, Donka & Stockwell, Robert. 2009. *English Words: History and Structure*. Second edition. Cambridge: Cambridge University Press.

Mohamed, A. Mohamed. 2001. *Modern Kiswahili Grammar*. Nairobi: East African Educational Publishers.

Plag, Ingo. 2002. *Word-formation in English*. Cambridge: Cambridge University Press.

Rubanza, Yunus I. 1996. *Mofolojia ya Kiswahili*. Dar es Salaam: The Open University of Tanzania.

Schadeberg, Thilo C. 1992. *A Sketch of Swahili Morphology*, 3rd edition. Köln: Rüdiger Köppe Verlag.

Spencer, Andrew. 1991. *Morphological Theory: An Introduction to Word Structure in Generative Grammar*. Oxford: Blackwell.

Resources cited:

Ashton, Ethol O. 1944. *Kiswahili Grammar (Including Intonation)*. London: Longmans.

Ayres-Bennett, Wendy & Carruthers, Janice. 2001. *Problems and Perspectives: Studies in the Mordern French Language*. Essex: Pearson Education Limited.

Battye, Adrian, Marie-Anne Hintz & Paul Rowlett. 2000. *The French Language Today: A Linguistic Introduction*. London: Routledge.

Bauer, Laurie. 2001. *Morphological Productivity*. Cambridge: Cambridge University Press.

Bolozky, Shmuel. 1999. *Measuring Productivity in Word Formation*. Leiden: Brill.

Booij, Geert. 1992. Compounding in Dutch. *Rivista di Linguistica,* 4(1): 37-59.

Contini-Morava, Ellen. 1983. *Tense and Non-tense in Swahili Grammar: Semantic Asymmetry between Affirmative and Negative*. Doctoral thesis. Columbia: Columbia University.

Contini-Morava, Ellen. 1989. *Discourse Pragmatics and Semantic Categorization: The Case of Negation and Tense-aspect with Special Reference to Swahili*. Berlin: Mouton de Gruyter.

Contini-Morava, Ellen. 1994. *Noun Classification in Kiswahili*. Publications of the Institute for Advanced Technology in the Humanities, University of Virginia. Research Reports, Second Series.

Contini-Morava, Ellen. 2007. Kiswahili morphology. In: Kaye, Alan S. (ed.). *Morphology of Asia and Africa*, vol. 2. Winona Lake and Indiana: Eisenbrauns. pp. 1129-1158.

Denning, Keith & Leben, William R. 1995. *English Vocabulary Elements*. Oxford: Oxford University Press.

Dixon, Robert M.W & Aikhenvald, Alexandra Y. 2002. (eds). *Word: A Cross-linguistic Typology*. Cambridge: Cambridge University Press.

Dixon, Robert M.W & Aikhenvald, Alexandra Y. 2002. Word: A typological framework. In: Dixon, Robert M.W & Aikhenvald, Alexandra Y. (eds.). *Word: A Cross-linguistic Typology*. Cambridge: Cambridge University Press. pp. 1-41.

Fagyal, Zsuzsanna, Douglas Kibbe & Fred Jenkins. 2006. *French: A Linguistic Introduction*. Cambridge: Cambridge University Press.

Fox, Anthony. 2000. *Prosodic Features and Prosodic Structure: The Phonology of Suprasegmentals*. Oxford: Oxford University Press.

Fox, Anthony. 2000. *Prosodic Features and Prosodic Structure: The Phonology of Suprasegmentals*. Oxford: Oxford University Press.

Gambarage, Joash J. 2011. Mkanganyiko wa dhana ya mzizi, kiini na shina katika mofolojia ya Kiswahili. *KISWAHILI Journal of the Institute of Kiswahili Studies,* vol 74: 12-24.

Katamba, Francis. 2003. Bantu nominal morphology. In: Nurse, Derek & Philippson, Gérard (eds.) *The Bantu languages.* London: Routledge. pp. 103-120.

Kihore, Yared M. 2011. Majibu kwa makala "Mkanganyiko wa dhana ya mzizi, kiini na shina katika mofolojia ya Kiswahili na Joash J. Gambarage". *KISWAHILI Journal of the Institute of Kiswahili Studies,* vol 74: 25-27.

Lin, Hua. 2001. *A Grammar of Mandarin Chinese.* Munchen: Lincom Europa.

Massamba, David P.B. 1996. *Phonological theory: History and development.* Dar es Salaam University Press.

Massamba, David P.B. 2004. *Kamusi ya Isimu na Falsafa ya Lugha.* Dar es Salaam: Institute of Kiswahili Research, University of Dar es Salaam.

Massamba, David P.B. 2007. *Kiswahili Origins and the Bantu Divergence-Convergence Theory.* Dar es Salaam: Institute of Kiswahili Research.

Mathews, P.H. 2002. What can we conclude? In: Dixon, Robert M.W & Aikhenvald, Alexandra Y. (eds). *Word: A Cross-linguistic Typology.* Cambridge: Cambridge University Press. pp. 266-281.

Mgullu, Richard S. 1999. *Mtalaa wa Isimu: Fonetiki, Fonolojia na Mofolojia ya Kiswahili.* Nairobi: Longhorn Publishers.

Möhlig, Wilhelm J.G. & Kavari, Jekura U. 2008. *Reference Grammar of Herero (Otjiherero).* Köln: Rüdiger Köppe Verlag.

Plag, Ingo. 1999. *Morphological productivity: Structural Constraints in English Derivation.* Berlin: Mouton de Gruyter.

Rubanza, Yunus. 2007. Discrimination through Language. *Occasional Papers in Linguistics,* No.3. pp. 97-105.

Simpson, Paul. 1997. *Language through Literature: An Introduction.* London: Routledge.

Stonham, John. 2004. *Linguistic Theory and Complex Words: Nuuchahnulth Word formation.* New York: Palgrave Macmillan.

Storch, Anne. 2004. *The Noun Morphology of Western Nilotic.* Köln: Rüdiger Köppe Verlag.

Strothmann, F.W. 1935. The influence of aspect on the meaning of "Nomina Agentis" in Modern German. *The Journal of English and Germanic Philology,* vol. XXXIV (2): 188-200.

TUKI (Taasisi ya Uchunguzi wa Kiswahili). 2001. *Kamusi ya Kiswahili-Kiingereza.* Dar es Salaam: Institute of Kiswahili Research.

TUKI (Taasisis ya Uchunguzi wa Kiswahili). 2004. *Kamusi ya Biolojia, Fizikia na Kemia (English-Swahili Dictionary of Biology, Physics and Chemistry).* Dar es Salaam: TUKI/UNESCO/SIDA.

Exercise One

Study carefully Kiswahili data given in Set A and Set B below:

Set A

piga	hit
tumewapiga	we hit them
hajapigwa	s/he is not hit
pigana	hit one another
tumepigwa	we have been hit
walipigana	they hit one another
hawatapiganishwa	they will not be caused to hit one another

Set B

soma	read; study
somesha	teach; cause to read
someshea	teach for/at; cause to read for/at
amewasomesha	s/he taught them; s/he made them read
hajasomeshwa	s/he is not taught; s/he is not made to read

After examining the data above, try to attempt the following questions:

1. Define the terms *root* and *stem*. Then mention the *roots* of the two Kiswahili *stems* in Sets A and B above.

2. What do you understand by the notion *morpheme*? Make boundaries by a dash [-] sign to demarcate the morphemes in words: *walipigana* 'they hit one another' (Set A) and *amesomesha* 's/he taught them; s/he made them read' (Set B).

3. Based on your definition of the term *morpheme* above, what are the functions of four morphemes -*esh*-, -*wa*-, -*me*- and -*a* in the whole range of Kiswahili data given in the two sets above?

4. Following Katamba, F. (1993) *Morphology*. Oxford: Blackwell, the morpheme *ha-* has a specific name. Name and define it?

2 Word-Building

2.1 Introduction

One significant and pervasive linguistic phenomenon is that each language adds a new word to the lexicon of its grammar. This is a natural process available in any language. However, the way languages add words to their lexicons differ. Such different processes are introduced in this chapter. Since various languages use different means of building new words either from the existing ones or in-bringing quite new words which never existed in such languages, then it becomes necessary to synthesize together these processes. One important point to note is that there are about twelve ways of word-building attested across world languages.

Most students of linguistics, however, at least in Tanzania if not all over East African countries, tend to lean their thinking about strategies of word-building in Kiswahili to the experiences they have from English (or perhaps French) mechanisms. This is a very wrong approach because languages differ in their ways of word-buildings.

In linguistics, **word-building processes** (also called means of word-formation) traditionally refer to the natural means of creation of new words. This is an area which seems to be tackled from two assumptions as Bauer (1983: 7) long noted: 'any discussion of word-building makes two assumptions: that there are such things as words, and that at least some of them are formed'. Since the notion **word** is covered previously, the discussion in this chapter surrounds only around word-formation processes.

This chapter is envisaged in order to provide a summary of the facts surrounding the main word-formation processes attested across the world languages. The intent is to allow readers to have a quick glance at all the word-formation processes attested in the world languages before dwelling into the details of each and the way they work mainly in English and Kiswahili (and to a lesser extent in French). Comparatively, however, there would be only a fewer processes employed by Kiswahili speakers as ways of forming new words in the language. This is so because an individual language usually selects a fewer means to generate new words.

The processes used in building words in languages such as English and French, which are about twelve, are listed in (1) below. Of these, as will be the case in the subsequent chapters in this book, only the first five mechanisms are common in Swahili: affixation, compounding, borrowing, reduplication and calque.

(1) i.   *Affixation (derivation and inflection)*
     ii.   *Compounding*
     iii. *Reduplication*

iv.	Borrowing (loan words)
v.	Calque or Loan Translation
vi.	Clipping
vii.	Blending
viii.	Coinage
ix.	Back-formation
x.	Conversion
xi.	Neologism
xii.	Acronym

A look in literature suggests that some of these word-building processes are treated as major, namely affixation, reduplication, compounding and borrowing in languages like English, Dutch, Nootka and Mandarin Chinese. The rest are minor word-formation processes (Bauer 1983; Lin 2001; Booij 2002; Stonham 2002). In Kiswahili, four major word-building processes attested include affixation (derivation), reduplication, compounding, and borrowing.

2.2   Productivity in word-building

In word-building processes, as an important branch of morphology, **productivity** (which is the process of creating new words from other words and recycling existing ones to create newer bases) is given very significant considerations. This is evidenced by the fact that there are books of morphology that provide a broad section to discuss it (see e.g. Booij 2002) and some morphology books set an entire chapter to discuss the notion productivity and its related processes and results (see e.g. Bauer 1983 [Chapter Four]; Bauer 2003 [Chapter Five]; Katamba & Stonham 2006 [Chapter Four]). Also, some authors have devoted an entire book to present several issues revolving around productivity in morphology (see e.g. Plag 1999; Bauer 2001). In the present book, the degree of productivity is discussed in detail in the light of discussions offered for the individual word-building processes in each of the subsequent chapters.

In the list of characteristics of the human languages, productivity is given some equal weight amongst the twelve features mentioned in the literature for introduction to linguistics. In the perspective of natural language features, **productivity** is used to refer to the ability of human beings to generate several other novel structures from the existing ones. This means that (native) speakers of the given language are creatively able to generate newer utterances which have never been used before. Thus, **creativity** is a synonymous word to productivity.

May be the definition of creativity provided above is narrower because productivity also involves using the existing structures to form other structures. To expand its essence, we need to introduce another term, i.e. **recycling**. In the introduction to linguistics courses offered to first year students of linguistics, productivity (creativity) is regularly referred to as **recycling** in the sense that speakers of languages like Kiswahili and English may use the existing utterances to generate newer utterances as well.

Katamba and Stonham (2006) partly look at productivity as some kind of **open-endedness** in the lexicon of a language. This means that speakers of a language can add newer words to the existing lexicon. However, they caution 'until recently, word-building rules have tended to be seen as being largely passive in the sense that they are basically used to analyse existing words rather than to create new ones' (Katamba & Stonham 2006: 67). In the course of the presentations in the present book, on the one hand, this would be found true with processes like derivation, reduplication, compounding etc. across the three focal languages, but untrue for other processes like borrowing and calquing in Kiswahili. In this language, these two word-creation processes bring into the target languages quite new words.

In this line, therefore, creativity (productivity) in morphology is used to refer to the processes which involve creation of newer words, say in Kiswahili, either from the existing words [in other cases word-forms] and parts of words (affixes and roots), as in derivations such *pa* 'to give' > *mpaji* 'giver', inflectional processes like *mzazi* 'parent' > *wazazi* 'parents', compounded words like *mwananchi* 'citizen' [< *mwana* 'child' and *nchi* 'country'] etc. or from completely foreign structures as in borrowed words such as *posta* 'post office' and *ikulu* 'state house' in Kiswahili.

One is likely to succinctly predict that since we have productivity in word-building then unproductivity should prevail. This assumption is correctly reflected in natural languages. However, unproductivity refers to the degree of productivity in that some processes are very productive because they apply across several languages and in various word categories while some are less productive because they apply to a less number of languages and strictly to a few word-categories. Put in other words, we should be able to maintain that some productive processes are more **prolific** (very productive across languages and words), e.g. derivational processes while other productive processes are **blocked** (unproductive in a way). In the light of making sense of productive and unproductive processes as well as prolific and blocked productive processes, Booij (2005: 68) has captured this notion rightly as follows:

> When we call a morphological pattern **productive**, we mean that this pattern can be extended to new cases, can be used to form new words. When we say that a morphological pattern is **unproductive**, this means that it is not used for coining new words [...] Within the class of productive morphological templates, we find differences in **degree of productivity**. Morphological patterns are not used to the same degree. [...] The degree of productivity of a word-building pattern thus refers to the degree to which the structural possibilities of a word-building pattern are actually used. [Emphasis mine]

From the foregoing discussion, we are able to deduce that Geert Booij seems to underscore, of course succinctly, the application of the same mechanism of word-formation across several other words in a way of creating new words.

The same is captured in some more detailed manner by Katamba and Stonham (2006) who view productivity simply as a matter of **generality** and say that there are two key points required to understand the notion productivity:

(i) Productivity is a **matter of degree**. It is *not* a dichotomy, with some word-formation processes being productive and others unproductive. Probably no process is so general that it affects, without exception, *all* the bases to which it could potentially apply. The reality is that some processes are *relatively* more general than others.

(ii) Productivity is subject to the **dimension of time**. A process which is very general during one historical period may become less so at a subsequent period. Conversely, a new process entering a language may initially affect a tiny fraction of eligible inputs before eventually applying more widely. (Katamba & Stonham 2006: 69). [Emphasis, in italics by authors, in bold mine].

From this explanation, we interpret that these authors underline the degree of the applicability of the strategy across word categories. (I would add also that it applies across several languages). Also, they highlight the significance of time over the nativisation of the process as an actual and realistic means of forming new words in a given language.

We find that what is captured as the contexts for productivity above is realised differently in other literature. Based on French language, Ayres-Bennett and Carruthers (2001: 351) have the following to offer, I quote:

The productivity of a particular process of lexical creation is highly depended on the level of formality of the discourse, on sociolinguistic factors and on domain. .... With derivation, a small number of suffixes are more frequent used than in standard French, e.g. *clodo* 'tramp, begger' and *cinoche* 'movies, cinema". .... Types of suffixation not normally found in standard vocabulary are attested, e.g. *duraille* and *seulebre*" [translations mine[5]].

The scholars cited above introduce the question of the level of formality and socialinguistics as factors that could be used to determine the productivity of the mechanism in question. This informs us that productivity may be pervasive in informal languages but not accepted in the standard dialect.

All in all, *productivity* involves the power of a particular process to form new words. For instance, for the major word-building processes in English, French and Kiswahili, derivational processes, e.g. verbal derivations, are prolific in productivity than acronyms in creating new words. The same applies to reduplication pattern which is very productive in some languages like Kiswahili and Nookta than compounding pattern in these languages. This will be revealed in detail in the course of the discussion of the various chapters of this book.

2.3   Processes involved across world languages

In this section I offer a description of the individual word-building processes. Two things should be noted. Firstly, since I avoid to prepare examples from all languages of the world, most of our examples are from only selected languages, namely English, Hausa, Tagalog, French, Mandarin Chinese, Kiswahili, and Arabic.

---

5 Thanks to Nelius Neckemia, French Unit, Dar es Salaam University College of Education.

Secondly, what is referred to as major word-building processes in this book entails that the word-building processes are productive in several languages and across world's languages. These include affixation (derivation), compounding, reduplication and loanwords. Minor word-building processes (the rest in 1) are productive only in a number of languages and apply only to a fewer words.

2.3.1 Major word-building processes

The main morphological process that is attested across several languages of the world is **affixation** (see Bauer 1983; Booij 2002; Schadeberg 2003; Katamba & Stonham 2006; Minkova & Stockwell 2009). The affixation process is both derivational and inflectional and basically involves attachment of affixes at the initial position (prefixation), insertion within stems (infixation), and placing affixes at final position (suffixation). The focus in most books, particularly on Indo-European languages (Bauer 1982; Booij 2005) and Bantu languages (Rubanza 1996; Schadeberg 2003) is on prefixation and suffixation. Ayres-Bennett and Carruthers (2001: 344) succinctly summarized the differences between the two as follows:

> At basic level, suffixes and prefixes are distinguished by their position in the word [...] Suffixes generally change the grammatical class of the word, where as prefixes do not. ... Two exceptions in French: prefix *anti-* turns a noun into an adjective, for example *tache* [N] 'stain, dirty' *antitache* [Adj] 'anti-stain, dirty-repellent' [...] Suffixation in Indo-European languages is for marking case and category.

This process involves the attachment of affix(es) to a word which brings derivation, i.e. forming a new word as in *ktb* 'write' to *kitaab* 'book' in Arabic, or it involves inflectional processes such as tense and aspect marking like the perfective marker *-me* in Kiswahili, as in *jenga* 'build' to *a-me-jeng-a* 's/he (had) built'. Chapters 3 and 4 of this book are meant to discuss the whole affixation processes in English, French and Kiswahili, a process highly acknowledged as a very productive means of word-building in the language.

Another major word-building strategy is **reduplication**, i.e. repetition or copying of all or part of the stem to the base, is widely used as a means of forming new words in Creole languages as well as in other languages. For example, Indonesian reveals total reduplication as in *rumah* 'house' *rumahrumah* 'houses' while Tagalog shows partial reduplication as in *bili* 'buy' *bibili* 'will buy' (see Katamba 1993). As evidenced in Chapter 5 of this book, this is a highly productive process in Kiswahili. Some examples include *polepole* 'slowly' [< *pole* 'slow'] and *lialia* 'cry frequently' [< *lia* 'cry'].

Borrowing refers to a process in which a word (or words) is imported from another language and gets localised in the receiving language. The borrowed words are called **loan words**. Facts show that even important languages like German has a large and increasing number of borrowings, especially from English e.g. *handy* 'cell phone'. English itself is well-known for its mixed vocabulary and overall affinity for foreign words. A number of words in this language are from Latin and Greek, e.g. *strata, street, bishop* etc. It has loanwords from Bantu too, e.g. *tsetse (Setswana)* and *safari (Swahili)*.

As it will be evident in this book, words of foreign origin become integrated into the target language. For instance, based on French, Ayres-Bennett and Carruthers (2001: 324) record that:

> Borrowed words are integrated linguistically into the host language (phonologically, morphologically and syntactically) [...] e.g. *babyboomer* and *body building* from English [...] Loanwords may be seen as more fully assimilated in that, in addition to having undergone phonological, morphological and syntactic adaptation, they remain relatively frequently, are widely used in the speech community, and have achieved a certain level of recognition or acceptance, if not normative approval.

In the same spirit, for instance, Kiswahili has English loan words like *shati* 'shirt' and *kiosk* 'cabin shop'. In Mandarin Chinese English loan words are many, e.g. *jiānádà* 'Canada' (Lin 2001: 52). Loanwords in French include *walkman* 'walkman', *conteneur* 'container' etc. (Ayres-Bennett & Carruthers 2001: 325). Chapter 6 of this book is dedicated to discussion on borrowing in English, French and Kiswahili.

Compounding leads to **compounds** which are multiple-morpheme words that we identify as consisting of two or more parts that make a single word. In a compound, several free morphemes are combined together; resulting in a word that often derives its meaning from the combination of its components. In English, compounds are often not written as single words e.g. *classroom*, separated words e.g. *light bulb*, or combined by a hyphen e.g. *book-keeping*. In Mandarin Chinese several compounds are attested to the extent that it might be true to say that this is a language of compounded word, e.g. *mǎimai* [buy-sell] 'trade' and *hǎodai* [good-bad] 'in any case' (Lin 2001: 62-63). Compounding in English, French and Kiswahili leads to words like *garimoshi* 'train' and *batamzinga* 'turkey'. This is the subject matter under discussion in chapter 7 in this book.

2.3.2 Minor word-building processes

A number of word-building processes are minor. These are minor because they occur less frequently in French, Kiswahili and English languages. Also, they apply to a few words in any language they occur. In this book, these will only be captured altogether in this section.

Calque (Loan-translation) – this refers to borrowing a word or phrase from another language by literal, word-for-word or root-for-root translation (Batibo 1987). A good example is an English phrase **to lose face**, which is a calque from Chinese language. This also involves semantic loan, i.e. the extension of the meaning of a word to include new, foreign meanings. Kiswahili employs a lot of this in its term development projects (Batibo 2010).

Acronym entails words which are formed from the initials of several words. This is possible in English whereby even very newer initials are used as complete words, e.g. *HIV* (Human Immune Virus), *RAM* (Random Access Memory), *CD* (Compact Disk) etc.

Back-formation refers to the extraction of a word out of a larger word. In other words, back-formation is the removal of an element (say an affix) from a word in order to form a new word, e.g. *edit* from *editor*, *peddle* from *peddler*, and *televise* from *television*. Since nothing of this kind of word-building process happens in Kiswahili, then this is all what this process is offered in this book.

Blending – a process of creating a new word by combining the parts of two different words, usually the beginning of one word and the end of another, e.g. *motel* (motor and hotel) and *brunch* (breakfast + lunch) in English. In Kiswahili we have words like *chajio* 'brunch' which comes from *chakula cha jioni* 'an evening meal'. Nonetheless, this is a very less significant topic thus it is not dealt with in this book.

Clipping – a process of creating new words by shortening parts of a longer word particularly in English, e.g. influenza – *flu*, refrigerator – *fridge*, doctor – *doc* etc. Readers of this book should not confuse clipping with back-formation and affixation. It should be known that clipping in Kiswahili and other Bantu languages seems to be not prolific. It means that this process is not productive in Kiswahili, as in other Bantu languages[6] hence it will not be attended at in this book.

Another minor word building process is **neologism**. It involves bringing into a language a completely new word, e.g. *quack* in English. This is related to **coinage**, the art of labelling and nativisation of the labels as words, e.g. *asprin* in English.

The last means of forming new words is through reversing the meaning of the word without changing its morphology as in *lower* 'adjective' vs. *to lower* 'verb' technically called **conversion**.

Swahili words are also involved in **conversion**. Perhaps the following examples will help to exemplify this point[7]:

(2)   a.   *Meza*   *chakula!*
              swallow   7.food
              'Swallow the food!'

       b.   *Niletee*   *meza*
              I-bring   table
              'Bring me the table'

(3)   a.   *Paka*   *rangi*
              paint   colour
              '(You) should paint'

       b.   *Tu-me-mu-ona*   *paka*
              we-PST-OM9-see   9.cat
              'We saw the cat'

(4)   a.   *Ki-atu*   *kipo*   *juu*   *ya* *paa*
              7-shoe   is   top   of 5.roof
              'The shoe is on top of the roof'

---

6   Some students at University of Dar es Salaam once kept on mentioning Bantu words which underwent affixation and de-affixation as if were undergoing clipping.

7   Thanks to my students, namely Jonathani Abayo and Ojijo George, for pin pointing these examples.

b.   *Paa   juu*
     fly   up
     'Fly high'

The examples above are illustrative of conversion in Kiswahili. While (2a) indicates *meza* as a verb, i.e. swallow, in (2b) the same word *meza* refers to a tool (noun), i.e. table. (3a) has the word *paka* 'paint' as a verb, while in (3b) it refers to a name, i.e. cat. Likewise, the word *paa* 'roof' is a noun in (4a) and a verb in (4b), i.e. *paa* 'fly'. It underscored here that it is such kind of derivations which take place without any morphological adjustment within words, which is refered to as zero derivation by Katamba (1993), which Kiswahili words above demonstrate here.

Resources cited:

Ayres-Bennett, Wendy & Carruthers, Janice. 2001. *Problems and Perspectives: Studies in the Modern French Language*. Essex: Pearson Education Limited.

Batibo, Herman. 1987. The challenge of linguistics in language development: The case of Kiswahili in Tanzania. *LASU Conference Proceedings, Harare*. pp. 39-46.

Batibo, Herman. 2010. Challenges of term standardisation, dissemination and acceptance. *Terminology Development for the Intellectualisation of African Languages*. Proceedings from the SANTED Terminology Development Workshop held on 11–12 May 2009. PRAESA Occasional Papers No. 38. pp. 22-25.

Booij, Geert. 1992. Compounding in Dutch. *Rivista di Linguistica*, 4(1): 37-59.

Booij, Geert. 2002. *The Morphology of Dutch*. Oxford: Oxford University Press.

Inkelas, Sharon & Zoll, Cheryl. 2005. *Reduplication: Doubling in Morphology*. Cambridge: Cambridge University Press.

Katamba, Francis. 1993. *Morphology*. London: Macmillan.

Lin, Hua. 2001. *A Grammar of Mandarin Chinese*. Munchen: Lincom Europa.

Plag, Ingo. 1999. *Morphological productivity: Structural Constraints in English Derivation*. Berlin: Mouton de Gruyter.

Exercise Two

2.1 The notion productivity is bound to cyclicity condition. Discuss.

2.2 Differentiate minor word-building processes in French and English.

2.3 Discuss major word formation processes in Kiswahili.

3 Derivation

3.1 Introducing derivation

One of the major topics which appear at least in each volume of linguistic morphology, perhaps because it is pervasive across languages, is **derivation**. Its significance in analysing inflecting languages such as English and French as well as agglutinative languages like Kiswahili cannot be under-estimated. This chapter, therefore, explores the importance of derivation, as one of the word-formation processes, in these languages. This function is in the line with Booij's (2005: 51) view that 'the basic function of derivational process is to enable the language user to make new lexemes.'

It is major word categories, i.e. nouns, verbs and adjectives, which undergo derivation in several languages. Associated with this process are the alterations of the senses in these major word categories which tend to derive other nouns, a number of verbs, some adjectives, as well adverbs. This is illustrated in (1) below. Examples in (1a) show formation of other meanings of English adjectives after attaching the suffix *-ful*, while French examples in (1b) show derivation by addition of suffixes *-aire* and *-ée*. The examples in (1c) show nominalisation of verbs in Kiswahili by addition of an affix *-aji*.

(1)   a.   *power* [Adj]   *powerful* [N]
              harm [Adj]   *harmful* [Adj]
              great [Adj]   *greatful* [Adj]

    b.   *consul* [V]   'diplomat'   *consulaire* [N] 'ambassador, consular'
              arriver [V]   'arrive'   arrivée [N]   'arrival'

    c.   *cheza* [V]   'play'   *mchezaji* [N]   'player'
              zungumza [V] 'talk'   *mzungumzaji* [N] 'speaker, spokesperson'
              chunga [V]   'to herd'   *mchungaji* [N]   'herder, priest'

The data in (1) above helps us to understand the meaning of the notion *derivation* which is said to involve morphemes which alter the meaning and/or word-category of the base (Katamba 1993). The former explanation will involve elements in English which are engaged in change in meanings while maintaining the word-category of the bases (1a). The latter definition involves French and Kiswahili examples which are engaged in alteration of both meanings and word-classes of the bases.

In this line, currently, Katamba and Stonham (2006) put it as:

> Derivational affixes which alter the meaning or grammatical category of the base... Derivational morphemes form new words either by changing the meaning of the base to which they are attached, for example, *kind* vs. *un-kind* (both are adjectives but with opposite meanings), *obey* vs. *dis-obey* (both are

verbs but with opposite meanings)… Or by changing the word-class that a base belongs to, for example, the addition of -ly to the adjectives *kind* and *simple* produces the adverbs *kindly* and *simply*. As a rule, it is possible to derive an adverb by adding the suffix -ly to an adjective base in English. (Katamba and Stonham 2006: 46, 49).

In order to deal seriously with how derivational processes manifest across our focal languages, this book presents basically three derivational processes: noun derivation processes (nominalisation), verbal internal derivations (verbalization), and adjectival derivations (adjectivisation) (for terms, see also Booij 2005). The choice of these subject matters emanates from the essence derivation itself (as shown below), as well as the characteristics of the morphologies of the target languages (inflecting and agglutinating).

Firstly, all three languages demonstrate nominal derivation which covers the formation of nouns from stems of other nouns, verbs and adjectives. The nominal derivations in these languages appear to be associated with the major semantic roles, i.e. agentive, instrument and patient. (This is discussed in detail in section 3.2 below).

Secondly, adjectival derivations are closely related to nominal derivations and in most cases nouns turn to adjectives and adjectives become nouns in the process. Thus, this chapter provides a detailed analysis of the various adjectival formations in the representative languages.

Thirdly, as will be evident in the course of the discussion, English language reveals a good deal of verb-forming derivations by attaching affixes, e.g. *woman - womanise, character - characterise, beauty - beautify, solid - solidify* etc (see Plag 2002).

Verbal system in African languages, however, reveals a good deal of derivational processes, those which do not involve the formation of the nominals, but the ones attached to the verbs and to form new essences of the verbs. Such derivational processes make a broad topic in Niger-Congo family, in which the new essences of verbs are formed. This is well captured by Hyman (2007: 150) who mentions verb extensions which have a wide distribution within Niger-Congo and other derivations associated with affixation.

Just to make things straight here, the notion derivation will also be used to mean the process of addition of certain morpheme or morphemes to the specific root position of the nominal morphology, verbal system as well as adjectival morphology which change both of them in both form and meaning.

3.2   Nominal derivations (nominalisation)

The essence of this wide topic known as *nominal derivation*, technically also known as **nominalisation**, is to cover the formation of various noun stems from other nouns, verbs, adjectives and other word-categories. Also, under this topic, the specification of the classes with which the noun stems may be associated with in the formation of nouns is offered.

The nominalisation processes appear to involve affixation in all three languages. In fact, suffixation is more pervasive than prefixation in such derivations. Nominalisation by suffixation is shown in words like *capital* [N] – *capitalism* [N] and *cheza* [V] 'play' – *mchezaji* [N] 'player' in English and Kiswahili respectively.

According to Payne and Olsen (2009), nominalization is classically considered a derivational process, meaning that it correlates with either a change in part-of-speech and/or a substantive change in meaning. As we can see, this point of view (i.e. change in meaning and/or word-class) is also maintained by Katamba (1993). Some derivational forms may be idiosyncratic in meaning (only referring to specific notions and words), but others may be quite consistent in their meaning contribution (applying to several words and giving similar effects) (Payne & Olsen 2009: 151).

Basically, the morphologies of world's languages like Kiswahili, English and French permit major types of nouns which result from derivations. In the existing literature (at least for African languages, (Schadeberg 1984; Newman 2000; Seidel 2008; Payne & Olsen 2009)), the following clusters of resulting words are obvious:

- The first group encompasses what is known in Latin as **nomina agentis** which involve nouns which are associated with instigators or doers of actions or events embedded in the verbs in question, e.g. *piga* 'hit' – *mpigaji* 'hitter' in Kiswahili as well as *build* – *builder* in English.
- The second group is made up of **nomina instrumenti** which embraces all nouns which perform the instrument roles in the constructions, e.g. *fagia* 'sweep' – *fagio* 'broom' in Kiswahili as well as *cook* – *cooker* in English.
- The other group is made up of **nomina pantis**, i.e. nominals associated with semantic roles, namely themes, patients and the like, e.g. *uza* 'sell' – *muuzaji* 'seller' in Kiswahili.

At this juncture, therefore, it would be better to dwell into the details of each nominalisation process in order to have a better understanding of each process in these languages.

3.2.1 Nominalisation in English

As for nominalisation in English, three points are worth discussing before any further description.

Firstly, although a number of derivational affixes are employed to create new nouns in English, usually a specific number of affixes is employed for that purpose. This is because affixes, as grammatical entities, are not prone to borrowing. This is in line with Plag (2002) who discusses the function of about 22 tokens of derivational suffixes in English (see details below). This informs us that nominalisation in English takes only suffixes for both typical word-changing derivation and meaning-changing derivation.

Thus, it is informative to suggest that derivation is mostly characterised by suffixation in English.

Furthermore, the word-class that results from nominal derivation is usually not opaque because each suffix either produces a given word-category or changes the meaning of the base. In this spirit, Williams (1981: 248) suggests 'it is generally the case that a suffix determines the category of a word of which it is a part'. Examples of English nominalising suffixes are offered in (2) (Ibid):

(2)

	Source words		Suffix			Resulting words
N	*race*		-ism	>	N	*racism*
V	*commune*		-ist	>	N	*communist*
V	*revolve*		-ion	>	N	*revolution*
V	*write*		-er	>	N	*writer*
Adj	*happy*		-ness	>	N	*happiness*

Secondly, prefixation is not pervasively associated with derivations which alter word-classes in English, rather it focuses on deriving new meanings (Katamba 1993). Thus, nominal derivation in English is least prefixal. Plag (2002) has completely forgiven the nominalisation by prefixation in the language. Hammond (1993: 562) accentuates this phenomenon as he says 'whereas there is a plethora of category-changing suffixes, there are only a few category-changing prefixes'. Look on how the prefix *counter-* maintains word-class in (3) (Ibid).

(3)   *counter + revolution*$_N$ >   N

       counter + sink$_V$ >   V

       counter + productive$_A$ >   A

Thirdly, on the classification of nouns as per semantic roles, it seems that English is not a right candidate as for typical nomina-agentis nouns. This is because the language seems to take both **nomina-agentis (agentive nouns)** and **nomina pantis (active-participant nouns)** by deriving them by affixes. It means that some suffixes in English are characteristic of deriving agentive nouns from other word categories. The main derivative suffix of this nature is *-er* (with its variants: *-or, -r*). A few examples given below show formation of nouns from verbs:

(4)   -er

	build	*builder*
	eat	*eater*
	mark	*marker*
	buy	*buyer*
	sell	*seller*

       -or

	govern	*governor*
	compress	*compressor*
	direct	*director*
	act	*actor*
	conduct	*conductor*

       -r

	dance	*dancer*
	drive	*driver*
	take	*taker*

Such **nomina instrumenti (instrumental nouns)**, formed through addition of a nominalising suffix *-er* and *-or* in English, semantically denote instrumental roles. This process is attested in the language, as illustrated in (5).

(5)   -er   *cook*   *cooker*
                    heat   *heater*
                    wipe   *wiper*
                    revolve   *revolver*

         -or   *connect*   *connector*
                    radiate   *radiator*

In Table 1 below, a list of the remaining nominalising suffixes in English are offered, with some illustrative words provided. (For further details, see Plag 2002; Minkova & Stockwell 2009).

We see that suffixes in English function to derive several nouns with a variety of classifications. This is in line with Plag (2002: 109) who categorically says nominal suffixes are often employed to derive abstract and personal nouns from verbs, adjectives and nouns. Such abstract nouns can denote actions, results of actions, or other related concepts, but also properties, qualities and the like. Nouns derived by suffixes in English have also meanings are extended to other, related senses so that practically each suffix can be shown to be able to express more than one meaning (Ibid).

Table 1: Nominalising suffixes in English

Suffixes	Function	Examples
-al	Abstract nouns derived denote an action or result of an action	*removal, arrival, refusal, renewal, survival*
-ist	It derives nouns denoting persons	*Marxist, communist, fascist, populist*
-ant	count nouns referring to persons or to substances	*applicant, defendant, deviant*
-acy	Nouns derived involve: 'the fact that something converges'	*adequacy, animacy, intimacy*
-age	Derived nouns express an activity, some nouns indicate quantity	*coverage, voltage, orphanage*
-dom	It derives a kind of 'state of being X' nouns	*kingdom, freedom, studentdom*
-ance/ -ancy	It creates action nouns	*dependency, abundance, alliance, emergence*
-ess	Derives nouns for female humans and animals	*waitress, actress, hostess, lioness*
-ee	Derived nouns involving events of non-volitional participants	*consignee, employee, payee*
-eer	Derives nouns with the feature: X deals in, X is concerned with	*mountaineer, auctioneer*
-ful	It derives measure partitive nouns	*handful, skilful*
-hood	Derived nouns show: state and collectivity	*adulthood, childhood, Christianhood*

-ion	It denotes events or results of processes	*division, erosion, colonization*
-an/-ian	Some derived nouns are for 'belongingness' while others show: X having to do with Y	*Chomskyan, Tanzanian, historian, technician,*
-ing	Nouns derived by deverbal suffix denote processes	*sleeping, begging, running, sleeping*
-ism	Form abstract nouns from other nouns and adjectives	*conservatism, Marxism, minimalism*
-ment	derives action nouns denoting processes or results	*assessment, involvement, treatment*
-ity	Derives nouns denoting qualities, states or properties	*solidarity, curiosity, productivity*
-ness	Derives abstract nouns	*goodness, happiness, kindness*
-ship	It derives nouns denoting state or condition	*citizenship, friendship, membership,*

3.2.2 Nominal derivation in Kiswahili

Generally Kiswahili derives nouns from other nouns, verbs and adjectives (and these words fall into specific clusters). However, each cluster has internal morphologies. For instance, nouns derived from nouns would be associated with prefixation, a change pervasive in the noun-classes in Niger-Congo. Nouns derived from verbs are basically allied to both prefixation and suffixation, i.e. created by addition of nominalising prefixes and suffixes. Adjectives loose their inherent properties and become nouns in Kiswahili once they are assigned with new noun prefixes. Thus, since each nominal source behaves separately, in what follows, we treat each in its independent section.

3.2.2.1 *Noun-noun derivations in Kiswahili*

A number of nouns are formed through noun-to-noun derivation. The process is conclusively **prefixation** as it involves a shift of noun classes through substitutions of the respective noun class prefixes which ultimately result into changes in meanings. The result of the changeover of the noun prefixes is a new noun which follows the singular-plural pairing and semantic classification of the new class. This process is very rich across Bantu languages (see Schadeberg 2003; Seidel 2008).

The derivations involved revolve around a selected number of classes in Kiswahili, as it is also a case in other Bantu languages. The common resultant noun-classes mostly include: (a) dimunitives as in *mtoto* 'child' [cl.1] » *kitoto* 'small child' [cl.7], (b) agumentatives such as *mto* 'river' [cl.3] » *jito* 'huge river' [cl.7], (c) derogatives like *mbwa* 'dog' » *kijibwa* 'bad small child' [cl.7], and (d) abstractions as in *mtu* 'person' [cl.1] » *utu* 'humanity' [cl.14].

This derivational process is quite productive because these new nouns can be derived from different classes. The following examples in Table 2 will help us have a better understanding of how pervasively nouns derive from other nouns in Kiswahili.

Table 2: Nouns derived from other nouns in Swahili

1. **Dinumitives**

shoka	'axe'	3	*kashoka*	'small axe'	13
mdudu	'insect'	1	*tuvidudu*	'small insects	14
wazee	'elders'	2	*tuzee*	'little elders'	14
nyumba	'house'	9	*kanyumba*	'small house'	13
ukuta	'wall'	11	*kaukuta*	'small wall'	13
visima	'wells'	8	*tuvisima*	'small wells'	14
kiti	'chair'	7	*tuviti*	'small chairs'	13

2. **Augumentatives**

shoka	'axe'	3	*lishoka*	'a big axe'	3
mdudu	'insect'	1	*jidudu*	'a big insect	5
wazee	'elders'	2	*zee*	'a big elder'	5
nyumba	'house'	9	*mjumba*	'a big house'	3
ukuta	'wall'	11	*kuta*	'a big wall'	5
visima	'wells'	8	*sima*	'a big well'	5
kiti	'chair'	7	*mkiti*	'a big chair'	3

3. **Derogatives**

mtu	'person'	1	*jitu*	'giant, ghost'	5
bibi	'grandmother'	5	*kibibi*	'mistress'	7
gari	'car'	5	*kigari*	'a bad car'	7

4. **Abstract nouns**

dini	'religion'	9	*udini*	'religiousness'	11
mzalendo	'patriot'	1	*uzalendo*	'patriotism'	5
wazee	'elders'	2	*uzee*	'elderlyhood, old age'	11
nyumba	'house'	9	*unyumba*	'sex'	5
nyama	'meat'	10	*unyama*	'animosity'	5

It seems that some significant facts could be deduced from data in Table 1 above. For the purpose of clarity, three points shall be discussed in the following paragraphs.

One, the first two resultants (dimunitives and augumentatives) are common semantic classifications across Bantu languages (see Schadeberg 2003). Kiswahili data above show that dimunitives are widely formed by addition of the noun class prefixes of classes 12 and 13. Schadeberg (2003: 83) seems to suggest that these classes have the inherent semantic feature of smallness. Augumentatives are widely formed by assigning nouns to noun-classes 3 and 5 in Kiswahili. These classes have the inherent semantic feature of largeness.

Two, the third row of resultant nouns, i.e. derogative, is not widely reported in the literature (see Schadeberg 1994; Mohamed 2001). However, Kiswahili data above show that derogatives are widely formed by addition of the noun class prefixes of classes 5 and 7. It is a plausible assumption that the classes are associated with size in that the former refers to big size (hugeness, supernaturalness) while the latter entails small size (tininess).

Three, as we see in examples, abstract nouns fall into class 11 in Kiswahili. Although some nouns are formed by prefixation of noun class 5/6 in the language, the main resulting noun class is 11.

3.2.2.2   Adjective-noun derivation in Kiswahili

The second nominal derivation in Kiswahili involves adjectives. In fact, a number of tokens show that there are possibilities of deriving nouns from adjectives in the language. Usually, nouns formed from adjectives in the language result into abstract nouns. Though there are several nouns which are formed through this derivational process in this language, perhaps the examples in Table 3 will help to summarise this point.

Table 3: Abstract nouns derived from adjectives in Swahili

Adjective		Noun	
zuri	'beautiful'	uzuri	'beauty'
baya	'bad'	ubaya	'badness'
dogo	'small'	udogo	'smallness
kubwa	'big'	ukubwa	'oldness'
kale	'old'	ukale	'oldness'
eusi	'black'	weusi	'blackness'
pole	'gentle'	upole	'politeness'
rembo	'pretty'	urembo	'decoration'
kali	'fierce'	ukali	'hushness'
janja	'crafty, canny'	ujanja	'deceit'
jinga	'silly'	ujinga	'stupidity'

Here we see that in examples of abstract nouns above, all resulting nouns fall into class 11 in Kiswahili. There could be other nouns formed by prefixation of other noun classes for such a process but I would content here that in the language, the main resulting noun class is 11.

3.2.2.3   Verb-noun derivation in kiswahili

Kiswahili permits derivation of nouns from verbs and this process is rather pervasive in the language thus its productivity is very high. This means that verbal stems are attached with nominalising affixes which then change the inherent property of verbs from verb-category into noun-category. In the literature, it follows, the other term used is **deverbal nouns** which in fact refers to nouns formed from verbal stems and roots.

In all cases, nouns derived through deverbal processes involve addition of a nominalising final vowel to a verb stem. Thus, it is through **suffixation**, particularly of derivational vowels, that we get nominals from verbs in Kiswahili. This could be obtained in words like *tega* 'to trap' [V] » *mitego* 'traps, snares' [N], *gawa* 'separate, divide' [V] » *mgawo* 'division' [N], *piga* 'hit' [V] » *mpigaji* 'striker, beater' [N], and *vaa* 'wear, put on' » *vazi* 'clothing, dress' [N].

Two important morphological issues need to be mentioned. The first issue is that each deverbal noun does carry either an overt noun class prefix like *m-* and *mi-* above or a zero noun class prefix as in *ø-vazi* 'clothing, dress'. This is because in Bantu languages like Kiswahili the noun class system is a formal characteristic of its nouns thus any noun derived from verbs is assigned with a noun-class prefix of its subsequent class.

Another issue is that deverbal nouns are associated, in most cases, with the use of two main derivational suffixes namely applicative and causative extensions. For example, the verb *enda* 'go, walk' can be causitivized by *-esh-* first hence becomes *endesha* 'drive, control' and then nominalised by suffixation to form the noun *mwendeshaji* 'administrator'. For the applicative, we may use another example here. The verb *hama* 'emigrate, evacuate, move' can be applicativized by *-i-* to generate *hamia* 'immigrate, move to' and then get nominalised by suffixation to form the noun *mhamiaji* 'emigrant, immigrant'.

It is claimed that suffixal derivational process which is highly productive in Kiswahili language, is plorific in other Bantu languages as well (see e.g. Kahigi 2005 [Sisumbwa]; Seidel 2008 [Shiyeyi]). In what follows I articulate the different kinds of nominalisation through suffixation in Kiswahili.

Nomina agentis (Agentive nouns): Although Bauer (2004) does not include it in the list of morphological terminologies, the literature on nominalisation by suffixation in some Indo-European languages tend to use the label nomina agentis rather commonly (see Strothmann 1935 [German]; Pultrová 2007 [Latin]). It is also found in Bantu nominalisations. For instance, this label, nomina agentis, is an expression which Seidel (2008a: 133) employed in the study of Shiyeyi. Schadeberg (1984: 5) uses agentive noun for Kiswahili while Schadeberg (2003: 80) utilizes the expression **agent nouns** for Bantu languages. I would not involve myself is search of proper term here because the essence of agent nouns (agentives) is related to how derbal nouns are formed in any language where nomina agentis is used.

All in all, nomina agentis is associated with the formation of nouns through suffixation of affixes which in turn change the verbs into agentive-like nominals. In Bantu languages, the notion nomina agentis revolves around the fact that the primary kind of agent nouns are derived from verbs by adding the nominalising suffix *-i* (also suffix *-aji*, as we will see below) attached to verbal stems and the resultant nouns are basically assigned to class 1/2 for humans (Schaderbg 2003: 80).

Kiswahili permits the suffixation of the nominaliser *-i* to its verbs to form nouns. Such resultant nouns indicate agents or doer of the actions embedded in the source verbs. Most of these deverbal nouns are assigned prefixes for noun-classes 1/2. Probably the following examples would help us have a better understanding of the notion nomina agentis in Kiswahili. Notice from these examples that the nomina agentis *-i* appears at the end of each nominal and the noun-class prefix is for 1/2.

(6)   *Nomina agentis in Kiswahili by suffix -i*

Source verb		Resultant nominal [cl.1/2]	
soma	'study, read'	*msomi*	'educated person, scholar'
shona	'sew'	*mshoni*	'tailor'
tema	'cut, chop'	*watemi*	'chiefs, rulers'
pika	'cook'	*mpishi*	'a cook'

This process has undergone some modification with time. Schadeberg (1984: 85) reports that the nominaliser -*i* triggers changes of the preceding consonants in Kiswahili. My data show the following nouns which have undergone morphophonological modifications once the nominaliser -i has been attached to them.

(7)   *Nomina agentis in Kiswahili through suffix -i and morphophonological changes*

Source verb		Resultant nominal [cl.1/2]	
jenga	'to build'	*mjenzi*	'masonry, builder'
tunga	'compose'	*mtunzi*	'composer'
penda	'love, like'	*mpenzi*	'lover'
penda	'love, like'	*mpenzi*	'lover'

Nomina agentis in modern Kiswahili is very productive but it has changed and recently the use of the nominalising suffix -*aji*, which does not trigger morphophonological changes of the preceding consonant, is rather pervasive. Schadeberg (1984: 5) claims that 'these changes are no loner productive; modern derivations may leave the consonant unchanged. The suffix -aji is is highly productive'.

My observation is that suffix -*aji* is pervasive in Kiswahili, as shown in (8), but in most cases it is attached to verbs associated with the causative and applicative suffixes (as described above). This might be the reason that the preceding consonant is not affected. The following words are examples of nominals formed through suffixation of -*aji* in Kiswahili. This is also shown in (9) below.

(8)   *Nomina agentis in Kiswahili by suffix -aji*

Source verb		Resultant nominal [cl.1/2]	
panga	'to rent'	*mpangaji*	'renter'
funga	'tie, score'	*mfungaji*	'scorer'
tunga	'compose'	*mtungaji*	'composer'
tenda	'to do'	*mtendaji*	'administrator'
imba	'sing'	*waimbaji*	'singers'
iga	'imitate'	*waigaji*	'imitators'
panda	'sow'	*wapandaji*	'planters'
pa	'give'	*wapaji*	'givers'
chunga	'herd, graze'	*wachungaji*	'priests'
kimbia	'run'	*wakimbiaji*	'athletes, runners'

(9)   *Nomina agentis in Kiswahili by suffix -i/-aji and verbal extensions*

Source verb		Resultant nominal [cl.1/2 and 11]	
zaa	'to give birth'	*mzalishaji*	'producer'
zunguka	'rotate'	*mzungushaji*	'cheater'
hama	'emigrate'	*wahamiaji*	'immigrants'
zaa	'to give birth'	*mzalishaji*	'producer'
zaa	'to give birth'	*uzazi*	'offspring'

Nomina pantis (Active-participant nouns): This is also a term that Bauer (2004) does not include in the glossaries of morphological terms. However, it is found in Bantu nominalisations because nomina pantis is used by Seidel (2008a: 135) in the study of Shiyeyi. Schadeberg (1984: 4) uses active participants for Kiswahili.

Such kinds of nouns are formed through addition of a nominalising suffix -a in Kiswahili. These nouns are created from verbs which typically denote patient (undergoer) of the action embedded in verbs. Most of the nouns in this group take noun class 1/2 prefixes, as shown in (10). Some nouns fall into noun classes 7/8, as indicated in (11).

(10)   *Nomina pantiis in Kiswahili by suffix -a [cl.^{1}/$_2$]*

Source verb		Resultant nominal	
uza	'sell'	*mwuza*	'seller'
enda	'go, walk'	*mwenda*	'walker'
wiwa	'go, walk'	*wawia*	'creditors'

(11)   *Nomina pantis in Kiswahili by suffix -a [cl.7/8 and 6/7]*

Source verb		Resultant nominal	
chaa	'to dawn'	*kichea*	'brightness after cloudness'
goya	'to hook'	*kigovya*	'fruit hook'
kula	'eat'	*chakula*	'food'
oa	'to marry'	*ndoa*	'marriage'

Several nouns in this category are derived from verbs which received the passive morpheme -w- in Kiswahili. Such kinds of nouns are formed through addition of a nominalising suffix -a after the passive -w- in Kiswahili, as pointed out in (12).

(12)   *Nomina pantiis in Kiswahili by suffix -a after a passive -w-*

Source verb		Resultant nominal	
funga	'tie, enclose'	*wafungwa*	'prisoner'
tuma	'send'	*mtumwa*	'slave'
pachika	'tuck, insert in'	*kipachikwa*	'affix '
zaa	'to give birth'	*wazawa*	'natives'
zaa	'to give birth'	*mzaliwa*	'native'
penda	'love'	*wapendwa*	'beloved ones'
wia	'to owe'	*wawiwa*	'debtors'

Nomina instrumenti (Instrumental nouns): Bauer (2004) has not included this in the glossary for morphology. However, it is found in Bantu nominalisations because nomina instrumenti is used by Seidel (2008a: 136) and Schadeberg (1984: 5) uses instrument nouns for Kiswahili.

Suffix -*o*: Some nouns are formed through addition of a nominalising suffix -o in Kiswahili. This is pervasive in the language, though it is not typical instruments, as illustrated in (13) whereby various nouns are formed but they don't function as instruments. These nouns are created from verbs which signify actions and essences which fall into noun-classes 3/4.

(13)   *Nomina instrumenti in Kiswahili by suffix -o*

verb		nominal		class
enda	'go, walk'	*mwenendo*	'manner'	3
zoza	'talk'	*mzozo*	'conflict'	3
dunda	'beat'	*mdundo*	'drumbeat'	3
gawa	'divide'	*migawo*	'divisions'	4
panga	'arrange'	*mipango*	'plans'	4

But there are nouns which are created from verbs which typically signify instruments. These derived nouns fall into numerous noun-classes, as exemplified in (14). Furthermore, in the language, the causative form -*iz*- (Lodhi 2002) plays a vital role in designating these nouns, as illustrated in (15).

(14)   *Nomina instrumenti in Kiswahili by suffix -o*

verb		nominal		class
tega	'to trap'	*mitego*	'traps'	4
zaa	'to give birth'	*uzao*	'offspring'	11
zaa	'to give birth'	*mazao*	'products'	6

(15)   *Nomina instrumenti in Kiswahili by suffix -o and causative* -iz-

verb		nominal		class
angalia	'watch'	*angalizo*	'warning'	4
chota	'to fetch'	*chetezo*	'censer'	7

Nominalisation by suffixes -*e* and -*u*: A couple of nouns in Kiswahili are derived through suffixation of -*e* and -*u*. Such nouns fall into numerous classes, as shown below.

(16)   *Nomina instrumenti in Kiswahili by suffix -e and -u*

verb		nominal		class
kata	'to cut'	*mikate*	'breads'	4
tulia	'to calm'	*utulivu*	'calmness'	14
tulia	'to calm'	*mtulivu*	'gentle person'	1
angalia	'to watch'	*waangalifu*	'careful people'	2
angalia	'to watch'	*uangalifu*	'carefulness'	11

zama	'to dive'	*uzamivu*	'PhD studies'	11
potea	'be lost'	*upotevu*	'loss, vandalism'	11
potea	'be lost'	*wapotevu*	'wasteful persons'	2

Nouns derived through infinitives in Swahili: In Kiswahili, and across Bantu family, infinitives are used as nouns and such nouns have the shape *ku*-stem-*a*. Schadeberg (2003: 80) says, 'from a morphological point of view, infinitives are nouns by virtue of having a nominal prefix, but also have verbal characteristics such as the possibility to include an object concord as well as a limited range of inflectional morphemes in pre-stem position…'. A couple of infinitival nouns in Kiswahili are shown in (17).

(17)   *Infinitival nouns in Swahili*

kulala	'sleeping'
kucheka	'laughing'
kulima	'to cultivate'
kukata	'to cut'
kulia	'to cry, a crying'
kuzama	'to dive'
kupotea	'to be lost'

3.3   Verbal derivational processes (verbalisations)

Mechanisms of deriving new verbs are pervasively attested in these languages. In order to offer a detailed examination of this process, in this section, we describe the various **verbalisation** processes in English and Kiswahili.

3.3.1 Verbalisation in English

Both prefixation and suffixation are involved in this process in English. However, only a couple of prefixes and suffixes are derivational in the language. Estimates in this book suggest that only 7 affixes are verbalising in the language. This is in line with Plag (2002: 116) who says 'there are four suffixes which derive verbs from other categories (mostly adjectives and nouns), *-ate, -en, -ify* and *-ize*'.

Even derivational prefixes seem to be few in English. Hammond (1993: 563) suggests that even the three category-changing prefixes in English are restricted in such a way that some relevant structures cannot be raised. He mentions the verbalising prefixes as follows: *en-, de-* and *be-* (Ibid: 564). Also, he underscores that these three prefixes are restricted and they append only to morphologically underived bases (Ibid).

The observations by Plag and Hammond above are not unique because other scholars also found that only a few affixes are involved in verbal derivation in English. For example, contemporary sources such as Dixon (2008: 32) stipulate that we should mention that there are a number of minor processes for verb derivation. In a way of capturing these facts, the verbalising suffixes in the language are captured in Table 4 while verbalising prefixes are offered in table 5.

Table 4: Verbalisation by suffixation in English

Suffix	Functions	Examples
-ate	Latinate suffix that derives heterogeneous verbs	*regular – regulate, hyphen – hyphenate, orchestra – orchestrate, vaccine - vaccinate*
-en	Germanic suffix functional to monosyllabic adjectives	*black - blacken, broad - broaden, quick -quicken, ripe – ripen, strength – strengthen, smooth – smoothen, wide – widen*
-ify	This suffix attaches to several base words	*solid – solidify, simple - simplify, class – classify, glory – glorify*
-ize, -ise	suffix that derives heterogeneous verbs	*computer – computerize, colony – colonize, memory - memorise, item - itemise*

Table 5: Verbalisation (category-changing) by prefixation in English

Prefix	Functions	Examples
en-	It creates verbs from bases (mainly adjectives)	*rich - enrich, gender – engender, able - enable, danger - endanger, courage - encourage*
be-	It makes verbs from mainly other verbs and nouns.	*come - become, fit - befit, fall - befall, friend - befriend, witch - bewitch*
de-	It forms verbs from mainly other verbs and nouns.	*grade - degrade, value – devalue, rail – derail, brief – debrief, bug - debug*

3.3.2 Verbal derivations in Kiswahili

Niger-Congo languages, particularly Bantu languages like Kiswahili construct new senses of the verbs by the use of various **verbal extensions** (see e.g. Rugemalira 1995; Lodhi 2002; Hyman 2003) and such verbal extensions have a variety of functions (Hyman 2007: 149), among others: (a) increase valence e.g. causative and applicative, (b) decrease valence e.g. passive, reciprocal, and stative, and (c) (re-)orient action e.g. reversive. Put in other words, in Bantu languages, the conceptualization of the term verbal extensions seems to involve some verbal suffixes which add new participants, like the applicative and causative which introduce a participant in a construction. Other extensions reduce participants which are passive, reciprocal, and stative tend to reduce the argument structure of the verb in question (cf. Lusekelo 2012).

Forms of verbal extensions in Bantu languages: The use of the different morphological shapes of the same verbal extension is manifested in several Bantu languages. For our purpose here, the forms of the verbal extensions in Kiswahili are provided below.

(18) a. Applicative *-i/il-*[8] *lim-i-a* 'cultivate with/for'
              som-e-a 'read at/for'
              vu-li-a 'fish with/for'

---

8 We show only the basic shapes of the extensions. In fact, some morphemes, i.e. applicative, causative, stative and reversive are raised into different forms, mainly -e/el-, -ez/esh-, -ek- and -o- respectively (cf. Lodhi 2002 for details).

b.	Causative	-ish/iz-	kat-ish-a	'cause to cut'
			wek-esh-a	'install, make to put'
			kat-iz-a	'interrupt, cause to cut'
c.	Stative	-ik-	fany-ik-a	'be done/doable'
			sem-ek-a	'be said'
d.	Reciprocal	-an-	pig-an-a	'fight'
e.	Positional	-am-	in-am-a[9]	'bend down, be bent'
			fung-am-a	'be fixedly bound'
f.	Contactive	-at-	fumb-at-a	'enclose with hands'
g.	Reversive	-u-	fung-u-a	'open'
			chom-o-a	'withdraw, draw out'
h.	Passive	-w-	pig-w-a	'be beaten'
			chuku-liw-a	'be taken'
i.	Inceptive	-p-	nene-p-a	'fatten, get fat'
			ogo-p-a	'fear'
j.	Intensive	-ili-	sik-ili-za	'listen attentively'
			pot-ele-a	'be lost for ever'

It should be born in mind that data in (18) above presents only the basic morphological realizations of the main extensions in Kiswahili. Reference to Lodhi (2002) would be necessary for readers who will prefer to get a deeper understanding of the different morphological manifestations of these extensions in Kiswahili. What is seen significant to represent in this book is the derivational power of these extensions.

Causative: The semantic contribution of the causative form -ish/iz- in Kiswahili, and in other Bantu languages as well, is to 'make/help/oblige someone (to) do something' and/or 'to make someone become somehow'. The syntactic function of the causative is to add a causee argument to the verb in question. Perhaps examples in (19) below will help to illustrate this point.

(19)   a.   *Watoto wanacheza mpira*

         Wa-toto   *wa-na-cheza*   *m-pira*

         2-child   SMpl.-PRES-play   3-ball

         'The children play soccer'

     b.   *Walimu wanawachezesha watoto mpira*

         Wa-limu   *wa-na-wa-chez-esh-a*   *wa-toto*   *m-pira*

         2-teacher   SMpl.-PRES-OM2-play-Caus-FV   2-child   3-ball

         'Teachers caused children to play soccer'

---

9 I should mention here that verbs, e.g. *inama* 'bend' carrying the positional form -*am*- in Kiswahili manifest in a fused way, i.e. decomposed behaviour of the affix hence it occurs as one unit.

The examples above show that a verb *cheza* 'play' takes one argument known as *mpira* 'ball' in (19a). The causative has added another argument of the same verb, i.e. *vijana* 'youth' hence now the verb has two arguments (19b).

Applicative: From a syntactic point of view, across Bantu languages, the applicative is succinctly assumed that it makes intransitive verbs transitive and transitive verbs super-transitive. On the other hand, as for thematic roles, the applicative provides several semantic functions to the verb. Lodhi (2002) offers various alternative semantic roles connected to applicative. In the following examples, the applicative licenses argument structures connected to the following semantic roles: as a beneficiary/benefactive which is shown by *vijana* 'youth' in (21), goal or location as indicated by *chumbani* 'in the room' in (22), as well as motive, purpose or reason illustrated by *hela* 'money' in (23).

(20) *Wageni wamewalipia ada.*
      Wa-geni   wa-me-wa-lip-i-a   ada
      2-guest   SMpl.-PST-OM2-pay-Appl-FV   fee
      'Guests have paid fees (for them)'

(21) *Wageni wamewalipia vijana ada.*
      Wa-geni   wa-me-wa-lip-i-a   vi-jana   ada
      2-guest   SMpl.-PST-OM2-pay-Appl-FV   8-youth   fee
      'Guests have paid for the youth fees'

(22) *Walinzi wamebebea matunda chumbani.*
      Wa-linzi   wa-me-beb-e-a   ma-tunda   chumba-ni
      2-guard   SMpl.-PST-carry-Appl-FV   6-fruit   7.room-Loc
      'Guards have carried fruits into the room'

(23) *Walinzi wamebebea matunda hela.*
      Wa-linzi   wa-me-beb-e-a   ma-tunda   hela
      2-guard   SMpl.-PST-carry-Appl-FV   6-fruit   money
      'Guards have carried fruits for money'

In detransitivization, verbs get affected through reduction of the number of the arguments. Therefore, ditransitive verbs become monotransitive and transitive ones change to intransitive when attached with some verbal extensions.

Reciprocal: It reduces the arguments of the verb by binding two of them together. The basic fact about the reciprocal across Bantu languages is that reciprocal verbs require more than one agent, and the agents are at the same time mutual patients of their action (Schadelberg 2003). Put in other words, reciprocal extension implies that the action of the predicate is carried out either together with or against each other. In Kiswahili example in (24b), the reciprocal brings together two arguments of the verb, i.e. the subject and object called mwananchi 'citizen', to function as one subjective plural argument, i.e. wananchi 'citizens'.

(24) a. *Mwananchi alimpiga mwananchi.*
          mw-ananchi   a-li-m-piga   mw-ananchi
          1-citizen   SMsg.-PST-OM1-hit   1-citizen
          "Citizen hit (another) citizen"

b. *Wananchi walipigana.*
   wa-nanchi   wa-li-pig-an-a
   2-citizen   SMsg.-PST-OM1-hit-Recip.-FV
   "Citizens hit one another"

Stative: This is one of the arguments reducing extension in Kiswahili, as well as in other Bantu languages. The notion stative is denoting a state-of-affairs (in fact as opposed to dynamic, denoting an action). It is expressing existence rather than an action. Said differently, the stative verb extension in stative verbs describes a state.

Functionally, it is said that the stative makes an argument (an object noun phrase) to be the subject but not an agent in a construction. Put in other words, the stative involves promotion of the object noun phrase to the subject position and completely suppression of the subject and deletes the agentivity. In fact, statives are incompatible with agentive action, i.e. it is impossible to specify an agent and adjuncts that imply agency, and in particular instruments and purpose adjuncts, are also ruled out (Seidl & Dimitriadis 2003; Mchombo 2004). Khumalo (2009: 166) puts it as:

> The stative indicates an intransitive state or condition without any special reference to an agent determining that condition. This is because the suffixation of the stative eliminates the subject NP, making it inexpressible in the syntactic structure, while converting the object NP of the input verb into the subject.

This is shown in Kiswahili whereby the stative morpheme does not allow the suppressed agent to be re-introduced in the by phrase. This is shown in (25b) whereby the object vibanda 'kiosks' has become the subject of the sentence which is related to (33a) in which the same noun e occurred as an object. Notice that the subject of (25a) is deleted.

(25) a. *Wamachinga wamejenga vibanda vizuri*
         wa-machinga   wa-li-jenga   vi-banda   vi-zuri
         2-trader   SMpl.-PST-build   8-kiosk   8-good
         'Small traders build good kiosks'

      b. *Vibanda vilijengeka vizuri*
         vi-banda   vi-li-jeng-ek-a   vi-zuri
         8-kiosk   SMpl.-PST- build-Stat.-FV 8-good
         'Kiosks were well built'

Some extensions are involved in argument re-orientation. The passive extension re-orients the position of the subject and object noun phrases of the unmarked affirmative sentence. It permits the object to be subjectivized and the subject to appear in the oblique. Scholars say that the passive is derivational in Bantu languages (Schadeberg 2003: 78). In Kiswahili, the passive construction allows the object to appear in the subject position and the subject to move to the oblique position as in (26b). In some cases speakers of Kiswahili may optionally omit the subject, as shown in (26c).

(26) a. *Mjomba alinunua kitabu.*
        m-jomba   a-li-nunua   ki-tabu
        1-uncle   SMsg.-PST-buy   7-book
        'Uncle bought a book'

      b. *Kitabu kilinunuliwa na mjomba.*
        ki-tabu   ki-li-nunu-liw-a   na   m-jomba
        7-book   SMsg.-PST-buy-Pass.-FV   by   1-uncle
        'The book was bought by uncle'

      c. *Kitabu kilinunuliwa.*
        ki-tabu   ki-li-nunu-liw-a
        7-book   SMsg.-PST-buy-Pass.-FV
        'The book was bought'

Reversive: Generally, in Kiswahili, as in other Bantu languages, the reversive extension gives the opposite meaning to the verb expressed in the simple form, either in transitive or intrasitive verbs (Schadeberg 2003)[10]. Recent studies have pointed out that semi-productive extensions like the reversive as well as non-productive extensions do indeed occur closer to the root and have implications to the order of the other less derivational extensions which occur away from the verb-root (Anderson & Kotzé 2008; & Kotzé 2008). A fewer verbs below show the reversivization of the actions embedded therein.

(27) *panga*   'arrange'   *pang-u-a*   'disarrange'
      funga   'tie'   *fung-u-a*   'untie'
      ezeka   'thatch'   *ez-u-a*   'up-roof'
      tandika   'spread out'   *tand-u-a*   'roll on'
      tega   'trap'   *teg-u-a*   'untrap'
      choma   'pierce'   *chom-o-a*   'up-root, remove'
      tata   'tangle'   *tat-u-a*   'disentangle'

Sequencing of verbal extensions: Generally, Bantu verbal complexes allow concatenation of several morphemes which function to designate both inflectional functions and derivational goals. Such verbal affixes are ordered in a way that they form some specific fashion of occurrences which are obeyed in order to maintain grammaticality. There are sequences of derivational patterns in Bantu languages (see Rugemalira 1995; Hyman 2003). Therefore, one of the contributions of this book is to look into the details of the possibilities of sequencing of all derivational affixes in Kiswahili.

Looked at a close range, the morphological template that fixes the preferred order of the derivational morphemes on the basis of principles independent of syntactic derivation or semantic composition can be traced back to the work of Hyman (2003) who noted a recurrence of the order Causative-Applicative-Reciproca-Passive (CARP). The reconstructed proto-Bantu forms are shown below.

---

10 A number of verbs in Kiswahili seem to show opposite meanings but it becomes impossible to parse the forms, e.g. *vaa* 'put on' : *v-u-a* 'put off' [instead of *vuwa*] and *tia* 'put into': toa 'put out' [?*towa*].

(28)	Causative	Applicative	Reciprocal	Passive	[Hyman 2003: 66]
	*- ịc- »	- ịd- »	-an- »	-u-	

Perhaps a fewer examples from Kiswahili will help to illustrate this template[11]. The examples in (28) above present all the extensions in Hyman's (2003) CARP template and demonstrates that the order of the extensions in Kiswahili could be reciprocal-causative-applicative-passive. One differing order shown is that of the reciprocal preceding the causative.

(29) *Ma-harusi*[12]   *hawa*   *wa-li-fung-an-ish-i-w-a*   *Karimjee*
      2.bridal couple 2.these 3plSM-PST-tie-Rec-Caus-Appl-Pass-FV Karimjee
      'These bridal couple were made to wed each other in the Karimjee (hall)'

(30) *Ma-jogoo wa-wili*   *wa-ta-pamb-an-ish-i-w-a*   *hela*
      6-rooster 2-two   3plSM-FUT-?fight-Rec-Caus-Appl-Pass-FV 9.money
      'The two roosters will be made to fight for money'

That is not the only templatic paradigm available for Bantu languages. Generally, their findings demonstrate that Bantu languages have strict patterns of ordering of these extensions. However, their investigations concentrate on the co-occurrences of few extensions. For example, Hyman (2003) deals only with four productive extensions, namely the causative, applicative, reciprocal and passive hence his postulation of CARP template. In addition to the extensions investigated by Hyman (2003), addition of the stative -ik- is made in some studies, e.g. Rugemalira (1995) who examines the ordering of five productive extensions in Runyambo. Nonetheless, frozen and semi-productive verbal extensions are left out even in these studies. This book, therefore, investigates the ordering of the frozen verbal extensions, semi-productive extensions as well as productive extensions in Bantu languages with special reference to Kiswahili.

Very current studies of the Bantu verbal extensions which focus on the sequencing of more extensions produce interesting results. For example, in their computational approach, Anderson and Kotzé (2008) and Kotzé (2011) examine the co-occurrences of almost 20 extensions in the Northern Sotho [Lesotho] from a computational point of reference. They recognized that all Bantu extensions do occur in four slots within the verbal complex in the language. Thus, they established the templatic order summarized, for the purpose of discussion and argumentation in this book, in (31).

(31) Order of all extensions in Northern Sotho (Kotzé 2011: 31)

P1	P2	P3	P4
Root-attached	**Medial**	**Penultimate**	**Pre-final vowel**
Contactive -ar-	Reversive -ol/olog-, -og-	Causative -is-	Passive -w-
Positional -am-	Associative -agan/akan-	Aplicative -el-	

---

11 The materials discussed hereunder were also presented at the *Conference of the 50 Years of Kiswahili as a Language of Unity, Liberalization and Renaissance* at Blue Pearl Hotel, Dar es Salaam, organised by the Institute of Kiswahili Studies, 4-6 October 2012.

12 Both *arusi* and *harusi* 'wedding' are available in Kiswahili lexicon (see TUKI 2001).

Intensive -agal-	Reciprocal -an-
Dispersive -alal-	Neutro-passive -eg-

Following Anderson and Kotzé (2008) and Kotzé (2011), the motivation for examining almost all verbal extensions in Kiswahili arose due to three reasons. One, the reversive in Northern Sotho occurs in a tier closer to the verbal root. This entails that reversivization is a derivational process which takes place before other derivations. The same needs to be investigated in Kiswahili. Two, though frozen or lexicalized verbal extensions seem to occur very close to the verb-stem in Northern Sotho, their derivational power is neglected in previous studies. Thus, this book looks into the analysis of the derivational power of the frozen extensions in Kiswahili. Three, it seems that the grammar of Northern Sotho separates the passive form -w- from productive extensions into inflectional slot. This is also observed in other Bantu languages like Kagulu [Tanzania] (Petzell 2008) whereby the passive form functions more like a tense and aspect marker rather than a derivational morpheme. It follows therefore that Hyman's (2003) templatic order needs re-examination with regard to the status of the passive in Bantu languages.

In these analyses, the distinction between frozen, semi-productive and full productive extensions is not made. It will be evident in the discussion herein that the positional, contactive and intensive are lexicalized extensions because their semantics depend on the entire stem and finding their underived counterparts in the language is an endeavour that yields no results. The reversive seems to fall into the semi-productive extension because it occurs in a fewer verb-roots in Kiswahili. The rest of the extensions are pervasive in the grammar of the language. Having said that, in what follows, I present the restrictions of distributions of the Kiswahili verbal extensions.

In Kiswahili, the lexicalized extensions, namely positional -am- and contactive -at- always occur closer to the verb-roots than semi-productive and productive extensions and never otherwise. (32) is illustrative of this case. In (32a) the positional occurs before the reciprocal -an- while in (32b) the contactive precedes the causative -ish-. As indicated in (32c) and (32d), such orders are strictly observed in order to maintain grammaticality.

(32) a. *fung-am-a* 'be squeezed'   *fung-am-an-a* 'be allied together'

　　 b. *fumb-at-a* 'grasp in a hand' *fumb-at-ish-a* 'cause to enclose with hands'

　　 c. **fung-an-am-a*

　　 d. **fumb-ish-at-a*

Although Kihore et al. (2003) do not stipulate, it seems that Standard Kiswahili allows the stative form -ik- to precede productive extensions. The examples in (41) illustrate this point. In (33c) the stative -ek- precedes the causative -ez- and in (33d) the stative precedes both the causative and reciprocal. This suggests that Hyman's (2003) CARP needs to be expanded in order to include the stative which is a very productive extension in Kiswahili.

(33) a. *pend-a*   'like'

　　 b. *pend-ek-a*   'be liked'

　　 c. *pend-ek-ez-a*   'recommend'

　　 d. *pend-ek-ez-an-a* 'recommend each other'

Co-occurrences of all verbal extensions: The first issue to be addressed in this section revolves around ordering of productive extensions in Kiswahili. Bantu languages allow several extensions to be concatenated (cf. Rugemalira 1995; Hyman 2003; Schadeberg 2003). As for Kiswahili, the maximum number of extensions co-occurrnces is not yet fully explored. Kihore et al. (2003) seem to imply that Standard Kiswahili permits four levels of combinations of verbal extensions. Following the co-occurrence of the highly productive extensions (Rugemalira 1995; Krüger 2006) or penultimate positioned extensions (Anderson & Kotzé 2008; Kotzé 2011), Kiswahili may permit up to four extensions. This is illustrated in (34).

(34) *Mabondia hawa*   *ha-wa-ta-pig-an-ish-i-w-a*   *Karimjee*

     2.boxer   2.these   Neg-3plSM-FUT-hit-Rec-Caus-Appl-Pass-FV   Karimjee

     'These boxers will not be made to fight each other in Karimjee (hall)'

The Kiswahili monotransitive verb piga 'hit' in (33) above accommodates four extensions ordered as follows: reciprocal-causative-applicative-passive. This order seems to apply, except for the reciprocal preceding the causative, to CARP templatic order. Kihore et al. (2003) suggest that reciprocalization precedes causativization for semantic reasons: an action of hitting each other should be manifested first before other actions. This entails that intended semantics plays a vital role in dictating order of extensions.

The reciprocal in Kiswahili seems to appear closer to the root because in some verbs, semantics associated with the reciprocal tend to be lexicalized in some verbs. Mkude (2005) shows that some verbs tend to demonstrate lexicalized extensions which could hardly be separated from the core-roots. Such verbs will eventually dictate the reciprocal to precede other productive extensions hence disturb the CARP templatic order. Perhaps an example in (35) will help to illustrate this point.

(35) *Ma-jogoo wa-wili wa-ta-pamb-an-ish-i-w-a*   *hela*

     6-rooster   2-two   3plSM-FUT-?fight-Rec-Caus-Appl-Pass-FV   9.money

     'The two roosters will be made to fight for money

As shown in (35) above, the verb pambana 'contest [one another]' seems to have the reciprocal form -an- which of course provides the reading contest or fight each other. While TUKI (2001) list it as a lexical entry, Mkude (2005) suggests that such verbs have lexicalized reciprocals. I will argue here that the reciprocal which precedes the causative in Kiswahili has either being lexicalized or is in the process of being lexicalized. Also, I will term such extensions, for convenience purposes, semi-frozen extensions. This argument is backed up by evidence that several verbs in Kiswahili tend to support the CARP templatic order by permitting the reciprocal to appear after the causative, as shown in (37). In fact, the order we get typically fits the CARP template. Therefore, lexicalization of the reciprocal has implications to the four positions of verbal extensions provided by Anderson and Kotzé (2008) and Kotzé (2011).

(36) Vi-jana   hawa   wa-li-pang-ish-i-an-a   vyumba

8-youth   2.these   3plSM-PST-rent-Caus-Appl-Rec-FV   8.room

'These teenagers made to rent for each other the rooms'

(37) Wa-chezaji   wa-na-in-am-ish-i-an-a   ukuta-ni
2-player   3plSM-PRES-?bend-Pos-Caus-Appl-Rec-FV   11.wall-LOC
'The players make each other lean on the wall'

(38) Vi-jana ha-wa-wezi   ku-fumb-at-an-ish-i-an-a   hadhara-ni
8-youth Neg-3plSM-be Inf-?hold-Cont-Rec-Caus-Appl-Rec-FV   public-LOC
'The teenagers cannot make to enclose in hands each other in public

(39) Wa-fungwa   wa-li-fung-u-li-an-a   mi-lango
2-prisoner   3plSM-PST-open-Rev-Appl-Rec-FV   4-door
'The prisoners opened the doors for each other'

One may notice the different positioning of the applicative in examples above. Another topic for discussion in this section revolves around concatenation of Apart from the contradicting results for the ordering of semi-frozen and productive extensions mentioned above; typically frozen extensions co-occur with productive ones. The question posed above, i.e. what would be the upper limit constraints for the co-occurrence of the frozen, semi-productive and productive extensions in Kiswahili is to be answered now. In fact, data points towards the fact that Kiswahili verbs may allow up to four levels. May be the following examples will help us have a better understanding of this point.

At this point, the four levels of concatenation of the extensions in Kiswahili provided in Kihore et al. (2003) are maintained even when frozen, semi-frozen and productive extensions are used. This is shown in (37) where the positional form -am- co-occurs with the causative, applicative and reciprocal and in (38) whereby the contactive -at- co-occurs with the semi-frozen reciprocal, causative, applicative and productive reciprocal.

Moreover, in the order of all the extensions in Kiswahili, the reversive extension tends to precede productive extensions hence it follows under semi-frozen extensions. One example above is illustrative of the fact that the reversive occur before the applicative and reciprocal in Kiswahili.

The reversive in Bantu languages, e.g. Northern Sotho, occurs in a tier closer to the verbal root (Anderson & Kotzé 2008; Kotzé 2011). This has implications to the ordering of the frozen and productive extensions in Kiswahili. In fact it entails that reversivization is a derivational process which takes place before other derivations, namely causativization, applicativization, reciprocalization as well as passivization. Also, the frozen or lexicalized verbal extensions seem to occur very close to the root. Their lexicalization is arrived at because either no verbs which occur without them in daughter languages or the meanings of the verbs associated with them seem to point towards productivity that resulted from the attachment of the extensions.

So far, the order of the frozen and reversive extensions points towards another issue, i.e. slots for the extensions. In fact, for Kiswahili, at this juncture, I will propose the template in (449). This has been arrived at following the discussion above.

(39) **Frozen**   **Semi-frozen**   **Productive**
   Positional *-am-*   Reversive *-u-*   Causative *-ish-*
   Contactive *-at-*   Applicative *-i-*
                                                     Reciprocal *-an-*
                                                     Passive *-w-*

3.4   Adjectival suffixes (adjectivisation)

3.4.1 Adjectivisation in English

Plag (2002) argues that adjectival suffixes of English are used either to derive **relational adjectives,** i.e. relate the noun the adjective qualifies to the base word of the derived adjective, e.g. *algebraic mind* means 'a mind having to do with algebra' or **qualitative adjectives,** i.e. expresses specific concepts like *grammatical*.

The following table offers a list of 12 tokens of adjectivising affixes in the language.

Table 6: Adjectivising affixes in English

Affix	Explanation	Examples
-able	Append to transitive and intransitive verbal bases	*perishable, fashionable, breakable, knowledgeable*
-al	It attaches exclusively to Latinate bases	*accidental, colonial, cultural, institutional*
-ary	It attaches to nouns	*complement – complementary, evolution - evolutionary, moment - momentary*
-ed	It appends to compounds or phrases	*empty-headed, fair-minded broad-minded*
-esque	It appends to common and proper nouns	*picturesque*
-ful	It creates adjectives meaning 'having X	*forgetfull, beautiful, purposeful, tactful*
-ic	It attaches to foreign bases	*economic – economomical, historic -historical, magic - magical*
-ish	This suffix can attach to adjectives	*clearish, freeish, sharpish, childish*
-ive	It forms adjectives mostly from Latinate verbs	*connective, explosive, offensive, passive, preventive, primitive*

-less	It derives adjectives from nouns	*hopeless, speechless, thankless*
-ly	It derives adjectives from nouns	*brotherly, fatherly, womanly*
-ous	It derives adjectives from nouns	*erroneous, homogeneous, ambiguous,*

3.4.2 Adjectivisation in Kiswahili

Kiswahili language, as other Bantu languages, has a few words which are core (typical) adjectives, a few examples are offered in (40). Since thre is only a restricted number of adjectives in Kiswahili, only a few of them denote colour hence colour-adjectives (40a). A few other adjectives denote age (40b), while some designate size (40c). Other adjectives show some characteristics, e.g. human prospensity (40d).

(40)   a.   *-eupe* 'white'

                -eusi 'black'

   b.   *-kuu* 'old, big'

                -zee 'old'

   c.   *-refu* 'tall'

                -fupi 'short'

   d.   *-zuri*   'beautiful'

                -baya   'bad'

A number of adjective related modifications, however, are made possible through the use of verbal expressions which are derived into adjective-like words. This is a property of Bantu languages because studies also show that nominal expressions function to designate adjectival roles in Bantu languages (Shembuli 2010).

The suffix -fu: Several verbs can be adjectivised using the suffix *-fu* in Kiswahili (Lodhi 2001). Several of these adjectives become stative adjectives perhaps because they are created from stative (intransitive) verbs by suffixation of *-fu*, as in (41a). Some verbs of Arabic origin become adjectives after affixation (Shembuli 2010), as in (41b).

(41)   **Verbs**   **Adjectives**

   a.   *sumbua* 'to trouble'   *msumbufu* 'stubborn'

             changamka 'be jovial'   *mchangamfu* 'jovial'

             punguka 'be reduced'   *upungufu* 'deficiency'

             angalia 'take care'   *angalifu* 'careful'

   b.   *amini* 'believe, trust'   *uaminifu* 'truthfulness, honesty'

             haribu 'destroy '   *haribisu* 'destructive'

             baini 'realise'   *bainifu* 'evident'

             zini 'fornicate'   *zinifu*   'adulterous'

             sahau 'forget'   *sahaulifu* 'forgetful'

The suffix -vu: Some original Kiswahili verbs can be adjectivised using the suffix -*vu*, as shown in (31). Such derived adjectives show the state.

(42)

Verbs	Adjectives
iva 'to ripen'	*bivu* 'ripe' [mbivu 'ripe']
oza 'to rote'	*bovu* 'rotten'
uma 'be enjured, hurt'	*maumivu* 'pain'
legea 'be loose'	*legevu* 'slackness, weakness'

There are a few words which seem to behave like ajectives after suffixing -*o*. However, analysis suggests that a few Kiswahili verbs can be nominalised using the suffix -*o*, as shown in (43) to denote 'state'.

(43)

Verbs	Nominal expressions
fukuta 'burn without flame'	*fukuto* 'burning heat'
poromoka 'fall'	*maporomoko* 'water falls'

3.5   Other prefixes and their functions

A number of other affixes perform derivational work. This section is therefore offering illustrations of these affixes. First, we begin by describing the origin of most of these affixes before we turn to their functions.

English affixes have three places of origin. First, in many literatures, the mentioned English suffixes of Latin origin include: -*ant*; -*able-*, -*ible*, -*fy*; and -*ous*. Also, Latinate prefixes in English comprise: *de*, *di-*, *dis-*, *ex-*, *extra-*, *im-* (English *in-*), *inter-*, *pre-*, *sub-*, and *trans-* (Bauer 1983; Plag 2002; Minkova & Stockwell 2009).

Second, a number of prefixes in English are native. This means that several prefixes in the language are indigenous and were not borrowed from other languages, e.g. *in-* (Bauer 1983; Plag 2002; Minkova & Stockwell 2009).

Other affixes in English are of French origin. Zbierska-Sawala (1989) presents some 20 tokens of the French suffixes in Middle English. She offers some examples which appear to be used in contemporary English as well: -*able merciable*, -*al colonial*, -*ance ignorance*, -*ise sacrefise* etc.

Other clusters of English prefixes can be deduced based on semantics. Plag (2002: 123-124) says prefixes of English can be classified semantically into the following groups.

Quantifying prefixes: e.g. 'one' (*uni-*, *unilateral*, *unification*), 'twice or two' (*bi-*, *bilateral*, *bisyllabic* and *di-* *disyllabic*, *ditransitive*), 'many' (*multi-*, *multi-purpose*, *multi-lateral* and *poly-*, *polysyllabic*, 'half' (*semi-*, *semi-conscious*, *semi-desert*), 'to excess' (*hyper-*, *hyperactive*, *hypermarket* and *over-*, *overestimate*, *overtax*), 'not sufficiently' (*undernourish*, *underpay*) etc.

Locative prefixes: e.g. around' (*circumnavigate*, *circumscribe*), *counter-* 'against' (*counterbalance*, *counterexample*), *endo-* 'internal to X' (*endocentric*), *inter-* 'between' (*interbreed*, *intergalactic*), *intra-* 'inside' (*intramuscular*, *intravenous*), *trans-* 'across' (*transcontinental*, *transmigrate*) etc.

Temporal prefixes: 'before' (*pre* and *fore-*) *predetermine, premedical, forefather, foresee*), 'after' (*post-, poststructuralism, postmodify, postmodern*), or 'new' (*neo-, neoclassical, Neo-Latin*).

Prefixes expressing **negation**: e.g. *de-, dis-, in-, non-, un-* as in demerit, disadvantage, nonsense etc.

Table 7: Prefixes of negation in English

Prefix	Examples
a-	*asexual* 'without sex', *ahistorical* 'without history
anti-	*anti-war, anti-abortion, anti-capitalistic*
de-	*decolonize*
dis-	*disqualify, disassemble, dismantle, disagree*
in-	*Intolerable, implausible, incomprehensible*
mis-	*mispronounce, misreport, mismatch*
non-	*non-returnable, nonscientific,*
un-	*uncork, unwind, unwrap*
ir-	*irregular*
il-	*illegal*

Resources used:

Anderson, Winston. M. & Kotzé, Albert E. 2008. Verbal extension sequencing: An examination from a computational perspective. *Literator,* 29(1). pp. 43-64.

Dixon, Robert M.W. 2008. Deriving verbs in English. *Language Sciences,* vol. 30: 31–52.

Hammond, Michael. 1993. On the absence of category-changing prefixes in English. *Linguistic inquiry,* vol. 24(3): 562-567

Hyman, Larry M. 2003. Suffix ordering in Bantu: A morphocentric approach. In: Booij, Geert & Marle, Jaap van (eds.). *Yearbook of Morphology.* Dordrecht: Kluwer Academic. pp. 245-281.

Hyman, Larry M. 2007. Niger-Congo verb extensions: Overview and discussion. In: Payne, Doris L. and Jaime Peña (eds.) *Selected Proceedings of the 37th Annual Conference on African Linguistics.* Somerville, MA: Cascadilla Proceedings Project. pp. 149-163.

Katamba, Francis. 2003. Bantu nominal morphology. In: Nurse, Derek & Philippson, Gérard (eds.) *The Bantu languages.* London: Routledge. pp. 103-120.

Kotzé, Albert E. 2011. Lexical generality as a determinant of extension position in Northern Sotho. *South African Journal of African Languages,* 31(1): 30-40.

Krüger, Caspar J.H. 2006. *Introduction to the Morphology of Setswana.* Muenchen: Lincom Europa.

Lodhi, Abdulaziz Y. 2001. The suffixes *-fu* and *-vu* in Swahili: A preliminary analysis.

Africa & Asia, vol. 1: 35-39.

Lodhi, Abdulaziz Y. 2002. Verbal extensions in Bantu: The case of Swahili and Nyamwezi. *Africa & Asia,* vol. 2: 4-26.

Lusekelo, Amani 2012. *Inflectional and Derivational Morphology in Optimality Theory: Multiple Object-nouns and Co-occurrence of Verbal Extensions in Kinyakyusa.* Doctorla thesis, University of Botswana.

Maho, Jouni. 1999. *A Comparative Study of Bantu Noun Classes.* Gothenburg: Acta Universitatis Gothoburgensis.

Newman, Paul. 1990. *Nominals and Verbal Plurality in Chadic.* Dordretch: Foris Publications.

Nurse, Derek & Philippson, Gérard. (eds.) (2003). *The Bantu Languages.* London: Routledge.

Payne, Doris L. & Derek Olsen. 2009. Maa (Maasai) nominalization: Animacy, agentivity and instrument. In: Matondo, Masangu, Fiona Mc Laughlin, and Eric Potsdam (eds.). *Selected Proceedings of the 38th Annual Conference on African Linguistics.* Somerville, MA: Cascadilla Proceedings Project. pp. 151-165.

Petzell, Malin. 2008. *The Kagulu Language of Tanzania: Grammar, Texts and Vocabulary.* Köln: Rüdiger Köppe Verlag.

Rugemalira, Josephat M. 1995. Verb extensions in Runyambo. *Afrikanistische Arbeitspapiere (AAP),* 41: 51-87.

Schadeberg, Thilo. 1984 [1992]. *A Sketch of Swahili Morphology.* Dordrecht: Foris Publications.

Schadeberg, Thilo C. 2003. Derivation. In: Nurse, Derek and Gérard Philippson. (eds.). *The Bantu Languages.* London: Routledge. pp. 71-89.

Seidel, Frank. 2008. *A grammar of Yeyi. A Bantu Language of Southern Africa.* Köln: Rüdiger Köppe Verlag.

Shembilu, Musa M.S. 2010. Mabadiliko ya kifonolojia na kimofolojia wakati wa utohoaji maneno ya Kiarabu katika Kiswahili: Mifano kutoka Kamusi ya Kiswahili Sanifu (TUKI 2004). *KISWAHILI: Journal of the Institute of Kiswahili Studies,* vol. 73: 45-57.

Strothmann, F.W. 1935. The influence of aspect on the meaning of "Nomina Agentis" in Modern German. The Jornal of English and Germanic Philogogy, vol. xxxiv (2) 188-200

Williams, Edwin. 1981. On the notions 'lexically related' and 'head of a word'. *Linguistic inquiry,* vol. 12(2): 245-274.

Zbierska-Sawala, Anna. 1989. On the status of the French derivational suffixes in Early Middle English. *Studia anglica posnaniensia,* XXII: 91-99.

Exercise Three

3. 1. How many derivational affixes are there in English language?
        Mention them.

    2. Providing relevant examples, differentiate the derivational affixes
        mentioned in (3.1) above into those occupying prefixal position and
        suffixal position in English words.

3.2 It is established by various linguists that Bantu languages are very rich in
     verbal affixes which are derivational in nature (cf. Lodhi 2002; Hyman 2003;
     Schadeberg 2003; Lusekelo (2012). Select one Bantu language of your choice
     and investigate its verbal extensions. Then provide a short essay to describe the
     derivational verbal affixes in that language.

4 Inflection

4.1 Defining inflection

There is a close relationship between morphology and syntax because syntax requires morphology to bring certain things such as agreement devices for syntactic operations to work. Likewise, some morphological changes target syntactic demands. Focal languages in this book demonstrate a broad pattern of inflectional systems which interact with syntax. This means that several mechanisms are employed in order for the speakers of these languages to accommodate the whole required information during their conversations. Even beyond the target languages in the book, the inflectional features are several and differ from language to language. Using French, Battye et al. (2000: 121) say:

> In summary, words like *avocates* 'advocate', *grande* 'big' and *voit* 'see' are bundles of linguistic information. Besides its dictionary meaning, each contains units of **grammatical meaning**. In the case of nouns and adjectives this relates to **gender** and **number**; in the case of finite verbs it relates to **subject agreement** features and **tense**. Units of meaning, whether dictionary meaning or grammatical meaning, are called morphemes, and are the minimal units of grammatical analysis.

One major point which is inflection is composed of a kind of affixation that involves change of word-forms. Again, using French, Battye et al. (2000: 124) say:

> We saw number and gender making on nouns and adjectives, as well as subject agreement and tense marking on finite verbs. Morphological processes adding grammatical meaning are inflectional morphology. ... Apart from the meaning added, inflectional morphology can be recognized in two other ways. First, it doesn't change the word category: *advocates* 'promoter' and *advocat* 'promoter' are both nouns.... Second, inflectional morphology is productive, generally applying in all suitable contexts.

If we could consider only one language, say French as in above, then the notion of inflection would be to some extend narrower or detailed because each language has some kind of language-specific ways of marking inflectional morphology. In this line, Bauer (2004: 55) has provided the following view:

> **Inflection** or **inflectional morphology** is the morphology which provides different forms of the same word to show the role that word plays in a sentence.

These different forms are traditionally set out as **paradigms**. Inflectional morphology is the most syntactic relevant type of morphology, which is obligatory in a particular syntactic construction and which typically has a form associated with every cell in a paradigm. [emphasis hers]

This is the first part which is very essential for the analysis of inflectional morphology in Kiswahili because it hints on the paradigmatic approach to morphology.

Secondly, various functions of the inflectional morphology are captured in the definition of Bauer (2004), as she says:

Inflection can be divided into 'contextual' inflection, which is the morphology demanded by the construction in which the word occurs..... and 'inherent' inflection, which is the inflectional morphology that is not due to agreement, but which is usually chosen independent of the syntactic construction.... (Bauer 2004: 55).

Using Indo-European languages like Italian and French, she mentions that the former (contextual inflection) is associated with case and agreement patterns while the latter (inherent inflection) is connected to tense and aspect.

This book, therefore, offers a brief discussion of the broad topical issues about the syntactic features surrounding the inflectional morphology. In fact, the grammatical features (given in order of presentation here) in (1) are dealt with and their coverage provides a background to the broad spectrum of the inflectional morphology in the world's languages.

(1) i.   *Number*
     ii.   *Negation*
     iii. *Tense, aspect and modality (mood)*
     iv.   *Gender*
     v.   *Agreement and concord patterns*
     vi.   *Case*

4.2   Inflections in Kiswahili

4.2.1 Number (singularity-plurality distinctions)

Number is one of the main inflectional features manifesting in the morphology of African languages. Bauer (2004: 79) says that number is a morphological category, usually marked on a noun or pronoun, but also shown by agreements with verb, adjectives and determiners, which shows how many entities are perceived as being involved. In what follows, I offer the results of the survey of the various number marking strategies.

Number is one of the inflectional features marked in Kiswahili. Two important ideas are worth noting for the number system in Kiswahili. First, Kiswahili makes use of two-way-distinction of number. This means that nouns and adjectives are either in singular or plural. The singular number involves individual items (single entities) while the plural counts from two onwards to many items.

Second, the noun class system provides both singular and plural pairings of the nouns in the language. This is a very important means of encoding number in Kiswahili, as well as in other Bantu languages. Table 1 below shows the correspondences between singular and plural in Kiswahili nominal system. Notice that only noun classes 1 to 13 can occur in singular-plural pairings.

Table 1: Singular-plural pairings in Kiswahili

Singular			Plural		
class	Example		class	Example	
1	*mume*	husband	2	*waume*	husbands
	muuguzi	nurse		*wauguzi*	nurses
	mvulana	boy		*wavulana*	boys
	mzazi	parent		*wazazi*	parents
3	*mnazi*	coconut tree	4	*minazi*	coconut trees
	mzabibu	grape vine		*mizabibu*	grape vines
	mzizi	root		*mizizi*	roots
	mbuni	coffee tree		*mibuni*	coffee trees
5	*jiwe*	stone	6	*mawe*	stones
	jino	tooth		*meno*	teeth
	tawi	branch		*matawi*	branches
	wimbi	wave		*mawimbi*	waves
7	*kiti*	chair	8	*viti*	chairs
	kiongozi	leader		*viongozi*	leaders
	kipofu	blind person		*vipofu*	blind persons
	kikombe	cup		*vikombe*	cups
	kitoto	bad child	8	*vitoto*	bad children
	kimeza	bad table	8	*vimeza*	bad tables
9	*ng'ombe*	cow	10	*ng'ombe*	cows
	nyama	meat		*nyama*	meat
	nyumba	house		*nyumba*	houses
11	*ubao*	wood	10	*mbao*	boards
	ubale	slice		*mbale*	slices
	ubawa	wing		*mbawa*	wings
	ubavu	rib		*mbavu*	ribs
	ubati	small whip		*mbati*	small whips
12	*katoto*	small child	13	*tutoto*	small children
	kakiti	small chair		*tuviti*	small chairs
	kameza	small table		*tumeza*	small tables

As for Kiswahili, in fact the same applies to all Bantu languages, Table 1 above shows how nouns in singular (first column) undergo morphological changes through prefixation when they turn into plural form (second column). However, this is a simplified way of indicating singular-plural distinctions in Swahili[13]. There are number of nouns which show features of one class but may fall in another class. Further, some nouns fit in several patterns.

This description is also accepted by scholars such as Schadeberg (2001: 11) and Kihore et al. (2003: 97-98) who argue that Kiswahili permits singular-plural distinctions for nominals which are from the same noun class. Said in another way, change of the shape of the noun class tends to indicate either singularity or plurality of the nominals in the language. Also, the change of the agreement forms in the verbal complex may denote singularity or plurality of the construction in question.

4.2.2 Negation in Kiswahili

As one of the grammatical functions discussed under inflectional morphology, **negation**, particularly in Bantu languages in general manifests in diverse ways though the following three strategies available in the literature: lexical words, particles and verbal affixes (see Beaudoin-Lietz 1999; Güldemann 1999; Ngonyani 2003; Nurse 2008).

In addition, negation formatives in Bantu languages occupy slot of the verbal complex (see Meussen 1967: 108; Maho 2007: 215-216; Nurse 2008: 31). Thus, these formatives co-exist with other markers of functional categories including tense, aspect and mood. It is established that any negation morpheme may be constrained by the TAM of the verb under consideration (see Swilla 1998; Beaudoin-Lietz 1999; Tanda & Neba 2005).

Furthermore, it is noted that negation in Bantu languages is associated with phonological and morphological modifications (Tanda & Neba 2005). The interaction between phonological and morpho-syntactic processes lead to the influence that the negation affix may replace functional categories in a construction. Therefore, there is a need to carefully treat the morphological processes associated with these formatives in order to come out with a clear picture of what is attested in the language.

The main mechanism for negation is associated with the presence of a negative formative which is used regularly in Bantu language to express negation (Guthrie 1967: 40). This formative occupies pre-initial, post-initial and post-final positions. Many Bantu languages make use of pre-initial negative with a proto-form *-ka- (Güldemann 1999).

Some Bantu languages make of use a post-initial negative with a proto-form *-ti- (Güldemann 1999). Moreover, in a number of Bantu languages, the use of post-final (post-verbal) negation marker is attested.

The second strategy used to mark negation involves lexical items which occur in the final position in a sentence. These words which perform negation function do occur as particles in Bantu languages like Chingoni (Tanzania) which has a particle *lepa* 'no' (Ngonyani 2003) and Matuumbi (Tanzania) which has the particle *liili* 'not' (Odden 1996).

In addition, some Bantu languages make use of lexical entries which are not particles in order to encode negation. Guthrie (1967: 41) found that in some Bantu languages there are negative elements to which an abstracted meaning only can be assigned because they

---

13 These prefixes show two functions, demunitive and number, however, at this juncture I will not go into intricate issues of this case.

occur in negative verbals for which there is no parallel affirmative verbal. A good example is Kiswahili which has some of the following words which are used for negation: *hakuna* 'deny', *hapana* 'don't have', and *pasipo* 'without' (see Beaudoin-Lietz 1999; Schicho 1992).

In this section, details about negation strategies in Kiswahili have been explored. As evident in what follows, two studies are used to uncover what transpires in the languages as regards to this grammatical function.

Ngonyani (2001: 18, 21, 23) mentions that there are four strategies for expressing sentential negation in Swahili: (i) negation in tensed clauses which uses the marker *si-* (for first person singular) and *ha-* (for the rest), (ii) the prefix *-si-* used in prohibitive forms and in relative clauses, (iii) the negative copula *si* which replaces the affirmative copula *ni*, and (iv) the use of *kuto-* in gerundive and infinitival clauses.

On the other hand, it is claimed that three negation markers are associated with the verbal complex in Kiswahili. Beaudin-Lietz (1999: 213) mentions the formatives *ha-*, *-si-* and *-to-*. These negation markers are distinguished in the verbal construction by a number of mechanisms. The formatives *ha-* and *-to-* can only occur as bound morphemes while a morpheme *-si-* occurs as a free morpheme.

All in all, negation in Kiswahili involves all the strategies mentioned by these two scholars. In what follows, examples are provided to substantiate the different patterns of negations in the language.

(2)   a.   *Hajafika nyumbani.*
            ha-ja-fika   *nyumba-ni*
            SM3sg.Neg-PRES-arrive 9.home-Loc
            'She/he has not arrived home'

      b.   *Hatofika[14] nyumbani.*
            ha-to-fika   *nyumba-ni*
            SM3sg.Neg-FUT-arrive 9.home-Loc
            'She/he will not arrive home'

      c.   *Sitofika nyumbani.*
            si-to-fika   *nyumba-ni*
            SM1sg.Neg-FUT-arrive 9.home-Loc
            'I will not arrive home'

      d.   *Umasikini si kilema.*
            u-masikini   *si*   *ki-lema*
            14-poverty   Neg   7-disability
            'Poverty is not disability'

Examples in (2) show various negation affixes in Kiswahili. It is necessary to underscore two important points herein. One, as Beaudin-Lietz (1999) cautions, these formatives cannot co-occur in the same simple verbal construction and not one of the three markers can co-occur with either of the other two in the same verbal construction.

---

14 The form -*ta*- is also used for negation in Kiswahili, thus (2b), for instance, could also read *Hatafika nyumbani* 'She/he will not arrive home'.

Two, the formative *ha-* seems to perform two grammatical functions in Kiswahili. On the one hand *ha-* and *si-* designate the subject which has the features person (third person) and number (singular). On the other hand, it embeds negations in itself. Such kind of morphemes which embrace several inflectional functions in them are technically called **portmanteau morphemes**. Katamba (1993) calls such elements which have two or more grammatical functions as **portmanteau morph**. Bauer (2004: 86) defines it as 'any morph which through cumulation realizes more than one morphosyntactic property....'. Therefore, since *ha-* has two features, then if qualifies to be a portmanteau morph in Kiswahili.

4.2.3 Tenses, aspects and modality in Kiswahili

A number of studies have tried to analyse the tense, aspect and modality system in Kiswahili using different approaches and theoretical orientations. For example, Contini-Morava (1983, 1989) analyses tense and aspect in Kiswahili from a pragmatic point of view, while Beaudoin-Lietz (1999) and Hewson and Nurse (2000) use a cognitive (Guillaumean) model. Lindfors (2003) categorically employs the linear dimension (Reichenbach) model to capture tense/aspect of Kiswahili. However, for a morphological purpose, this section treats these elements as inflectional features embedded in the Kiswahili verbal complex.

Tenses (time frame of an event, action or situation (Nurse 2008)): Kiswahili has three kinds of tense distinctions, namely past, present and future tenses. Perhaps the following examples will illustrate this point.

(3) a. *Nilisoma kitabu jana.*

      ni-li-soma   *ki-tabu*   *jana*

      I-PST-read   7-book   yesterday

      "I read the book yesterday'

  b. *Ninasoma kitabu leo.*

      ni-na-soma   *ki-tabu*   *leo*

      I-PST-read   7-book   today

      "I read the book today'

  c. *Nitasoma kitabu kesho.*

      ni-ta-soma   *ki-tabu*   *kesho*

      I-FUT-read   7-book   tomorrow

      "I will read the book tomorrow'

Using these examples we find that past tense is marked by a morpheme *-li-* and it indicates an event described by the verb group before speech time. It co-occurs with temporal adverbials like *jana* 'yesterday'. The future tense is marked by a morpheme *-ta-* and it describes events that are assumed to follow speech time and has a temporal adverbial *kesho* 'tomorrow'. Lastly, though it may use the form *-na-* and adverbials like *leo* 'today', the present tense is difficult to classify due to the fact that present tense is not primarily a deictic temporal reference. This is observed in several works associated with tense and aspect in Bantu languages (Nurse 2008).

Aspects (the level of completion of the event/situation embedded in the verb (Nurse 2007): Three distinct aspects are attested in Kiswahili, namely perfective aspect which marks the terminated actions (4a), progressive aspect which indicates the continuation of the event (4b) and habitual aspect that denotes a habit (4c).

(4)   a.   *Nimesoma kitabu asubuhi.*

         ni-me-soma   *ki-tabu*   *asubuhi*

         I-perf-read   7-book   morning

         "I have read the book in the morning."

   b.   *Ninasoma kitabu sasa.*

         ni-na-soma   *ki-tabu*   *sasa*

         I-prog-read   7-book   now

         "I am reading the book now"

   c.   *Ninasoma kitabu mara nyingi.*

         ni-na-soma   *ki-tabu*   *mara nyingi*

         I-hab-read   7-book   several times

         "I read the book several times"

Thus, the morpheme *-me-* is used to mark perfective aspect. It is used with both past and future time. The form *-me-* marks the completion of an event. Habitual, as an imperfective aspect, is marked by *-na-*. Also, progressive aspect is marked by the same morpheme *-na-*.

Modality revolves around the idea that in many Bantu languages different shapes of the final vowel encode aspect (and **mood**) (Nurse & Philippson 2006: 156). Beaudoin-Lietz (1999: 182) categorically analyses modality in Kiswahili by observing the various readings associated with the finals *-a, -e* and *-i*. This section offers only a quick glance to moods in Kiswahili. A detailed study of modality in Kiswahili appears in Beaudoin-Lietz (1999) and readers are strongly advised to refer to that document.

Basically three morphemes are attested for modality (moods) in Kiswahili but generally two kinds of moods are attested in the language, namely imperative and subjunctive. The three suffixal formatives for modality, namely the imperative -a (which should not be equated to the default final vowel) as well as the subjunctive *-i*, are well represented in the Kiswahili constructions. See illustrations in (5) and explanation thereafter.

(5)   a.   *Sisi tunakula.*

         sisi   *tu-na-ku-l-**a***

         we   we-PRES-INF-eat-FV

         We are eating.

   b.   *Wewe, kula!*

         wewe   *ku-l-**a***

         you   INF-eat-Imper

         You, eat!

   c.   *Nasema, kuleni!*

         ni-na-sema   *ku-l-e-ni*

I-PRES-say   INF-eat-Imper

I say, you should eat.

d. *Nasema, sikupi*

ni-na-sema   si-kup-**i**

I-PRES-say   Neg-give-Imper

I say, I won't give you.

e. *Nasema, msome*

ni-na-sema   m-som-**e**

I-PRES-say   Neg-give-Subjunc.

I say, I should read.

We said that mood is marked as a suffix, and is always the final vowel in the verbal complex. The first sentence demonstrates how the final vowel -*a* could appear in an affirmative construction as just a default final (5a). This vowel could be referred to as indicative mood. But in (5b) the same final indicates imperative mood in Kiswahili. Beaudoin-Lietz (1999: 183) put it rightly as, "The affirmative imperative, expressing a command, is the form with the least number of morphemes. It consists of the verbal base and the final, occurring with final -*a*.

The other imperative mood is marked by the vowel -*e* which co-occurs with the formative -*ni* as in (39c). The sequence -*e*...*ni* is a kind of an imperative mood which provide an address of plurality. In (13d) the imperative for the negative constructions is provided and, as you can see, it is associated with the final -*i*.

Lastly, we have subjunctive mood which is indicated in (5e). As opposed to imperative mood, it obligatorily carries the subject marker. The final vowel changes its shape to -*e*. The subjunctive mood involves very polite requests given to another person. Beaudin-Lietz (1999) says that to express concepts such as 'almost to do' or 'just to do' which may be expressed in other Bantu languages by auxiliaries followed by forms in the subjunctive, these are expressed in Kiswahili by lexical words or phrases which are then followed by a verb with a subjunctive ending.

4.2.4 Agreement and concord patterns in Kiswahili

In general, *agreement* and *concord* are used herein to mean manifestations of the various grammatical properties (also called *phi*-features), namely, *gender, number, person* and *case* in various languages of the world (Baker 2008). The notion agreement refers to realizations of such features between the subject nouns, verbs and object nouns while concord entails the agreement within noun phrases (Ibid).

Specific to agreement, Seidel and Dimitriadis (1997) noted that Kiswahili verbs carry morphemes that agree with their subject and object in noun class. The agreement markers include information about *number, person* and *noun class*. To strengthen this point, Riedel (2009: 3) is worth quoting as she says 'Bantu languages are well-known for their agglutinative morphology. Especially the system of verbal inflections is rich. Bantu verbal complexes include morphemes which are co-referential with the subject and/or the object (or objects) of a verb.' Moreover, Hendersen (2006) and Lusekelo (2009a, 2013a) presents manifestation of such features in various determiners and modifiers in noun phrases in Kiswahili and other Bantu languages.

In what follows I provide a brief description of the agreement and concord paterns in Kiswahili. Readers should be aware that several ways of the object agreements in Kiswahili are covered in detail in works such as Wald (1979), Seidel and Dimitriadis (1997) and Riedel (2009). The concord and subject agreements for the language appear in several works (see Contini-Morava 1994; Mohamed 2001; Kihore et al. 2003; Hendersen 2006; Lusekelo 2009a, among many others). These markers, i.e. head markers in noun phrases as well as subject marker and object marker in verbs, have mainly *person* and *number* features hence they have typical inflectional properties in Kiswahili, as well as in other Bantu languages.

Concord in Kiswahili: The agreement of *number* feature is the main poperty of Kiswahili. Lusekelo (2013b: 23) provides the examples of noun phrases which show concord in number across word categories within a noun phrase. Examples in (6) show concord being manifested in affixes *m-* and *ki-* while in (7) plural number is indicated in morphemes *wa-* and *vi-*.

(6) a. *mzee yule mpole* 'that kind elder'
     b. *kijana wangu mmoja* 'one youngster of mine'

(7) a. *wazee wale wapole* 'those kind elders'
     b. *vijana wetu wawili* 'our two youngsters'

The concord provided above has influence on the syntax of agreement in Kiswahili. The feature *number* tends to manifest in verbs as well as the predicates of the verbs in the language. This is described below.

Head marking and subject agreement in Kiswahili: First we will examine the subject agreement patterns in Kiswahili. As in other Bantu languages, Kiswahili puts noun dependants to the right of the head noun (see Ashton 1944; Mohamed 2001; Kihore 2003; Lusekelo 2009a, among others). Since each Bantu language reveals some distinctness on the orders, Kiswahili has subject agreement patterns described below.

Ashton (1944: 46, 54) states that the adjective follows its noun and has concords as in *kisu kirefu* 'long knife' and *mtu mvivu* 'lazy person' and pronominal roots, namely, possessive, demonstrative, interrogative, o-reference and *-enye* can either carry concords to the noun or stand alone as pronouns. Polomé (1967: 143) confirms that nouns in Kiswahili occur initially but for non-proximity demonstratives may precede. Perhaps this could be illustrated with a few examples. In these examples, observe the manifestations of the noun class prefixes throughout the constructions.

(8) *Vikapu vyangu vidogo vimeanguka chini.*

vi-kapu	*vi-angu vi-dogo*	*vi-me-anguk-a* *chini*	
8-basket	8-mine 8-small	SM8-PST-fall-FV	down

'My small baskets have fallen down'

(9)   *Machungwa mabichi yalichumwa.*
       ma-chungwa   *ma-bichi*   *ya-li-chum-w-a*
       6-orange   6-raw   SM6-PST-pick-Pass-FV
       'The raw oranges were picked'

(10)   *Mjomba amefariki leo.*
       m-jomba   *a-me-fariki*   *leo*
       1-uncle   SM1-PST-die   today
       'Uncle has died today'

In order to have a better understanding of subject agreement and object concords discussed herein, readers are advised to refer to the nominal prefixes in Kiswahili. In fact, in the examples above, one notices the use of the noun prefixes for indicating concordial agreements between the head nouns, the nominal modifiers as well as the verbal complex. These noun class prefixes are used to designate the agreement patterns of the subject in Kiswahili.

Object agreement and noun phrases in Kiswahili: The other nominal agreement pattern involves noun phrases which appear in the object position in a sentence. Object agreement is associated with the cliticization of a morpheme in the prefix position of the Kiswahili verb. This morpheme has connection to the noun phrase in the object position in the sentence. Their relationship is accounted for through person and number as Riedel (2009: 46) rightly observes:

> In Kiswahili, object marking is obligatory with animate objects much more generally. This particularly holds for nouns referring to humans. In Kiswahili [....] object marking is obligatory for object nouns modified by a possessive that refer to a human....

Perhaps the following examples will help to illustrate the grammatical features covered by the object marker in Kiswahili. In these examples, the object markers which have similar features to the noun phrase in object position are inserted on the verbs where necessary. As will be shown below, this has several implications.

(11)   *Tulimuona mwalimu wake.*
       tu-li-mu-ona   *mw-alimu*   *wake*
       SM1pl-PST-OM1-see   1-teacher   Poss
       'We saw his/her teacher'

(12)   *Tuliwaona walimu wake.*
       tu-li-wa-ona   *wa-limu*   *wake*
       SM1pl-PST-OM2-see   2-teacher   Poss
       'We saw his/her teachers'

(13)   *Tuliona miti mingi.*
       tu-li-ona   *mi-ti*   *mingi*
       SM1pl-PST-OM1-see   4-tree   many
       'We saw many trees'

(14)   *Tuliiona ile miti.*
        tu-li-i-ona   *ile*   *miti*
        SM1pl-PST-OM4-see   Dem   4-tree
        'We saw those trees (the trees)'

Observing object marking in these examples, one notices four things. One, in example (11) the object noun has singular and human features which also appear in object marker -*mu*- which stands for the noun class 1 (human, singular). Two, the features in (12) refer to the plural features of the noun *walimu* 'teachers' which are also reflected directly in the object marker -wa- which is for noun class 2 (humans). Therefore, the first two examples show two features, namely the number (singular-plural distinctions) and humanness, a feature which is not covered herein. Three, in example (13) there is no object marking because the object now, i.e. *miti* 'trees' is not obligatorily triggering object marking because it is an inanimate noun. This feature is also not covered in detail here thus readers are advised to opt for the references mentioned above. Lastly, example (14) has an object marker despite the fact that the object noun is inanimate. The reason that triggers object marking in this context is nothing but definiteness and specificity. In fact this sentence is referring to the specific trees hence a definite reading is given.

For further and detailed syntactic and pragmatic functions of the agreement readers of this book are advised to contact the literature covering this area. In fact there is an extensive literature dealing with object marking in Kiswahili (see Seidel & Dimitriadis 1997; Bukuru 1998; Wald 1979, 1997, 1998; Riedel 2009).

Person in Swahili: Another grammatical feature embedded in subject agreement morphemes as well as object markers is person. With **person**, Bauer (2004: 83-84) defines it as "a morphological category which distinguishes the speaker from the addressee and from other individuals discussed. The first person refers to the speaker [...] 'I' or a group [...] 'we'. The second person refers to someone addressed directly [...] 'you'. The third person is used for other referents corresponding to [...] 'he, she, it' [...] ".

Person is denoted in Kiswahili through the agreement elements which appear in the verb, i.e. subject and object markers. Thus, in Kiswahili examples used for subject agreement and object marking above, we can use some to indicate person. In example (8) above, the form *vi*- on the verbal prefix marks third person while example (9) above has the form *ya*- which also marks third person (in plural).

The same is indicated with object nouns. For example, in (11) above it is illustrated that the object markers -*wa*- and -*mu*- show, among others, third person. The same is done for the object marker -*wa* which indicates third person too (10). Although we used the third person for all the examples here, any person can be shown this way in Kiswahili.

4.3   Inflections in English

English has eight basic inflections. This has been termed as a closed system in Bauer (1983, 2003) because only a few morphemes are employed to show grammatical functions. Only three morphological areas are affected by inflection. Bauer (2004: 103) says 'as far as English is concerned, inflectional morphology is taken to include verbal -s, -ed, -ing and nominal plurals, possibly comparative and superlative -er and -est.'

Following Bauer (1983), a list of all inflectional affixes in the language is provided in (15) below:

(15) a.   pastness: -ed   talk-talk-ed
      b.   progressive marking: -ing   dance-danc-ing
      c.   plural marker: -s   student-student-s
      d.   present simple tense: -s   talk-talk-s
      e.   possessive: -'s   John-John's
      f.   comparative: -er   tall-tall-er
      g.   superlative: -est   tall-tall-est
      h.   past participle: -en   write-writt-en

Verbal inflections involve indicators of pastness. The tradition suffix is -ed which surfaces in regular verbs, e.g. *walk-walked, jump-jumped, kick-kicked, thank-thanked* etc. a number of other verbs in English take -d, e.g. *fine-fined, file-filed* etc. some verbs are created into pastness by -ied, as in *try-tried.*

The progressive aspect (traditionally called continuous tense) is designated by -ing. This is also called the *gerund*. It occurs in works such as *buy-buying, cry-crying, put-putting, begin-beginning* etc.

Number is commonly shown in English nouns. So countable nouns such *as book, house* and *tree* take their plurals by affixing -s to get *books, houses* and *trees*. On pluralisation in English, Booij (2005: 110) says:

> Head marking in Indo-European languages can also be illustrated by quantifiers that denote a quantity higher than 1. These quantifiers require the plural form of the head noun if it is countable, as in English *two books*. This is a case of government in which the number of nouns (normally a case of inherent inflection) plays a role in contextual inflection.

Pluralisation is related to singularisation. The difference is that while the former is shown in nouns, the latter however, is designated in verbs. Thus, verbs like *cut-cuts, buy-buys* and *eat-eats* show singular-plural distinctions.

The possessive marker is also called genitive. Booij (2005: 106) says:

> Nouns may require a particular marking on their dependent. In the phrase *John's house* the dependent NP *John* is marked as such through the presence of the possessive marker *s*, whereas the head noun *house* is not marked for this syntactic relationship. In languages with **genitive** case, this case is typically used for marking relations between nouns.

Agreement is mentioned as another pervasive inflection process in English (Bauer 1983, 2003). Booij (2005: 107) says 'the second main type of contextual inflection besides government is agreement (also called **concord**). In many Indo-European languages attributive adjectives agree with respect to a number of morphosyntactic properties with their head nouns'.

In other languages, gender is shown in word-categories. Booij (2005: 107) says:

> For such languages, we only observe direct morphological effects of gender on the form of dependent adjectives and determiners. In French, the gender of a noun (masculine or feminine) manifests itself in the choice of the sg articles (indefinite *un* or *une*, definite *le* or *la*), and in the form of the adjective (suffix *-e* in feminine forms), but not in the inflectional form of the noun itself.

To sum up, both Kiswahili and English have pervasive inflectional systems which manifest mainly in the morphology of nouns, verbs, demonstratives and adjectives.

Resources cited:

Ashton, Ethol O. 1944. *Swahili Grammar (Including Intonation)*. London: Longmans.

Baker, Mark C. 2008. *The Syntax of Agreement and Concord*. Cambridge: Cambridge University Press.

Battye, Adrian, Marie-Anne Hintz & Paul Rowlett. 2000. *The French Language Today: A Linguistic Introduction*. Londo: Routledge.

Beaudoin-Lietz, Christa A. 1999. *Formatives of Tense, Aspect, Mood and Negation in the Verbal Construction of Standard Swahili*. Doctoral thesis, Memorial University of Newfoundland.

Bukuru, Denis. 1998. Object marking in Kirundi and Swahili. Master dissertation, University of Dar es Salaam.

Contini-Morava, Ellen. 1983. Tense and Non-tense in Swahili Grammar: Semantic Asymmetry between Affirmative and Negative. Doctoral thesis. Columbia: Columbia University.

Contini-Morava, Ellen. 1989. *Discourse Pragmatics and Semantic Categorization: The Case of Negation and Tense-aspect with Special Reference to Swahili*. Berlin: Mouton de Gruyter.

Contini-Morava, Ellen. 1994. *Noun Classification in Swahili.* Publications of the Institute for Advanced Technology in the Humanities, University of Virginia. Research Reports, Second Series.

Contini-Morava, Ellen. 2007. Swahili morphology. In: Kaye, Alan S. (ed.). *Morphology of Asia and Africa*, vol. 2. Winona Lake and Indiana: Eisenbrauns. pp. 1129-1158.

Guthrie, Malcolm. 1967. *Comparative Bantu: an introduction to the comparative linguistics and pre-history of Bantu languages.* Vol.1. Famborough: Gregg Press.

Güldemann, Tom. 1999. The genesis of verbal negation in Bantu and its dependency on functional features of clause types. In Jean-Marie Hombert & Larry M. Hyman (eds.) *Bantu historical linguistics: theoretical and empirical perspectives.* Carlifornia: CSLI Publications: 545-587.

Henderson, Brent. 2006. Multiple agreement, concord and case checking. In: Arasanyin, O. F. & Permberson, A. (eds.). *Proceedings of the 36th ACAL.* pp. 60-65.

Hewson, John & Nurse, Derek. 2001. Chronological staging of Swahili verbal system. *General Linguistics*, 38: 75-108.

Kamusi. *Kamusi ya Swahili-Kiingereza. http://africanlanguages.com/Swahili/.*

Katamba, Francis. 2003. Bantu nominal morphology. In: Nurse, Derek & Philippson, Gérard (eds.) *The Bantu languages.* London: Routledge. pp. 103-120.

Kihore, Yared, David P.B Massamba & Y. Msanjila. 2003. *Sarufi Maumbo ya Kiswahili Sanifu (SAMAKISA): Sekondari na Vyuo.* Dar es Salaam: Institue of Kiswahili Research.

Lindfors, Anna Y. (2003). Tense and aspect in Swahili. Uppsala: Uppsala Universitet, Institutionen for linguvistik.

Lusekelo, Amani. 2009a. The structure of the Swahili noun phrase: Evidence from fictional narratives. In: Burger, Willie & Marné Pienaar (eds.) *Die Tand van die Tyd: Opstelle opgedra aan Jac Conradie.* Bloemfontein: Sun Press. pp. 45-60.

Lusekelo, Amani. 2013b. DP-internal and V-external agreement patterns in Eastern Bantu: Re-statement of the facts in Eastern Bantu. *Journal of Linguistics and Language in Education*, vol. 7(1): 19-47.

Maho, Jouni. 2007. The linear ordering of TAM/NEG markers in the Bantu languages. *SOAS working papers in linguistics*, 15: 213-225.

Meeussen, Achille E. 1967. Bantu Grammatical Reconstructions. *Africana Linguistica*, 61 (3): 79-121.

Mohamed, A. Mohamed. 2001. *Modern Swahili Grammar.* Nairobi: East African Educational Publishers.

Ngonyani, Deo. 2003. Negation marking asymmetry in Bantu languages. *A Talk, World Congress of African Linguistics*, Rutgers University, 06, 18.

Nurse, Derek. 2007. The emergency of tense in early Bantu. Payne, Doris. L. & Peña, Jaime. (eds). *Selected Proceedings of the 37th Annual Conference on African Linguistics.* Somerville, MA: Cascadilla Proceedings Project. pp. 164-179.

Nurse, Derek. 2008. *Tense and Aspect in Bantu.* London: Oxford University Press.

Nurse, Nurse & Hinnebusch, Thomas J. 1993. *Swahili and Sabaki: A Linguistic History.* Berkeley: of California Publications in Linguistics.

Nurse, Derek & Philippson, Gérard. 2006. Common tense-aspect markers in Bantu. *Journal of African Languages and Linguistics* 27:155–196.

Odden, David. 1996. *The Phonology and Morphology of Kimatuumbi.* Oxford: Clarendon Press.

Petzell, Malin. 2010. Further analysis of negation in Kagulu. In: Legère, Karsten & Thornell, Christina (eds). *Bantu Languages: Analysis, Description and Theory*. Köln: Rüdiger Köppe Verlag. pp. 209-216.

Riedel, Kristina. 2009. *The Syntax of Object Marking in Sambaa: A Comparative Bantu Perspective*. Leiden: LOT Publications.

Rugemalira, Josephat. 2010. The -aga- TAM marker and the boundary between cliticization and affixation in Bantu. In: Legère, Karsten & Thornell, Christina (eds.). *Bantu Languages: Analyses, Description and Theory*. Cologne: Rüdiger Köppe. pp. 229-237.

Schadeberg, Thilo C. 2001. Number in Swahili grammar. *Afrikanistische Arbeitspapiere*: 7-16.

Schico, Walter. 1992. Non-acceptance and the negation in Swahili of Lubumbashi. *African Languages and Cultures*, 5(1): 75-89.

Seidel, Amanda & Dimitriadis, Alexis. 1997. The discourse function of object marking in Swahili. In *CLS 33: The Main Session*, 373–389. *des langues d'Afrique et universaux de la grammaire*, University Paris 8. Paris: L'Harmattan.

Spencer, Andrew. 1991. *Morphological Theory: An Introduction to Word Structure in Generative Grammar*. Oxford: Blackwell.

Storch, Anne. 2005. *The Noun Morphology of Western Nilotic*. Köln: Rüdiger Köppe Verlag.

Swilla, Imani. 1979. The noun class system and agreement in Chindali. In: *La civilisation des peuples des grands lacs: colloque de Bujumbura*, 4-10 Septembre. pp 379-393.

Swilla, Imani N. 1998. Tenses in Chindali. *Afrikanistische Arbeitspapiere*, 54: 95-125.

Tanda, V. Ambe & Ayu'nwi N. Neba. 2005. Negation in Mokpe and two related coastal Bantu languages of Cameroon. *African Study Monographs*, 25(4): 201-219.

TUKI (Taasisi ya Uchunguzi wa Swahili). 2001. *Kamusi ya Swahili-Kiingereza*. Dar es Salaam: Institute of Kiswahili Research.

Turuka, Ursus A.H. 1974. The grammar of place in Swahili. M.A thesis, University of Dar es Salaam.

Visser, Mariana. 2010. Definiteness and specificity in Xhosa determiner phrase. In: Legère, Karsten & Thornell, Christina (eds). *Bantu Languages: Analysis, Description and Theory*. Köln: Rüdiger Köppe Verlag. pp. 295-314.

Wald, Benji. 1979. The development of the Swahili object marker: A study of the interaction of syntax and discourse. In *Discourse and Syntax*, ed. Talmy Givón, 505–524. New York: Academic Press.

Wald, Benji. 1997. Verbal and the human/inanimate polarization of the Swahili object marker. In: G.R. Guy, C. Feagin, D. Schiffrin, and J. Baugh (eds.). *Towards a social science of language*. Amsterdam: John Benjamins.

Exercise Four

4. 1. How many inflectional affixes are there in English language? Mention them.

    2. Do we have prefixal inflections in English? Providing relevant examples, if any, mention them.

    3. Providing illustrative examples, differentiate inflectional affixes mentioned in (4.1).

4.2 It is established by various linguists that Bantu languages are very rich in nominal affixes which are inflectional in nature (cf. Schadeberg 2001; Riedel 2009; Lusekelo 2009b, 2013b). Select one Bantu language of your choice and investigate its nominal morphology. Provide a short essay to describe its inflectional affixes.

5 Reduplication

5.1 Introducing reduplication

5.1.1 Basics

Since this book is envisaged as a coursebook for students of linguistics, the intention of this chapter, therefore, is to help the readers to have a better understanding of the notion **reduplication**, one of the pervasive word-formation processes attested in most world's languages. It involves copying and repeating a segment or the whole base to generate a new word with somehow dissimilar meaning to that of the original base.

The first point to conceive here is that reduplication, according to Bauer (2003:30), is far more common across languages than the rare types of affixation. With this in mind, we will see in the course of the discussion in this chapter that at least all major word categories undergo reduplication across Eastern Bantu: nouns, verbs, adjectives, numerals and adverbs (cf. Odden 1996; Marlo 2002; Lusekelo 2009, among others).

This is also the same for Kiswahili Bantu. Rubanza (1997) and Novatna (2000) collected and analysed a good deal of reduplicants[15] in Kiswahili. In some grammar books, only pockets of this process are explored (cf. Ashton 1944:316-317; Mohamed 2001:20). Since reduplication is a natural word-formation process in this language, this chapter of the coursebook is meant to take the readers through the several ways this process is realised at least in other Bantu languages, namely, Kinande [DRC], Kinyakyusa [Tanzania/Malawi], Kikerewe [Tanzania], Subiya [Zambia/Malawi/Botswana], Lusaamia [Kenya/Uganda] and Wandya [Malawi/Botswana].

In two out of the three major reference languages of this book, however, i.e. English and French, reduplication is not a pervasive and plorific process. For instance, Minkova and Stockwell (2009) mention a few reduplication processes in English[16]. Bauer (1983) provides an outline of six word-formation processes in chapter seven (reduplication not listed): compounding, prefixation and suffixation, conversion, back-formation, clipping, and acronyms.

An important idea to bear in our minds is that reduplication is a mechanism of deriving new lexemes in natural languages. This happens because repeated segments (reduplicants), whether in full or partial reduplication, become part and parcel of the stems to which they

---

15 The **reduplicant** (abbreviated as RED) is the copied materials (Odden 1996; Marlo 2002; Downing 1999, 2003; Matondo 2006; Lusekelo 2009c). It is defined further in section 5.1.4 below. These materials which are copied are also referred to as *reduplicand* (abbreviated as *redup*) in other works such as Newman (2000) or *reduplicative* (Downing 2000).

16 Since English and French have less pervasive reduplication processes, as mentioned, much of the materials presented herein come from Kiswahili and other Bantu languages whose morphology permit prolific reduplication (Kinande, Kikerewe, Kinyakyusa, Lusaamia).

are attached (Mwita 2008:231). In cyclicity approach to analysis of word structures, this pattern entails that once reduplication has occurred, the element produced becomes an independent new word, readily available for another round of word-formation process in the language in question.

5.1.2 Alternative terminologies

The senses connected to the notion **reduplication** possibly could well be captured using other English words. In fact, linguists tend to employ other expressions when they refer to the senses associated with this word. For instance, in a linguistics workshop that covered reduplication which was held in Paris in France in June 2009, the alternative terminologies used freely by the participants to express the notion reduplication included **doubling, recurrence, repetition, copying** and **reiteration.** The term reiteration appeared even in the theme of the workshop, namely *International Workshop on Grammar of Reiteration*. The assumption is that such linguists have assigned the senses embraced by the term reduplication to senses carried by the alternative expressions which are used in general linguistics.

In fact, it seems true to a certain degree though that the concept reduplication is closely associated with the senses embedded in these alternative terminologies. Linguists, however, have assigned to the technical terminology reduplication some special process that functions to designate specific word formation process attested across world languages. As it will be evident in this chapter, such special functions tend to make this term more or less different from the other entries used by linguists specialising in linguistic morphology.

The aforementioned observations are also supported by remarks made by Kouwenberg (2003:1) who says 'the phenomenon is found in the literature as reduplication, **iteration** or reiteration, repetition and doubling'. Kouwenberg further articulates that these labels are used for a rather different array of linguistic forms which range from expressive vowel lengthening and verb doubling to morphological reduplication and repetition of the entire phrases.

As for the alternative terms, further evidence is found in the book by Inkelas and Zoll (2005) whose introductory chapter is full of expressions like repetition, reiteration, **duplication**, doubling, copying as well as reduplication. However, these authors employ these terms with caution because they are aware that such terminologies provide different interpretations as they are used in the analyses housed in dissimilar theoretical orientations. So far, based on several previous works, we have listed the following **eight** terminologies associated with the phenomenon described in this chapter:

(1)   *a.*   *reduplication*
      b.   *repetition*
      c.   *copying*
      d.   *reiteration*
      e.   *doubling*
      f.   *duplication*

g.   *iteration*
h.   *recurrence*

An important caution to be underscored here is that in case someone uses these alternative words, surfacing of the diverse and dissimilar linguistic notions embedded in the alternative terminologies cannot be under-estimated. It is the assumption of this book that for proper guidance to students of linguistics, it remains necessary, therefore, to stick to the term reduplication in this chapter in order to express precisely the phenomenon associated with it.

This choice is in the line with other works. For instance, in an article by Avran (2011) the technical words reduplication and repetition are used recurrently but selectively in order to draw a semantic boundary between them and other terminologies, i.e. doubling or iteration (for Avran but as well as others given in (1) above).

5.1.3 The definition of reduplication

The best way to perpetuate the delineation of the alternative terms in (1) above and then to introduce the proper definition of reduplication is probably by following the glossary book by Bauer (2004). In the course of defining the term, perhaps we should also make some comments about terminologies on the definition given by Bauer in the glossaries for morphology before proceeding to hint on the central concern embedded in the notion reduplication. Bauer (2004:90) says:

> **reduplication** is the repetition of some part of the **base** (possibly all of the base) as a **morphological process**. When disyllabic verbs take a plural subject in Samoan, one common way of showing this is to reduplicate the first consonant and vowel of the base, so *nofo* 'sit' gives *nonofo* in the plural, while *moe* 'sleep' gives *momoe* and *fasi* 'to beat' gives *fafasi*. In other languages, it may be the last part of a word which is reduplicated, with the **reduplicant** suffixed to the base. [emphasis by Bauer]

Three significant points need to be isolated and described here. The first point to note and underscore is the recurrent use of the term *repetition* in the definition of the terminology reduplication, a tendency common for several authors. It is the assumption of the present chapter that reduplication, as a word-formation process, involves repetition of the segment(s) from the base to the base itself. Perhaps the following Kiswahili verbal items in (2) and adjectival items in (3) will help to demonstrate how materials from the base (unreduplicated items) are repeated (in the reduplicated items):

(2) | **Unreduplicated** | **Reduplicated** |
|---|---|
| *piga* 'hit' | *pigapiga* 'hit repeatedly' |
| *kusema* 'to say, to talk' | *kusemasema* 'to rumour' |
| *cheza* 'play' | *chezacheza* 'play repeatedly' |
| *lima* 'cultivate' | *limalima* 'cultivate frequently' |
| *lia* 'cry' | *lialia* 'whimper' |

(3) **Unreduplicated**   **Reduplicated**
   fupi 'shot'   *fupifupi* 'fairly short'
   nene 'fat'   *nenenene* 'fairly fat'
   zuri 'good'   *zurizuri* 'slightly good'
   nyeupe 'white'   *nyeupenyeupe* 'whitish, pale'

In the illustrative examples in (2) and (3), each of the total bases is copied and then repeated to the bases in order to form another lexical item with somehow slightly different meaning. This pattern takes us to the second significant point to consider in the definition of the term reduplication.

The point is that such kind of a definition takes into consideration languages which permit partial reduplication, a topic we discuss in details below. As shown in examples in (2) and (3) above, also as it will be evident in the course of the presentation in this chapter, not all languages allow only partial reduplication rather other languages provide evidence of total reduplication as well. In this book, this is assumed to be an indicator that reduplication is not a narrow subject matter of discussion as it may appear in the definition rather it is a complex word-formation process.

The point which surrounds the use of the word repetition also needs further explanation. In offering further explanation, therefore, we borrow the distinction of the terms reduplication and repetition as from an important and authoritative volume by Newman (2000:509). It is succinctly presented that reduplication is a process that apply within a word rather than successive occurrence of the same word as in *very very tall* in English, which he terms repetition. Here we see that reduplication is word-internal while repetition is treated as word-external. The former is a word-formation process while the latter is a syntactic process.

In this book, therefore, we assume that, as one of the word formation processes attested in several languages, **reduplication** involves what looks-like an affix being realised by phonological material borrowed from the root or base. Such phonological materials are copied and repeated to the base which undergoes reduplication. This is in line with Katamba and Stonham (2006:180) who have reduced the meaning of reduplication to situations where the repeated part of the word serves some derivational or inflectional purpose(s) in the language that experiences the process in question.

The last point surrounds the fact that since reduplication manifests itself in different shapes, e.g. Samoan: *nofo* 'sit' - *nonofo* 'sit (pl.)' and Swahili: *lia* 'cry' - *lialia* 'whimper', the central concern of the phenomenon described in this coursebook revolves around copying and repeating the base materials. It should be understood that reduplication involves copying of linguistic materials (technically called reduplicant, a term introduced above and defined below) from the root or base of a word. Also reduplication involves applying such materials to the same root or base. The intention of the copying and repeating linguistic materials is to produce new words in the language in question, in this case of Samoan and Kiswahili.

Looking into the morphology of Kiswahili, in comparison with that for other languages mentioned above, this phenomenon involves the repetition of the part or whole of the word in order to form another word, as in *omba* 'beg' vs. *ombaomba* 'begger' (Mohamed 2001: 220) and *alialia* 'whimper frequently' (Ashton 1994: 316). In the same spirit, Rubanza (1997: 60) concludes that the definition of reduplication should also involve the semantics surrounding the reduplicated items in the language.

To sum up, it is reasonably fair to accept that the information provided in this section offers a narrow sense which fits only for the background to reduplication. It is plausibly argued, therefore, the definition given in this section is a kind of narrow approximation of the whole process of reduplication which could be understood well once someone reads the entire chapter of this book. This conclusive observation is also described by Inkelas and Zoll (2005:3) and Katamba and Stonham (2006:180) as narrower, which involves only the idea that reduplication is copying of the phonological materials from the base and repeating them to the base. The whole picture involves several other phenomena presented throughout this chapter.

5.1.4 Defining the reduplicant

It should be noted that the essence of reduplication aforementioned in this chapter of the book hinges also on the notion **reduplicant** (also known as **reduplicative** and in several sources abbreviated as RED (cf. Downing 2000; Marlo 2002)). This is a section of the base which is copied and repeated to the base in order to generate a new word with different semantic content, though related to sense of the base.

In some cases, though, the linguistic materials copied differ in morphological size thus propelling linguists to fail to identify the actual amount of the phonological materials needed to be copied. For Bantu languages, it seems that some agreement on the size of the reduplicant is established. Downing contends that:

> Striking confirmation that the reduplicative template is *minimally (as well as maximally) two syllables long* in all three languages [Bantu languages Siswati (Swaziland), Kinande (DRC) and Kikuyu (Kenya)] comes from the monosyllabic stems. In all three languages, monosyllabic stems are expanded to fill the two-syllable reduplicative template, but each language adopts a different strategy for expansion. (Downing 1999:65) [*emphasis mine*].

In order to offer proper explanation, perhaps we should make use of illustrative examples to substantiate the idea given by Downing. In (4) some illustrations on partial reduplication from Kinande [DRC] are given (Downing 2000a). Examples in (5) offer data for complete reduplication in Kiswahili (Novatna 2000).

(4) | **Unreduplicated** | **Reduplicated** |
|---|---|
| *eri-huma* 'beat' | *eri-huma-huma* 'to beat repeatedly' |
| *eri-swa* 'to drind' | *eri-swa-swa* 'to grind continuously' |
| *ery-esera* 'to play' | *ery-esera-sera* 'to play for' |

(5)   **Unreduplicated**   **Reduplicated**

tamu (Adj) 'delicious'   <u>*tamu*</u>-*tamu* (N) 'sweets'

pole (Adj) 'gentle'   <u>*pole*</u>-*pole* (Adv) 'slowly'

mbali (Adv) 'far'   <u>*mbali*</u>-*mbali* (Adj) 'various, different'

moto (Adj) 'warm, hot'   <u>*moto*</u>-*moto* (Adj) 'ardent'

The reduplicants have been underlined in the examples above, e.g *huma-* and *pole-* in Kinande and Kiswahili respectively. In (4) it is shown in Kinande that the element *eri-* (*ery-*) is not copied hence this kind of reduplication will be called partial reduplication. Kiswahili examples in (5) make use of full copying of the entire base hence it is complete reduplication.

5.1.5 Productivity of reduplication

The amount of productivity of reduplication differs across languages. Stonham (2004:121), for instance, reports that reduplication is a very prolific and important word-formation process in Nootka (indigenous American language). This entails that Nookta employs reduplication as one of its major word formation processes.

The productivity of reduplication is reported in several Niger-Congo languages of Africa, Kiswahili inclusive (cf. Odden 1996; Dowining 1999; Novatna 2000; Lusekelo 2009a; Mathangwane & Mtenje 2010, among others). Moreover, pidgins and creoles, like Nigeria Pidgin and Krio [Sierra Leone] make the widespread usage of reduplicants for both derivational and inflectional morphological functions (Ugot & Ogundipe 2011). This piece of information informs us that reduplication is a major word-formation process in African continent.

It seems the morphologies of Indo-European languages (English, French, German, Dutch etc.) have less pervasive reduplication. Boij (2005:59) says reduplication is 'an unusual word-formation process in Germanic languages'. Specifically, in Dutch, Booij (2002) seems to show that it does not fully work as he does not include it in his seminal work for the morphology of that language. Therefore, the prolific nature of reduplication is, however, highly questioned in the reference languages in this coursebook.

The preceding information does not rule out the possibilities of having words such as those listed in (6) for (mostly American) English (Ghomeshi et al. 2004:309).

(6)   a.   **Rhyme combinations**

super-duper

willy-nilly

pall-mall

okey-dokey

hanky-panky

b.   **Ablaut combinations**

flim-flam

zig-zag

sing-song

pitter-patter

riff-raff

mish-mash

A few tokens of reduplicants are mentioned in English. The status of these elements seems to trigger some doubts. We need, therefore, to delineate whether these are typical reduplication or not. This worry is in line with Booij (2005:22) who does not recognise **echo-word-formation** as a fully word-formation process as he says it is a kind of reduplication, as in English *zigzag, chitchat*, French *fou-fou* 'somewhat mad'.

In what follows, therefore, description of reduplication in Kiswahili is offered. This is assumed to pave way towards proper analysis of the Englisg reduplicated elements in (6). Also, it will enable us to tackle, with some precision, reduplication in French.

5.2 Characteristics of reduplication process

5.2.1 Features of reduplication in Kiswahili

The actual features of reduplication, as a pervasive word-formation process in Kiswahili (as well as in several other Bantu languages), needs to be addressed considering its characteristics across the Bantu family. The characteristics established, so far, seem to be five. In order to describe each feature in some details, the following examples from Kiswahili (7), Kikerewe [Tanzania] (Odden 1996) (8) and Lusaamia [Kenya/Uganda] (Marlo 2002, 2004) will be referred to in explanation.

(7)   **Base**   **Reduplicated word**

    cheusi 'black'   *cheusicheusi* 'darkish'

    warefu 'tall'   *warefuwarefu* 'fairly tall'

    kikubwa 'large'   *kikubwakikubwa* 'very large'

    cheka 'laugh'   *chekacheka* 'keep laughing'[17]

    piga 'hit'   *pigapiga* 'hit repeatedly'

    imba 'sing'   *imbaimba* 'sing frequently'

(8)   *gúmó* 'one'   *gumóó-gúmo* 'one by one'

    báná 'four'   *banáá-bána* 'four by four'

    mu-gází 'wide'   *mu-gazi-gází* 'kind of wide'

    i-bísi 'raw'   *i-bisi-bísi* 'kind of raw'

    ku-lima 'to cultivate'   *ku-lima-lima* 'to cultivate haphazardly'

    ku-bíba 'to plant'   *ku-bíbá-biba* 'to plant here and there'

---

17 Some speakers of Kiswahili will suggest that reduplicated words in the language might be assigned different meanings depending on context; therefore, *imbaimba* could be 'sing badly' and *chekacheka* 'giggle, silly laugh'.

(9) *oxu-sama* 'to bark' *oxusama-sama* 'to bark repeatedly'

oxu-fwaalula 'to undress' *oxu-fwaalula-fwaalula* 'to undress repeatedly'

kona 'sleep' *ßa-kona-kona* 'They sleep all the time'

5.2.1.1 *The amount of reduplicant*

Initially it was established by Bantuists that the amount of the material copied is at least minimally and perhaps maximally two syllables (see Downing 1999, 2000b). But the two-syllable doctrine established in some Bantu languages could partially work in other languages in the same family. Recently, it was found that other Bantu languages demonstrate only the minimality bisyllabic requirement. Thus, the copied materials in (7) through (9) above are at least two syllables in length.

This pattern of reduplication, i.e. a reduplicant being at least two syllables, is functionally confirmed for minimality only in Bantu languages. In other instances, however, Bantu languages permit reduplicants to be longer than two syllables as in Kiswahili, Kikerewe and Lusaamia data above. Also, it is found in Sukuma [Tanzania] (Matondo 2006) and Kurya [Kenya/Tanzania] (Mwita 2008). We will conclude, therefore, the minimality condition that requires reduplicants to be two-syllables long is satisfied while maximally non-finality condition is required.

In these examples, the illustrative examples such as *kona-kona* 'sleep all time' and *pigapiga* 'hit repeatedly' show that the amount reduplicated is at least two syllables. The other illustrations, e.g. *warefuwarefu* 'fairly tall' and *oxu-fwaalula-fwaalula* 'to undress repeatedly' demonstrate that the maximum amount of materials to be copied is unlimited. Generally, the former observation is what is called minimality condition of bisyllabic and the latter is known as maximality condition of non-finality.

Now we should probably compare the Lusaamia example *kona-kona* 'sleep all time' and an English token *zig-zaga*. The former shows that the base (unreduplicated element) is an independent lexical item, i.e. kona 'sleep' while the latter has no isolated unreduplicated element, i.e. *zig*.

5.2.1.2 *Resemblance between base and reduplicant*

Another main defining characteristic feature of reduplication, which remains stable, is associated with the nature of the linguistic material copied and repeated. Scholars such as Downing (1996), Kouwenberg (2003) and Katamba and Stonham (2006) underscore that the phonological shape of the materials copied must resemble the phonological form of the root or base from which they are taken from. This entails that similarities between the base and the reduplicant cannot be underestimated, otherwise the manifestation of reduplication could not be realised. In other words, the section of the word which is reproduced should be similar in at least sound pattern to the sound pattern of the source and not otherwise.

Perhaps we should also use illustrative examples given below to demonstrate this characteristic feature in the morphology of Bantu languages Kiswahili (10) (Rubanza 1997; Novatna 2000) and Kinyakyusa [Tanzania/Malawi] in (11) (Lusekelo 2009c).

(10) **Base (unreduplicated)**   **Reduplicated word**

    kulamba (V) 'to lick'   *kulambalamba* (V) 'to lick repeatedly'
    dogo (Adj) 'small'   *dogodogo* (Adj) 'very small'
    tamu (Adj) 'delicious, sweet'   *tamutamu* (N) 'sweets'
    tema (V) 'spit'   *tematema* (V) 'spit frequently'

(11) **Base (unreduplicated)**   **Reduplicated word**

    kulya 'to eat' [V]   *kulyakulya* 'eat repeatedly' [V]
    muno 'in here' [Adv]   *munomuno* 'just in here' [Adv]
    pagula 'break' [V]   *pagulapagula* 'break frequently' [V]

Since the primary purpose of the Kinyakyusa and Kiswahili example words above is to illustrate on phonological characteristic feature of the copied element and the base, we offer explanation which concludes as that both the base and the reduplicant have similarities in phonological segments.

To substantiate this, let us use one Kiswahili word to represent the rest of the data. From a typical phonological point of view, the word *kulamba* 'to lick' has a set of segmental elements known as consonants and vowels which seem to be divided as follows: *k-u-l-a-mb-a* hence we get the sequence of the segments *C-V-C-V-PreN-V*. In typical reduplication process, it is these segments of the base which are copied. In the process of copying, either the whole number of segments are copied and repeated or a fewer of them are reduplicated. In this way, one can easily judge that the phonological features of the word *kulambalamba* 'to lick repeatedly' provide the segments which looks as *k-u-l-a-mb-a-l-a-mb-a* hence we get the sequence of the segments *C-V-C-V-PreN-V-C-V-PreN-V*. It can plausibly be said that reduplication process here seems to satisfy its basic conditions because the features of the base, namely *kulamba* have been copied in the reduplicated word, i.e. *kulambalamba*. The kind of word formation process referred to as reduplication has been realised here.

Also, the characteristics of reduplication seem to be satisfied even in other words provided from Kinyakyusa in (11) above. For instance, the base word *muno* 'in here' which has the segmental phonological features *C-V-C-V* happens to be similar to the features of the reduplicated word *munomuno* 'right in here' with the segments *C-V-C-V-C-V*. Likewise, the segments of the Kiswahili base word *tamu* 'delicious, sweet' [CV-CV] appear in the reduplicated counter-part *tamutamu* (N) 'sweets' [CV-CV-CV-CV]. It is important to note at this juncture that these examples inform us of the main property of reduplication which is the similarity in phonology of the materials of the reduplicant to those of the base.

The examples described above do not provide a full picture of reduplication across Bantu languages as well as across other language phyla in the continent. The main problem lies on the fact that only segmental features are doubled while phonological features are divide into segmental features (consonants and vowels which we saw immediately above) and non-segmental elements or supra-segmental features which have not been discussed. In what follows, therefore, a foundation towards the analysis of the suprasegmental features in reduplication process is laid down. We begin asking the question whether reduplication is phonological or morphological and the copying of segments and supra-segments will lead us to the best conclusion.

5.2.1.3   Is reduplication morphology or phonology?

The classification of reduplication whether as involving phonology or morphology is another important point to discuss in this chapter. The evidence to enable a better classification comes from the findings across Bantu family. Such evidence is divided into two, i.e. scholars supporting reduplication to be phonological and those who ascribe reduplication to morphology.

Phonological evidence: It is established, on one hand, that reduplication in Bantu languages is phonological. The main argument in favour of this claim is that reduplication is prosodically constrained (see Odden 1996; Kula 2004). This means that the material copied must satisfy some prosodic conditions so as to create acceptable reduplicants and eventually produce acceptable new words. For instance, in Kikerewe data in (8) above, the reduplicant needs to be a two syllable material, say CV-CV. Also, a reduplicant in Kikerewe needs to carry at least low tones or low-high tone patterns. The tone patterns and the amount of syllabic content of the copied materials are analysable through prosodic approach.

It should be understood at this juncture that only tone has been mentioned as one of the supra-segmenatl features involved in the analysis of reduplicants. Other **suprasegmental features** commonly listed in seminal works like Fox (2000) include **length** (time involved in articulation of a segment in order to signal something (p. 12), **accent** (associated with stress, prominence, emphasis and force which bring about change in meaning (p. 114), **tone** (as an intrinsic property of a word, it has lexical or grammatical significance (p. 179)) and **intonation** which has meaning in itself (p. 269).

These suprasegmental features are characterised by the fact that they must be described in relation to other items (like consonant and vowel segments) in the same utterance. Also, from phonological point of view, supra-segmental features are often seen as modifications of segments in order to distinguish meaning (Ibid: 5). As will be evidenced in the course of the discussion below, this has implications to reduplication process which copies the section of a word or the whole entry in order to satisfy either derivational purpose or inflectional ends.

In all the reduplication processes, one important point must be emphasized here that the division of the segments and supra-segments intends to serve one purpose, i.e. to make sure that communication of the intended information is executed (Fox 2000). This means that reduplication has some semantic function (a topic discussed in detail in section 6.3 below).

It is a common agreement that reduplicated involves copying task which does not select only segmental features (consonants and vowels) but it takes supra-segmental features (e.g. accent and stress patterns) as well. The most common supra-segmental feature in the literature of African languages in general and Bantu languages in particular is tone (Hyman 2005). This is the main suprasegmental feature discussed in this chapter in redlation to reduplication.

In fact, tone plays a significant role in determining the status of the materials copied in Bantu languages (see Downing 2000b, 2003; Mwita 2008). Since Kinyakyusa and Kiswahili is not tonal (Ashton 1944; Felberg 1996; Kihore *et al.* 2004; Lusekelo 2007), then we will use illustrative examples from other Bantu languages. Examples (12) from Subiya (also called Chikuhane, spoken in Botswana, Zambia and Namibia) from Mathangwane and Mtenje (2010:178) also provides supporting data. In (13) we offer examples from Kikerewe (Odden 1996). These illustrative examples demonstrate how reduplication copies both segmental and supra-segmental features in Bantu languages.

(12) **Base**   **Reduplicated word**

    zíma (V) 'walk'   *zímazíma* (V) 'walk about aimlessly'
    lyá (V) 'eat'   *lyályá* (V) 'eat continuously'
    wáámba (V) 'talk'   *wáámbawáámba* (V) 'talk continuously'

(13) **Base**   **Reduplicated word**

    bábíli 'two'   *babili-bábíli* 'two by two'
    báná 'four'   *banáá-bána* 'four by four'
    mu-gází 'wide'   *mu-gazi-gází* 'kind of wide'
    i-bísi 'raw'   *i-bisi-bísi* 'kind of raw'

The words in (12) demonstrate that in Subiya the segments are copied because the reduplicated words have the forms which resemble the bases. In order to spare the reader energy to continue reading this book, I will avoid providing explanation for each example but show segmental copying in Subiya using only one verb. The segmental materials of the verb *zíma* 'walk', i.e. CVCV are repeated in the reduplicated verb *zímazíma* 'walk about aimlessly' hence we get CVCVCVCV. The same applies to the other verbs whereby all the segments are doubled to make a new word.

The segmental doubling is not the only process shown by these example verbs from Subiya. It is noted that even the supra-segments are also doubled. In the examples in (12) above, both high and lower tones are repeated. This means, the presence of the high tones in the base will also be realised in the reduplicated ones. Thus, the verb *zíma* 'walk' has the tone pattern high and low (H-L) which are repeated in the reduplicated verb *zímazíma* 'walk about aimlessly' to form a sequence of tones labelled H-L-H-L. The other verb, *lyá* 'eat' has the tone pattern H which is copied in the reduplicated verb, *lyályá* 'eat continuously' and result in a H-H pattern. This applies to the last word too. One important point to be accentuated here is that copying of the base involves all the phonological materials in Subiya.

The copying strategies for Subiya seem to be straightforward; copy both segments and supra-segments from the base into the reduplicated element. This pattern is not permitted in Kikerewe. Odden (1996) observes that the numeral reduplication is associated with alternation in tone patterns. Some numeral stems which contain two or more moras have reduplicants surfacing as toneless, e.g. *babili-bábíli* 'two by two' (p. 116). In other cases, Odden points out that in the reduplicated form, the rightmost token of the base lacks its lexical tone, as in *banáá-bána* 'four by four' (p. 118).

This pattern of Kikerewe seems to work only for numerals because Odden also claims that 'like number reduplication, the reduplicant in an adjective is toneless', e.g. *mu-gazi-gází* 'kind of wide' (Ibid: 120). This example shows that the entire of the first section of the reduplicated element does not bear any tone.

Likewise, other Bantu languages do not permit copying of the supra-segmental features but stick to reduplication of the segmental materials only (Downing 2003; Mwita 2008; Mathangwane & Mtenje 2010). It means, even if the language has tonological features, reduplication will always avoid copying tones in such languages. Perhaps the following examples from the Bantu language Wandya (spoken in Malawi and Tanzania) (Mathangwane & Mtenje 2010:179) will help make us have a better understanding of this reduplication behaviour.

(14) **Base**   **Reduplicated word**

    lúma (V) 'bite'   *lumalúma* (V) 'bite repeatedly'
    físa (V) 'hide'   *fisafísa* (V) 'hide continuously'
    nyamúla (V) 'pick up'   *nyamulanyamúla* (V) 'pick often'

Like adjectives in Kikerewe, examples in (14) above demonstrate that there is a major difference in the phonological features of the bases and those of the reduplicated words. In fact these data show that at segmental level all the materials of the base are copied but at supra-segmental level we find that tones are left behind. Take for instance the verb *lúma* 'bite' which has segmental features CVCV and supra-segmental features H-L. Its reduplicated counterpart, *lumalúma* 'bite repeatedly' has the segmental features similar to the base, i.e. CVCVCVCV but distinct tone patterns as it has L-L-H-L. This entails that the tone pattern of the base is not realised in the reduplicant.

Morphological evidence: So far, we have discussed features of reduplication which result into the conclusion that it is phonologically motivated. There is, however, another vast amount of literature which suggests that reduplication is morphologically motivated.

The first evidence for treating reduplication as a morphologically motivated process involves the insertion of the common final vowel in Bantu verb. For example, the inserted default vowel -a- in Kinande reduplicated words below (Downing 2000:1) supports the claim that this process is morphologically motivated.

(15)   a.   *eri-hum-**a**-humira* 'to beat to'
              *eri-hum-**a**-humirana* 'to beat for each other'
              *eri-tum-**a**-tumira* 'to send to'
              *eri-tum-**a**-tumana* 'to send each other'

b.   *eri-gamb-**a**-gambul-a* 'to talk'

       *eri-guluk-**a**-guluk-a* 'to fly'

Downing (2000) claims that 'morphological conditions on reduplication are best accounted for by defining the RED as a morphological constituent' (p. 2). She reiterates that that 'the fixed /a/ is best accounted for by defining the reduplicant as a morphological constituent' (p. 2). She argues that for the purpose of inflectional function, the default final vowel surfaces as *-a-* in reduplicated words in the language so as to fulfil the structure of the required morphological shape of these items (p. 6).

The other point which Downing (2000) develops emanates from the points we advanced in section items in section 6.2.1.2 that the base is required to be similar to the reduplicant. Examples in (15b) show that *-a-* is inserted on the RED which satisfies the minimality condition (pp. 11-12). The condition is that the RED should at least be CV-(C)V or (C)V-CV. Thus the default FV is inserted to accomplish the CV pattern required by this condition.

To sum up, the morphological choice of reduplication tends to incline to two facts which involve morphological modifications associated with reduplication. First, the insertion of the default FV and second the similarity between the RED and base. The reduplication which involves this phenomenon is also treated as compounding in some other works (e.g. Inkeles & Zoll 2005).

5.2.1.4 Prolific nature of reduplication

The other characteristic feature of reduplication is its productivity (creativity). The fact is reduplication is not a matter of repeating the materials from the base as a matter of fashion, rather it is a word-formation process. The amount of reduplication provided in the preceding sections suggests that it is one of the major word formation processes available in the Bantu family. Nonetheless, based on Katamba and Stonham (2006), its productivity is partly derivational and partly inflectional.

In Kiswahili, as well as in other Bantu languages (e.g. Kikerewe, Kinyakyusa, Lusaamia etc), this process is quite pervasive and it works in almost all major word-classes. Odden (1996), for instance, discusses reduplication in four word categories in Kikerewe, namely, numerals, nouns, adjectives and verbs. Lusekelo (2009a) offers the description of Kinyakyusa reduplications for numerals, adjectives, nouns, verbs and adverbs.

It is plausible to argue that in these languages, reduplication forms a central section of word formation processes which result into creation of new words with slightly different or completely new in semantic properties. In the line of Katamba and Stonham (2006), reduplication will be treated as derivational process.

Swahili shows that reduplication is associated with derivation because words undergo change in meaning once they are reduplicated. This is well illustrated by Swahili-words such as a verb *chekecha* 'sift' which turns into a noun *chekecheke* 'a sieve' after reduplication. (I deal in books with this issue in details in section 6.3 below).

In other languages such as Hausa (Newman 2000), however, reduplication is an inflectional process. In Hausa, reduplication functions to mark plurality, as shown in *jōjò* 'judge' - *jōjò -jōjò* 'judges'. Also, it gives intensification of adverbs such as *maza* 'quickly' - *maza-maza* 'very quickly'. (This is dealt with in a relatively deeper level in section 6.3 below).

The functions of reduplication mentioned above leads us to the questions whether reduplication provided in (6) for English is really one of the word-formation processes in the language or not. This is the main project we will turn to in the following section.

5.2.2 Characteristics of reduplication in English

Although reduplication per se is not a significant word-formation process in English and French, Ghomeshi *et al.* (2004) offer a description of a phenomenon of contrastive reduplication colloquial English (p. 307). They assert that contrastive reduplication targets word-classes such as nouns, verbs, adjectives, verb particles, and pronouns. Such elements have the semantic effect of focusing the denotation of the reduplicated element on a more sharply delimited, more specialized, range (p. 308).

Since sources appear to neglect it, the reduplicated elements in (American) English need to be examined at a very close range. In (16a-b) below, we offer meanings associated with the combinations from Ghomeshi *et al.* 2004:309). The rest of examples have been collected by the author:

(16)   a.   **Rhyme combinations**   **Origin/base and related meaning**

super-duper   [<*super*] adjective; of the greatest excellence, size, or

effectiveness

willy-nilly   [<*willing*] adverb; whether desired or not; without plan;

haphazardly

pall-mall   [<?] noun; game in which a boxwood ball was struck

with a mallet to drive it through an iron ring

okey-dokey   [<*okey*] sure, alright, sure thing

hanky-panky   [<?] noun; devious or mischievous activity;

illicit sexual activity

b.   **Ablaut combinations**

flim-flam   [<?] noun; nonsense; a deception; a swindle

[<?] verb; to deceive; to swindle

zig-zag   [<?] adjective; having short and sharp turns or angles;

crooked

sing-song   [<?] noun; verse, or a piece of verse

pitter-patter   [<?] noun; a rapid series of light tapping sounds

riff-raff	[<Middle English *riffe* and *raffe*, also *rif* and *raf*) noun; a rabble; a mob; persons of the lowest class in the community	
mish-mash	[<?] noun; collection or mixture of unrelated things; a hodgepodge.	

c. **Other reduplicated-like words**

hodgepodge	a heterogeneous mixture; jumble
mumbo-jumbo	complicated activity
bling bling	glittering
teeny weeny	very small

d. **Onomatopoeic words**

ding-dong	ring, peal (clock's tickling sound, sound ticking of a wall-watch)
flip-flap	sound given by sandals won by someone walking

Let us have a look at the example words provided in (16a-d) above. However, one should try to refer to reduplicated words in Kiswahili and other Bantu languages as well. This will guide the discussion.

One important thing we note is that such words are not treated as typical reduplicated elements even by the authors. For example, Ghomeshi *et al.* (2004:309-310) report that although global reduplication phenomenon is used to express such factors as plurality, diminutives, augmentatives, intensification etc. in other languages, contrastive focus meaning found in (American) English adds a new item to functions of reduplication. Thus, we ill accept their idea of adding contrastive focus of these elements which seem not to be true reduplicated words.

On the function of reduplication in English, the meanings associated with reduplication are vague. This is because it is said by Ghomeshi *et al.* (2004) that 'the use of a word or phrase often leaves open some vagueness, lack of precision, or ambiguity. Contrastive reduplication is used as one way to clarify such situations, by specifying a prototypical denotation of the lexical item in contrast to a potentially looser or more specialized reading.' (p. 311).

Perhaps we should also look into the structure of reduplicated items in English. It is reported that the contrastive reduplication in (American) English cannot be defined in prosodic terms rather it consists of more than a single word (Ghomeshi et al. 310-311). Our observation is that rhyme combinations seem to have source-words like those suggested in the list given in (16a) above (see the column for origin/base and related meaning). This substantiates that these elements satisfy the main feature of reduplication: the base must be similar to the reduplicant.

The ablaut combinations given in (16b) seem to lack the actual bases (originally unreduplicated words) for each. This is evidence that they violate the main feature of reduplication: the base should be similar to the reduplicant.

It is obvious that a number of items (which are very few) also appear to demonstrate the unproductivity of reduplication in English. To this number perhaps we should add the elements given in (16c), i.e. *hodgepodge* 'a heterogeneous mixture; jumble' and *mumbo-jumbo* 'complicated activity'.

Lastly, some onomatopoeic words in English look like reduplicated elements. These elements are given in (16d). likewise, they, however, do not seem to possess the unreduplicated bases as well.

5.3   Functional reduplication

5.3.1   Is reduplication inflectional or derivational?

In the foregoing discussion it was noted earlier that reduplication is a kind of word-formation process attested in Bantu language continent; perhaps less pervasive in English. However, we have to decide whether it functions as a derivational process (altering word meaning and/or word class) or inflectional (assuming grammatical roles) (Katamba 1993:46-47).

It is established that as a word-formation process, reduplication is both inflectional and derivational hence it remains central in morphological analyses of languages. Newman (2000:508) asserts that active reduplication refers to the word formation rules in which reduplicand functions as a synchronically recognizable derivational and inflectional process. Therefore, it is one of the ways through which derivational processes as well as inflectional mechanisms of deriving lexemes manifest.

Derivational function: Across Bantu family, a linguistic area where this phenomenon is highly productive, reduplication is associated with derivation because words undergo change in meaning once they are reduplicated. This is well illustrated by Kiswahili words such as a verb *chekecha* 'sift' which turns into a noun *chekecheke* 'a sieve' after reduplication. Another example is the noun *bia* 'corporation' which becomes a verb *biabia* 'work vigorously' after doubling.

In the literature, it is shown that reduplication is one of the word-formation processes attested in several languages of the world, e.g. Mandarin Chinetc.ese, Tagalog, Nookta (Katamba 1993; Lin 2001; Stonham 2004) and in Bantu languages, e.g. Kiswahili, Kinande, Kinyakyusa etc. (see Downing 2003; Contini-Morava 2007; Lusekelo 2009a). Put in other words, reduplication changes the meaning of the base (Kouwenberg & Darlene 2003).

Looking across the Bantu area, we find that reduplication is associated with several interpretations (Lusekelo 2009a). Therefore, the semantics revolving around these word-formation processes can be further discussed after the semantics surrounding reduplication in the following Kiswahili words from Rubanza (1997), Novatna (2000) and TUKI (2001).

(17) **Base**   **Reduplicated word**

tamu (Adj) 'delicious, sweet'   *tamutamu* (N) 'sweets'
pole (Adj) 'gentle'   *polepole* (Adv) 'slowly'
chokoa (V) 'poke, prod at'   *chokochoko* (N) 'quarrels, provocation'
geuza (V) 'change, alter'   *geugeu* (Adj) 'changeable, unstable'
chekecha (V) 'sift'   *chekecheke* (N) 'a sieve'
bia (N) 'corporation'   *biabia* (V) 'work vigorously'
jivu (N) 'ash'   *jivujivu* (Adj) 'grey'

(18) **Base**   **Reduplicated word**

moto (Adj) 'warm, hot'   *motomoto* (Adj) 'ardent'
bui (N) 'large spider'   *buibui* (N) 'spider'
dogo (Adj) 'small'   *dogodogo* (Adj) 'very small'
kubwa (Adj) 'large'   *kubwakubwa* (Adj) 'very large'
mbali (Adv) 'far'   *mbalimbali* (Adj) 'various, different'

Two senses of derivation described by Katamba and Stonham (2006:49) that either derivation changes the word-class that the base belongs to or change the meaning of the base to which they are attached to, are realised in data in (17) and (18) above. On the one hand, we see in the example (17) above that bases which fall under different word-categories namely adjective, verb and noun are transferred into different word-classes namely noun, adverb and verb. For example, an adjective pole 'gentle' becomes and adverb *polepole* 'slowly' and a noun *bia* 'corporation' becomes a verb *biabia* 'work vigorously'.

On the other hand, meaning of the data in (18) show that the kind of derivation involved here is typically of the change of meaning of the bases after reduplication. For instance, we see that an adjective *moto* 'warm, hot' remains in the same word-class after reduplication to *motomoto* 'ardent' but the meaning of the reduplicated word is changed. The same happens to a noun *bui* 'large spider' which remains a noun after reduplication but changes in meaning to *buibui* 'spider'.

The definition in Katamba and Stonham (2006:49) which uses either...or style faces a problem once other data are involved. We see an example of bata 'duck' batabata 'waddle, walk flat footed' in example (19) below that the word experiences both derivation by change of word class from noun to verb and derivation by change of meaning of the base. This is an area that Kiswahili data contributes to the better understanding of the fact that some morphological processes are language specific and my audience should be aware of the fact that not all processes cut across world languages.

(19) **Base**   **Reduplicated word**

bata (N) 'duck'   *batabata* (V) 'waddle, walk flat footed'
mbali (Adv) 'far'   *mbalimbali* (Adj) 'various, different'
fura (V) 'be enraged'   *furufuru* (Adj) 'copious, plenty'

However, this kind of analysis faces a problem once one considers another word given in (19) above. It is not very much clear whether the reduplicated word is typically a copy of the base. As will be explicitly uncovered in the discussion below, such kind of a question could be well answered using data which involves identification of the reduplicants through the analysis of both segmental and suprasegmental features in Bantu languages (Downing 2000b, 2003; Mwita 2008; Mathangwane & Mtenje 2010).

Inflectional function: The different remaining functions of reduplication fit altogether into the second way of word formation described in Katamba (1993) that they involve inflectional morphology. Booij (2005:99) says inflection involves morphological marking of the properties of a lexeme resulting into a number of forms of that lexeme, a set of grammatical words. These grammatical words function to delineate several inflectional roles.

Briefly, languages demonstrate at least one main inflectional property mentioned called *number* as in (20) below. In these functions, examples from languages are provided to illustrate such kind of inflectional process:

(20)   a.   Number marking (singular-plural distinctions) by reduplication

    Hausa: *àkàwu* 'clerk' > *àkàwu-àkàwu* 'clerks'

    àgōgo 'clock' > *àgōgo-àgōgo* 'clocks'

    Indonesian: *rumah* 'house' >*rumahrumah* 'houses'

    ibu 'mother'> *ibuibu* 'mothers'

    lalat 'fly' > *lalatlalat* 'flies'

  b.   Tense marking (time references)

    Tagalog: *bili* 'buy' >   *bibili* 'will buy'

    kain 'eat' > *kakain* 'will eat'

    pasok 'enter' > *papasok* 'will enter'

At this juncture, it can be concluded that the patterns of reduplication in these languages confirm that reduplication is an active process which is usually comparable in normal function to normal affixation process which brings about grammatical function like plurality and tenses.

5.3.2 The question of reduplication functions in Kiswahili

Beginning with verbs, data show that Kiswahili verbs undergo reduplication for **intensification** and **repeated** actions (Novatna 2000:64, 65). Schadeberg (1984:4 [1992]) pointed out that reduplicated verb stems in Kiswahili indicate **repetition** of action with low intensity. Examples given in (21) below are illustrative of this function. In fact most verbs in Kiswahili reduplicate in order to designate the repetition of the actions in the described in verbs.

(21)   **Base**   **Reduplicated word**

    hoji 'interrogate, examine'   *hojihoji* 'cross-examine'
    chapua 'speed up'   *chapuchapu* 'hurry up'
    cheka 'laugh'   *chekacheka* 'keep laughing'

piga 'hit'	*pigapiga* 'hit repeatedly'
imba 'sing'	*imbaimba* 'sing frequently'

In (21) above some verbs like *hoji* 'interrogate, examine' show intensification of the action described in the verb when they reduplicate to verbs like *hojihoji* 'cross-examine'. Other verbs show repeated actions such as *piga* 'hit' becomes *pigapiga* 'hit repeatedly'.

A mark of intensity and repetition is not the only function of reduplication attested in Kiswahili verbs. It is indicated that reduplication gives **focus** in Kiswahili (Lusekelo 2009). This is shown in examples below.

(22) **Unreduplicated forms**

i. *Mtoto a-na-m-pa mbwa chakula*
child SM-PRES-OM-R dog food
'The child gives the dog food'

ii. *Wazazi wa-na-wa-pa watoto hela*
Parents SM-PRES-OM-R children money
'Parents give children some money'

iii. *Mgeni a-na-tu-pa misaada*
Guest SM-PRES-OM-R help
'The guest gives us assistance'

(23) **Reduplicated forms (Focus on object-noun)**

i. *Mtoto a-na-m-pa-mpa mbwa chakula*
child SM-PRES-OM-R dog food
'The child gives the dog food carelessly'

ii. *Wazazi wa-na-wa-pa-wapa watoto hela*
Parents SM-PRES-OM-R children money
'Parents give children money recklessly'

iii. *Mgeni a-na-tu-pa-tu-pa misaada*
Guest SM-PRES-OM-R help
'The guest gives us assistance thoughtlessly'

(24) **Use of adverbials (Focused action)**

i. *Mtoto a-na-m-pa mbwa chakula mara kwa mara*
child SM-PRES-OM-R dog food several times
'The child gives the dog food often'

ii. *Wazazi wa-na-wa-pa watoto hela mara nyingi*
Parents SM-PRES-OM-R children money several times
'Parents frequently give children money'

iii. *Mgeni a-na-tu-pa misaada mara nyingi*
Guest SM-PRES-OM-R help several times
'The guest gives us assistance frequently'

In Lusekelo (2009c) it is stated that the unreduplicated forms of (22) the action is treated as a single one, i.e. doing it once at a defined moment. The reduplicated stems in (23) carry the object marker and denote recklessness and carelessness of the action but the focus is on 'the action of giving to specific object'. However, if Kiswahili speakers wish to accentuate the repetitiveness of the action, then the use of adverbials becomes the best option (24).

Furthermore, it is noted that throughout Bantu literature, verbal reduplication has semantic implications. For example, Lusaamia verbal reduplication indicates repetition, habitualness, and aimlessness (Marlo 2002:1); Bukusu verb stems reduplicate to give the meaning like 'repeatedly' or 'carelessly' (Downing 2003:73, 74); Kuria data demonstrates that verbal reduplication involves repetition, intensity, continuation and the lack of seriousness of the action or event (Mwita 2008:233); and in Kinyakyusa verbal reduplication is for intensification and repetition purposes (Lusekelo 2009). This function available in Kiswahili words reflects the similarity of Kiswahili and other Bantu languages.

On the question of nouns and adjectives, Kiswahili data shows that reduplication of these words is for intensification purposes. This is shown in examples in (25) below in which reduplicated nouns and adjectives give intensive readings.

(25) **Base**   **Reduplicated word**
  mbali (Adv) 'far'   *mbalimbali* (Adj) 'various, different'
  dogo (Adj) 'small'   *dogodogo* (Adj) 'very small'
  moto (Adj) 'warm, hot'   *motomoto* (Adj) 'ardent, passionate'

Data in other Bantu languages demonstrate that semantically full noun reduplication involves a process that accentuates the intrinsic semantic features of nouns and adjectives (Lusekelo 2009a). Also, the literature shows that as far as the function is concerned, noun and adjective (nominal) reduplication involves the semantic interpretation commonly known as 'the kind of N', i.e. the kind of Nominal meaning (see Odden 1996).

5.4 Types of reduplication

Though there are similarities in the patterns of reduplication in some language phylum, e.g. within Germanic languages or in Niger-Congo languages, patterns of reduplication also differ from one language to the other in the same phylum, e.g. between English and French or Kiswahili and Subiya. Studies, however, have established some clusters of various kinds of reduplication across the world.

For example, existing literature for Bantu languages indicates that reduplicative processes involve the commonest complete reduplication, partial (asymmetrical) reduplication as well as pseudo-reduplication that involves changes in the copied material, i.e. segmental reduplication (see Novatna 2000; Kula 2004; Atindogbé & Fogwe 2009; Lusekelo 2009a).

Looking into the word structures of Kiswahili, two types of reduplication attested in the language are obtainable in the previous works (see e.g. Rubanza 1997; Mnenuka 2010). The types include: one, complete reduplication, which involves copying of the entire word and repeating it, as in *maji-maji* 'somewthat wet' (Ashton 1944: 316), and two, partial reduplication which involves part of the base, as in *pepeta* 'sift' (Mohamed 2001: 220). This is one of the areas which are revisited in this chapter. In fact, data in Kiswahili point towards several mechanisms through which reduplication manifests itself in the language. Probably this lead to the third point discussed in this review.

A number of kinds of reduplication seem to be attested in other languages of the world. For instance, the picture described above, at least for Niger-Congo, is not obtained in several other languages available in African continent, e.g. Hausa and Amharic (Lesau 1995; Newman 2000) and Nigerian pidgin and Krio (Ugot & Ogundipe 2011). In these languages, several types of reduplication patterns are attested; varying from segmental copying on either side of the word through tonal alterations to full copy.

As it will be evident in the course of the discussions in this section, even the terminologies to denote the various types of reduplication differ from one language phylum to another which in fact indicates the different patterns therein. For example, right from the major titles, Newman (2000:509) uses the expression nature of the morphophonological processes to designate the different patterns of reduplication in Hausa. Other authors use the term types of reduplication (see Novatna 2000; Atindogbé & Fogwe 2009; Lusekelo 2009a).

5.4.1 Total reduplication or complete copy

The kind of reduplication called full copy refers to the process which copies the entire base-word and repeats it fully. In this case, even tone patterns are copied and repeated. Thus, the base and reduplicated element are similar in features, both segmental and auto-segmental.

Complete reduplication in Swahili: The kind of complete reduplication is attested in several word-classes in Kiswahili. As in other Bantu languages, perhaps across world languages, total or full reduplication involves copying of the entire base/stem (Odden 1996:113). This is illustrated by adjectives, verbs as well as adverbs reduplication given in examples in (26) below whereby the entire words are copied and repeated.

(26) **Base**   **Reduplicated word**

    dogo (Adj) 'small'   *dogodogo* (Adj) 'very small'
    moto (Adj) 'warm, hot'   *motomoto* (Adj) 'ardent, passionate'
    kubwa (Adj) 'large'   *kubwakubwa* (Adj) 'very large'
    moto (Adj) 'warm, hot'   *motomoto* (Adj) 'ardent, passionate'
    mbali (Adv) 'far'   *mbalimbali* (Adj) 'various, different'
    tinga (V) 'swing'   *tingatinga* (N) 'bridge made of timber'

In Kiswahili, as in other Bantu languages, there are cases in which adjectives take the agreement prefixes which are a copy of the noun to which they are attached (Lusekelo 2009a). In such a case Kiswahili adjectives undergo total reduplication as exemplified in (27) below.

(27) **Base**   **Reduplicated word**
    wazuri 'beautiful'   *wazuriwazuri* 'very beautiful'
    mdogo 'small'   *mdogomdogo* 'very small'

warefu 'tall'	*warefuwarefu* 'fairly tall'
kikubwa 'large'	*kikubwakikubwa* 'very large'
cheupe 'white'	*cheupecheupe* 'whitish'
cheusi 'black'	*cheusicheusi* 'darkish'

The same pattern of full reduplication is attested in Kiswahili monosyllabic verbs. In such verbs, the infinitive form ku- is copied together with the stem. It seems that very fewer monosyllabic verbs exist in Kiswahili because the dictionary lists only a couple of them which are exemplified below (TUKI 2001).

(28) **Base**   **Reduplicated word**

kufa 'to perish'	*kufakufa* 'to perish repeatedly'
kucha 'to be pious, rise (sun)'	*kuchakucha* 'to be pious often, rise often'
kuja 'to come'	*kujakuja* 'to come frequently'
kupa 'to give'	*kupakupa* 'to give frequently'
kuta 'to hit'	*kutakuta* 'to hit repeatedly'
kula 'to eat'	*kulakula* 'to eat frequently'

This is not the end of the phenomena described above because there are a number of other words which are formed through complete reduplication in Kiswahili.

(29) **Base**   **Reduplicated word**

taka (N) 'dirt, rubbish'	*takataka* (N) 'dirt, rubbish'
juu (Adv) 'on, over'	*juujuu* (Adj) 'arrogant, high up'
wima (Adv) 'erect, upright'	*wimawima* (Adj) 'upright'
wasi (N) 'disobedience'	*wasiwasi* (N) 'worry, anxiety'
hivi (Adv) 'this way'	*hivi hivi* (Adv) 'so so'

Total reduplication elsewhere: Mandarin Chinese demonstrates full reduplication. Lin (2001) has provided, among others, elements in (30) below. Examples in (30a) show a complete copy of both segment and autosegment features. On the contrary, examples in (30b) show copying of only segments (vowels and consonants) of words:

(30)   **Base**   **Reduplicated word**

a.	*hóng* 'red'	*hónghóng* 'quite red'
	pàng 'fat'	*pàngpàng* 'quite fat'
b.	*shì* 'try'	*shìshi* 'give it a try'
	kàn 'look'	*kaàkan* 'have a look'

Findings from Newman (2000) for Hausa present a phenomenon he calls full reduplication (also he identifies them as exact copy). Several fascinating patterns are attested in Hausa. Main patterns are presented below.

First, in this process, the underlying stem is repeated twice exactly as it is, i.e. the full stem serves as the reduplicand, as in *jōjì* 'judge' > *jōjì-jōjì* 'judges'. Second, there is a full reduplication with morphologically specified vowel shortening. Here there is full reduplication, including tone, but the final vowel of each component is shortened, as illustrated by *dōgō* 'tall' > *dōgo-dōgo* 'medium height' (Newman 2000:509).

Third, Newman (2000:510) mentions of the presence of full reduplication with a prespecified tone pattern and final vowel in Hausa. Here the process is full reduplication on a stem that takes tone-integrating suffix, e.g. *bugà* 'beat' > *bùge-bùge* 'beatings'. The fourth type is what he calls full reduplication with loss of final vowel in the first element, i.e. there is loss of the stem-final vowel in the first element, as shown by *wuri* 'quickly' > *wurwuri* 'very quickly'.

In Amharic, total reduplication of adjectives expresses either large number or selectivity. This is exemplified by *tǝru* 'good' > *tǝru tǝru* 'several good' for large number and *räǧǧim* 'all' > *räǧǧim räǧǧimun* 'just/only' for selectivity (Lesau 1995:175).

The nature of total reduplicative words in Dholuo offers the mitigating reduplication because the prefix, root and suffix are copied and results into word joined with -*a*- followed by a root and final -*a*- (Tucker 1994; Rubino 2005). This is shown in the following words:

(31)   **Base**   **Reduplicated word**

rech 'fish'   *rech-arecha* 'any, mere fish'
tedo 'cook'   *tedo-atédâ* 'just cooking'
nyóro 'yesterday'   *nyóro-anyórâ* 'only yesterday'

The foregoing discussion shows that complete reduplication is associated with copying all segments (and autosegments) and repeating them, as in Kiswahili and Mandarin Chinese. Other cases show that total reduplication is associated with copying the base materials and modifying them once repeated, as in Hausa and Mandarin Chinese. In Dholuo, full copy shows various morphological adjustments of the repeated elements.

5.4.2   Partial reduplication

This type of reduplication involves copying of a section of a base. In most cases, only a syllable is copied and repeated. Other literatures call it **syllabic copy** because only syllabic materials are copied from the bases. Moreover, partial reduplication in the literature for Bantu reduplication is also referred to as **asymmetrical reduplication**.

In Kiswahili Bantu, a large bunch of words which manifest partial reduplication include disyllabic and polysyllabic verbs. As shown in (32) below, such verbs involve copying of the stem only. It means that once the prefixes like the infinitive *ku*- is attached, reduplication involves only the stem.

(32)   **Base**   **Reduplicated word**

kuhoji 'to examine'   *kuhojihoji* 'to cross-examine'
kucheka 'to laugh'   *kuchekacheka* 'to keep laughing'
kupiga 'to hit'   *kupigapiga* 'to hit repeatedly'
kutembea 'to walk'   *kutembeatembea* 'to loiter'
kusambaza 'to scatter'   *kusambazasambaza* 'to scatter carelessly'
kunong'oneza 'to whisper to'   *kunong'onezanong'oneza* 'to whisper too frequently'

Partial reduplication in another Bantu language Kinyakyusa tends to select only derivational suffixes and reject inflectional prefixes (Lusekelo 2009c). This means inflectional prefixes like the infinitive *ku-* as well as the object marker are not copied, as illustrated in (33) while derivational suffixes like the causative form *-esy-* and reciprocal morpheme *-an-* are doubled, as shown in Nyakyusa examples in (34).

(33) **Base**   **Reduplicated word**

    kundililia 'to cry for him'   *kundililalilila* 'to cry for him often'
    kumpa 'to give him/her'   *kumpampa* 'to give him/her frequently'
    kubakoma 'to hit them'   *kubakomakoma* 'to hit them repeatedly'

(34) **Base**   **Reduplicated word**

    kusekana 'to laugh each other'   *kusekanasekana* 'to keep laughing at each other'
    kukomana 'to hit each other'   *kukomakomana* 'to hit each other repeatedly'
    kukinisya 'to cause to play'   *kukinisyakinisya* 'to cause to play repeatedly'

However, tense and aspect formatives, morphemes for negation as well as subject markers are not copied even in monosyllabic words in Kiswahili. This happens once the infinitive appears in the verbs. Such a pattern informs us that reduplicants are usually at least two syllables in the language. The following examples will help us have a better understanding of this behaviour.

(35) **Base**   **Reduplicated word**

    walikuja 'they came'   *walikujakuja* 'to come frequently'
    watawapa 'they will give them'   *watawapawapa* 'they will give frequently'
    hawakula 'they didn't eat'   *hawakulakula* 'they didn't eat frequently'

In examples in (35) above the tense and aspect markers *-li-* and *-ta-*, an object marker *-wa-* and the negation form *-ha-* do not surface in the reduplicated forms of the monosyllabic words. This situation happens because the minimally bisyllabic requirement is satisfied.

Moreover, in disyllabic and polysyllabic words in Kiswahili, the inflectional prefixes particularly the object marker, tense and aspect formatives, subject marker as well as the infinitive are not copied. Contrary to this behaviour, it is shown above that such forms, especially the object marker and the infinitive are doubled in monosyllabic words in Kiswahili. But in disyllabic and polysyllabic words, the infinitive, object marker as well as tense and aspect formatives are not copied. This is illustrated in (36) below where both the tense and aspect formatives namely -we- (immediate past) and -li- (remote past) and an object marker -wa- are not reduplicated.

(36) *kuwacheka* 'to laugh at them'   *kuwachekacheka* 'to keep laughing at them'
    kuwapiga 'to hit them'   *kuwapigapiga* 'to hit them repeatedly'
    wametembea 'they walked'   *wametembeatembea* 'they loitered'
    tulilala 'we slept'   *tulilalalala* 'we slept frequently'

This kind of pattern points towards the fact that Kiswahili permits minimal reduplication of two syllables. Downing (1999) and Mwita (2008) show that Bantu languages allow reduplication of at least two syllables hence the adjustment strategies, among others, involve copying of the inflectional forms like the object marker and the infinitive.

Furthermore, in some cases adjectives in Kiswahili undergo partial reduplication once they are attached with inflectional morphemes like the agreement forms. This is exemplified in (37).

(37) **Base**   **Reduplicated word**

    mdogo 'small'   *mdogodogo* 'very small'
    warefu 'tall'   *warefurefu* 'fairly tall'
    kikubwa 'large'   *kikubwakubwa* 'very large'
    cheupe 'white'   *cheupeupe* 'whitish'
    cheusi 'black'   *cheusiusi* 'darkish'

Partial reduplication in other languages: Tagalong (Austronesian language) makes use of partial reduplication. In the following examples, only the first CV-syllables are repeated from the base in order to express grammatical functions:

(38) *bili* 'buy'   *bibili* 'will buy'
     kain 'eat'   *kakain* 'will eat'
     pasok 'enter'   *papasok* 'will enter'

Newman (2000:510) mentions two patterns which seem to be typical partial reduplication types in Hausa. The first one is **rightward reduplication** of the final syllable of the stem, not including tone. It means that only segments of the final syllable are reduplicated. This is shown in the following word: *shāfā̀* 'wipe' > *shāffafē* 'wiped'.

In addition, Hausa has prefixal reduplication which is the process that involves **leftward copying** of the initial syllable from the stem without excluding tone. This is shown in the following examples: *santsī* 'smoothness' > *sassantsā* 'very smooth, slippery' and *tàmbayà̀* 'ask' > *tantambayà̀* 'ask often'.

Adjectives and verbs in Amharic provide evidence of partial reduplication. For instance, Lesau (1995: 175) reports that in adjectives, the second radical may be reduplicated and germinated, as in *tälləq* 'big' > *tälälləq* 'big' 'very big' and *mälkam* 'pretty' > *mälkakam* 'very pretty'. Idris (1981:18) reports reduplication in Amharic verbs, e.g. *mangər* 'to tell' > *mannəgagər* 'to discuss' and *manəgagər* 'to tell bit by bit' as well as *sibbir* 'he broke completely' > *sibirbirr* 'he smashed (broke into pieces)'.

To sum up, partial reduplication involves copying only basic materials from the base, as in Kiswahili. Other types of partial reduplication include reduplication which takes the form of the left-copying of syllables of the base, as in Tagalog, Amharic and Hausa. In other cases final syllables of the base are copied, as in Hausa.

5.4.3 Modified morpheme reduplication

Reduplication is not always a straightforward process rather in many instances it may involve processes which deviate from the norm. Usually abnormal reduplications do engage in modifications particularly of segments of the base resulting into somehow different in morphology of the reduplicant from the base. In this book I treat such instances of doubling as modified morpheme reduplication.

The kind of reduplication referred to here is called segmental reduplication in other works and is approached from templatic morphology (see Katamba 1993; Stonham 2004; Booij 2005; Mwita 2008, among others). In such languages as Tagalog (Philippines), Saho (Eritrea), Nuuchahnulth or Nootka (indigenous Canadian language) and Kinande (Democratic Republic of Congo) segmental reduplication involves copying of a segment like a consonant or vowel or an entire syllable (hence CV-template) and repeat it to the base to make a new word.

In Kiswahili, two cases that involve modification of the base once reduplicated are mentioned in Novatna (2000: 60-63). One, certain changes may occur in the act of reduplication. For instance, the final reduplicated form may be derived from an underlying form, usually a different kind of part of speech particularly verbs which lack the infinitive form ku- in their underlying forms. Two, we said that affixation is one of the major means of word formation in Kiswahili, and in other Bantu languages. Traditionally, in the process of assigning prefixes to some words change in meaning occur. However, reduplicated forms may also take prefixes hence their semantic properties usually changes change.

Several words are formed through this process in Kiswahili. Novatna (2000: 60-61) mentioned reduplicated verbs which lose their final vowel. Such verbs are exemplified in (39). In this instance it is only one segment namely the final vowel of the base which is replaced with another vowel of the reduplicated word.

(39) **Base**   **Reduplicated word**

chapua (V) 'speed up'   *chapuchapu* (Adv) 'hurry up'

geuza (V) 'change, alter'   *geugeu* (Adj) 'changeable, unstable'

fura (V) 'be enraged'   *furufuru* (Adj) 'copious, plenty'

zulu (V) 'be dizzy'   *zulizuli* (N) 'dizziness'

chokoa (V) 'poke, prod at'   *chokochoko* (N) 'quarrels, provocation'

pinda (V) 'bend, twist'   *pindupindu* (N) 'cholera'

tinga (V) 'swing'   *tingetinge* (N) 'bridge made of timber'

A couple of reduplicated words in Kiswahili undergo modification of the consonants. Such lexemes involve the deletion of a syllable of the base, usually the final one and then replacing it with another syllable in the reduplicated counterpart, as indicated in examples in (40) below.

(40) **Base**   **Reduplicated word**

kumbuka (V) 'remember'   *kumbukumbu* (N) 'records, remembrance'

chekecha (V) 'sift'   *chekecheke* (N) 'a sieve'

5.4.4 Pseudo-reduplication

The notion pseudo-reduplication (also written *pseudoreduplication* or *pseudo reduplication*) entails a kind of doubling of a limited set of materials from the base in order to satisfy certain conditions in the reduplicated forms. In the literature it is noted that in the process of forming new words through reduplication, a number of new words result from the copying of certain materials from the base to the reduplicated words in order to fulfil some morphological or phonological needs (Inkelas & Zoll 2005).

Pseudo-reduplication is common in creoles and pidgins of Arabic language like Nubi (Kenya and Uganda), Juba Arabic (Southern Sudan), Turku (Chad), Gulf Pidgin Arabic and Romanian Pidgin Arabic (Avram 2011). In these creoles and pidgins of Arabic, several pseudo-reduplicated words like those below are a commonplace because these are oral languages though lexicalization of these elements is also attested (see Avram 2011: 243). In (41) three case studies of the pseudo-reduplicated words are presented.

(41) **Pseudo-reduplicants in Arabic pidgins and creoles**

Pseudo-reduplicant	*Language*
'sim'sim 'sesame'	Nuba
simsim 'sesame'	Juba Arabic
semsem 'sesame'	Turku
sawasawa 'together'	Gulf Pidgin Arabic
sawasawa 'together'	Romanian Pidgin Arabic
semsem 'similar, identical'	Romanian Pidgin Arabic

The first word *simsim* 'sesame' is derived from an Arabic root which is common in Sudanese Colloquium Arabic while the second word *sawasawa* 'together' is etymologically derived from Arabic (Arvin 2011: 226, 242). Traditionally, in Arabic the word اعم means 'together, jointly, with each other, simultaneously' while the other word, مسمس means 'sesame'. However, the English word *sesame* is opted for by the speakers of these languages. But the word is modified through pseudo-reduplication in the borrowing languages. These are explicit instances whereby words are modified in order to fulfil some communicative purposes in some languages.

The third case involves pseudo-reduplication of the English word *same* in Romanian Pidgin Arabic. This is a case which provides an open ground for observing the question of pseudo-reduplication for non-Arabic speakers. The word is articulated as /se⊠m/ in English. Speakers of Romanian Pidgin Arabic have taken the sound and doubled it to produce the word *semsem* which means 'similar' or 'identical' in their language.

In literature for reduplication in Kiswahili (Novatna 2000), pseudo-reduplication is treated as not involving doubling of segments of the base but lack of the underlying base. In this book such approach is maintained because there are a great number of words which seem to be formed through reduplication of some of the syllables. Novatna (2000: 66) contends that such cases do not involve reduplication because of two reasons: (i) the words lack their underlying forms and reduplicated ones and (ii) they represent a single entity with intact meaning.

The following words, mostly nouns and adjectives, seem to be reduplicated but in fact they lack their base in Kiswahili.

(42)　*tongotongo*　'discharge from the eye'
　　　felefele　　'millet of an inferior kind'
　　　digidigi　　'kind of antelope, dik dik'
　　　hondohondo　'crowned hornbill'
　　　tepetepe　　'soft, tender'
　　　goigoi　　　'lazy, weak'
　　　konokono　　'snail'
　　　lengelenge　'blister'
　　　halahala　　'immediately, soon'
　　　wasiwasi　　'worry, confusion'
　　　hekaheka　　'struggle, confusion'

The case of nominal pseudo-reduplication is not an individual one in the language. The following verbal expressions seem to be pseudo-reduplicants in Kiswahili.

(43)　*vungavunga*　'crumple, crush'
　　　wayawaya　　'stagger, stumble'
　　　zongazonga　'confuse'
　　　tangatanga　'loiter, wander'
　　　gaagaa　　　'wiggle, jiggle '

Some two significant observations are worth mentioning here before proceeding to explain the notion of **pseudo-reduplication**. First, some words of English origin, e.g. *waya* 'wire' and *tepe* 'tape, braid' exist in Kiswahili lexicon (TUKI 2001). Such words should never be treated as base words for the reduplicants like *wayawaya* 'stagger, stumble' and *tepetepe* 'soft, tender' respectively. Second, word structures of the shapes like *vunga and *tongo seem to have a typical Kiswahili morphology and one may assume that they are roots for the words *vungavunga* 'crumple, crush' and *tongotongo* 'discharge from the eye' respectively. Nonetheless, such words do not exist in Kiswahili lexicon (TUKI 2001). These observations point towards the fact that words given above are typical instances of pseudo-reduplication.

In this book the case of reduplication discussed immediately above which are attested in Kiswahili is maintained as a kind of pseudo-reduplication because it is also described elsewhere in the literature. For instance, Zuraw (2002) says that in addition to various productive reduplicative morphemes, Tagalog (spoken in Philippines) has a large number of pseudo-reduplicated roots, as those in (44) below, i.e. roots of which one portion (the pseudo-reduplicant) is identical to another (the pseudo-base), but whose pseudo-base cannot stand alone, and which lack the morphosyntactic or semantic characteristics of a morphologically reduplicated Tagalog word.

(44)	*mismís* (N)	'remnants of food left after a meal'
	patpát (N)	'stick, piece of split bamboo'
	bunbón (N)	'dam for attracting fish; clear pond'
	lulód (N)	'shin'
	lulón (N)	'swallowing'

In Tagalog, Zuraw (2002) says, the pseudo-reduplicated words are not accidentally so because there are far more pseudo-reduplicated words than would be expected through random phoneme combination. Also, pseudo-reduplicated roots are phonologically exceptional in two ways. Firstly, it is rare to find two occurrences of the same consonant within a root except in pseudo-reduplicated words. It means that not just any root with two identical consonants is counted here as pseudo-reduplicated. Secondly, pseudo-reduplicated roots can contain consonant clusters that are otherwise rare or nonexistent root-internally.

Several reasons are established from a synchronic attempt that the roots above are not morphologically reduplicated but pseudo-reduplicated. Firstly, in Tagalog the minimal root is disyllabic; the only monosyllabic roots are clitics and loans. So if the words above were reduplicated, it would be from too-small roots like **lu*, **pat*, **bun* and **mis* which are not allowed in the language. Secondly, although Tagalog does have productive *CV*-reduplication, there is no productive *CVC-* reduplication. Thirdly, although many pseudo-reduplicated roots have a mimetic (imitation), there are no fixed meanings associated with the pseudo-reduplicating patterns.

Contrary to observations pointed out immediately above, the notion pseudo reduplication is treated rather differently by other scholars such as Newman (2000) for the Hausa reduplication patterns. He says that Hausa has a variety of reduplicative -*VCV* formatives, in which the *C* copies the consonant of the preceding syllable, as in the following elements (p. 511):

(45)	**Base**	**Reduplicated word**
	wurī 'place'	*wurầrē* 'places'
	damō 'lizard'	*dam-ầme* 'lizards'
	fuskằ 'face'	*fušakà* 'faces'
	zōmō 'rabbit'	*zōmầyē* 'rabbits'

It seems that Newman (2000) is irritated by scholars who treat it as reduplication as he says that in most studies, these are included as types of partial reduplication. He suggests that it is probably more accurate, however, to describe them as being simply affixes (rather than reduplicated elements), where the vowels (and usually the tone [tone is usually similar, i.e. high-low-high]) are fully specified but consonants are phonologically underspecified (p. 511).

Resources cited:

Atindogbé, Gratien G. & Chibaka, Evelyn Fogwe. 2009. Reduplication in Gunu: Segmental and prosodic description. In: Tanda, Vicent A., Henry K. Jick & Pius N. Tamanji (eds). *Language, Literature, and Social Discourse in Africa: Essays in Honour of Emmanuel Nges Chia*. Bamenda: Agwecams.

Avram, Andrei A. 2011. Pseudo-reduplication, reduplication and repletion: The case of Arabic-lexified pidgins and creoles. *RRL,* LVI, 3, Bucureşti. pp. 225-256.

Booij, Geert. 2002. *The Morphology of Dutch*. Oxford: Oxford University Press.

Contini-Morava, Ellen. 2007. Swahili morphology. In: Kaye, Alan S. (ed.). *Morphology of Asia and Africa*, vol. 2. Winona Lake and Indiana: Eisenbrauns. pp. 1129-1158.

Downing, Laura J. 1999. Verbal reduplication in three Bantu languages. In: Kager, René, Harry van der Hulst & Wim Zonnevald (eds.). *The Prosody-Morphology Interface*. Cambridge: Cambridge University Press. pp. 62-89.

Downing, Laura J. 2000a. Morphological and prosodic constraints on Kinande verbal reduplication. *Phonology*, vol. 17, pp. 1-38.

Downing, Laura J. 2000b. Satisfying minimality in Ndebele. *ZAS Papers in Linguistics*, vol. 19. pp. 23-39.

Downing, Laura J. 2003. Bukusu reduplication. In: Githiora, C., Littlefield, H. and Manfredi, V. (eds.). *Trends in African Linguistics 5*. Lawrenceville, New Jersey: Africa World Press. pp. 73-84.

Downing, Laura J. 2009. Linear disorder in Bantu reduplication. *A Talk at the Workshop on the Division of Labor between Morphology and Phonology & Fourth Network Meeting*. Amsterdam: Meertens Instituut.

Felberg, Knut. 1996. *Nyakyusa-English-Swahili and English-Nyakyusa Dictionary*. Dar es Salaam: Mkuki na Nyota Publishers.

Fox, Anthony. 2000. *Prosodic Features and Prosodic Structure: The Phonology of Suprasegmentals*. Oxford: Oxford University Press.

Ghomeshi, Jila, Ray Jackendoff, Nicole Rosen & Kevin Russell (2004). Contrastive focus reduplication in English (The Salad-Salad Paper). *Natural Language & Linguistic Theory*, vol. 22: 307-357.

Idris, Abdul A. 1981. The semantic structure of verbal reduplication: A case study of reduplication in Amharic, Hindi, Malay, Salish and Siroi. *Kansas Working Papers in Lingui*stics, 6: 17-42.

Inkelas, Sharon & Zoll, Cheryl. 2005. *Reduplication: Doubling in Morphology*. Cambridge: Cambridge University Press.

Kouwenberg, Silvia. 2003. Introduction. In: Kouwenberg, Silvia. (ed.). *Twice as Meaningful: Reduplication in Pidgins, Creoles and other Contact Languages*. London: Battlebridge Publications. pp. 1-6.

Kula, Nancy C. 2004. Domain variability in inflected reduplication. *MALILIME: Malawian Journal of Linguistics*, 4: 45-63.

Leslau, Wolf. 1995. *Reference Grammar of Amharic*. Wiesbaden: Harrassowitz.

Lin, Hua. 2001. *A Grammar of Mandarin Chinese*. Munchen: Lincom Europa.

Lodhi, Y. Abdulaziz. 2002. Verbal extensions in Bantu: The case of Kiswahili and Nyamwezi. *Africa and Asia*, 2. pp. 4-26.

Lusekelo, Amani. 2009c. A description of Kinyakyusa reduplication. *SKASE Journal of Theoretical Linguistics*. vol. 6(2). pp. 23-43.

Marlo, Michael R. 2002. Reduplication in Lusaamia. *Indiana University Working Papers in Linguistics Online* (Accessed: 15.10.2008).

Marlo, Michael. 2004. Prefixing reduplication in Lusaamia: Evidence from morphology. In Akinlabi, Akinbiyi (ed). *Proceedings of 4th World Congress of African Linguistics*. Cologne: Ruediger Koeppe Verlag. pp. .

Mathangwane, Joyce & Mtenje, Al. 2010. Tone and reduplication in Wandya and Subiya. In: Legère, Karsten & Thornell, Christina (eds.). *Bantu Languages: Analyses, Description and Theory*. Cologne: Rüdiger Köppe. pp. 175-189.

Matondo, Masangu. 2006. Tonal transfer in Kisukuma. In: Mugane, John, John P. Hutchison & Dee A. Worman. (eds.). *The Proceedings of the 35th Annual Conference on African Linguistics: African Languages and Linguistics in broad Perspective*. Sommerville, MA: Cascadilla Proceedings Project. pp. 125-135.

Mnenuka, Angelus. 2010. Dhima ya uradidi katika mawasiliano ya Kiswahili: Uimarishaji na udhoofishaji wa maana. *KISWAHILI: Journal of the Institute of Kiswahili Studies*, vol. 73: 32-44.

Mohamed, A. Mohamed. 2001. *Modern Kiswahili Grammar*. Nairobi: East African Educational Publishers.

Mwita, Leornard C. 2008. *Verbal Tone in Kuria*. Doctoral thesis, UCLA, Los Angeles.

Newman, Paul. 2000. *The Hausa Language: An Encyclopedic Reference Grammar*. New Haven & London: Yale University Press

Novatna, Jana. 2000. Reduplication in Swahili. *Afrikanistische Arbeitspapiere* (AAP), vol. 64. *Swahili Forum VII*. pp. 57-73.

Odden, David. 1996. Patterns of reduplication in Kikerewe. *OSU Working Papers in Linguistics*, 48: 111-149.

Rubanza, Yunus I. 1997. Dhana ya uradidi katika Kiswahili. *Kiswahili: Journal of the Institute of Kiswahili Research*, vol. 59: 53-62.

Rubino, Carl. 2005. Reduplication: Form, function and distribution. In: Hurch, Bernhard (ed.). *Studies on Reduplication*. Berlin: Mouton de Gruyter.

Rose, Sharon. 2003. The formation of Ethio-Semitic internal reduplication. In: Shimron, Joseph. (ed.). *Language Processing and Acquisition in Languages of Semitic, Root-based Morphology*. Amsterdam: John Benjamins. pp. 79-97.

Schluter, Kevin. 2008. Amharic internal reduplication and foot structure: A word-based approach. *Kansas Working Papers in Linguistics*, 30: 287-301.

Stonham, John. 2004. *Linguistic Theory and Complex Words: Nuuchahnulth Word formation*. New York: Palgrave Macmillan.

Tucker, Archibald N. 1994. *A Grammar of Kenya Luo (Dholuo)*. Köln: Rüdiger Köppe Verlag.

TUKI (Taasisi ya Uchunguzi wa Swahili). 2001. *Kamusi ya Swahili-Kiingereza*. Dar es Salaam: Institute of Kiswahili Research.

Ugot, Mercy & Afolabi Ogundipe. 2011. Reduplication in Nigerian Pidgin: A Versatile Communication Tool? *Pakistan Journal of Social Sciences Year*, 8(4): 227-233.

Zuraw, Kie. 2002. Aggressive reduplication. *Phonology*, vol. 19. pp. 395-439. [see also Zuraw, Kie (nd.). Aggressive reduplication. University of California, Los Angeles. Available at http://roa.rutgers.edu/files/790-1205/790-ZURAW-0-0. PDF (Accessed 03.02.2012)].

Exercise Five

5.1 In your opinion, is reduplication in Kiswahili derivational or inflectional?

5.2 Study carefully the following words from Kinyakyusa (Lusekelo 2009c).

lya 'eat' > *kulyakulya* 'eat repeatedly'
gwa 'fall' > *kugwakugwa* 'fall carelessly'
nwa 'drink' > *kunwakunwa* 'drink recklessly' **kunwanwa*
swa 'spit' > *kuswakuswa* 'spit repeatedly' **swakuswa*
nyasa 'spray' > *nyasanyasa* 'drizzle (of rain)'
lila 'cry' > *lilalila* 'cry recklessly'
tiima 'graze' > *tiimatiima* 'graze frequently'
lima 'cultivate' > *limalima* 'cultivate roughly'
seka 'laugh' > *sekaseka* 'giggle'
muno > 'in here' *munomuno* 'just in here'
kula > 'there' *kulakula* 'over there'
bwila > 'always' *bwilabwila* 'every day'
babilibabili 'two by two'
mitatumitatu 'three by three (trees, mats, etc.)'
jumojumo 'one by one'

1. Based on the data above, define the kind of reduplication demonstrated by these words.

2. In the list of the words provided above, what is the syllabic property of the words which undergo reduplication in this language?

3. Describe the semantics of the resulting words.

6 Lexical Borrowing

6.1 Lexical borrowing: Background information

Lexicons of natural languages tend to possess a large amount of indigenous words. This is what characterises a language into a given phylum. However, a lexicon of any language, no matter how isolated the language might be, contains a number of lexical entries which are of foreign origin. The phenomenon discussed in this chapter surrounds the characteristics of these words of foreign origin in three languages, namely English, Kiswahili and French.

Traditionally, two major languages have been donor languages, namely Greek and Latin for Indo-European zone. The Latinate (words of Latin origin) and Greek words appear in several technical issues in present day languages (e.g. French, English, German) because these two languages had been used in ancient civilisation endeavours (see Minkova & Stockwell 2009). Latinate words available in several Indo-European languages include words such as *agrarian* [ager], *vine* [vinum], *criminal* [crimen] and *arm* [arma] in English.

Currently, three major languages, namely French, English and Arabic have been mentioned in various books to be the main sources of loanwords in various world languages (cf. Newman 2000; Schadeberg 2009). Thus, a number of other languages have borrowed words from English, e.g. *hospitali* 'hospital', *blanketi* 'blanket' and *shati* 'shirt' in Kiswahili. Likewise, Arabic has influenced extensively the lexicon of several languages. This is exemplified by words like *algebra* [al-jabr], *sofa* [soffa], and *zero* [zero] in English.

In the Bantu family of Eastern Africa, Kiswahili is the main language which influences the lexicons of several Bantu languages in the area. Swilla (2000:301-302) mentions words such as *ichijiko* [<kijiko] 'spoon', *semanini* [<themanini] 'eighty' and *umwalimu* [<mwalimu] 'teacher' to be nativised in Chindali [Tanzania/Malawi].

Despite such observations, much attention has not been paid to borrowing in general linguistic morphology even in seminal works such as Bauer (1983), Booij (2005) and Katamba and Stonham (2006). The reason behind is that borrowing is not a natural word-formation process which emanates from words themselves, as for affixation or reduplication, rather it is some kind of imposition of words from other languages.

It is assumed, in this book, that the significance of loanwords upon the morphology of reference languages (French, Kiswahili and English), particularly the structure of numerous words, cannot be under-estimated. This will be shown by evidence in the course of the discussion herein. This decision will substantiate the necessity of dealing with borrowing, as an important process of word-formation.

The assumption above is in line with what is reported elsewhere with regard to other languages. For instance, a number of linguists have raised concerns on the different patterns in morphology of Bantu languages which have been none existent in such languages before but have been accommodated in a course of time after lexical borrowing. In the Eastern Bantu area, such observations appear in works such as Swilla (2000) [Chindali], Batibo (2002), Mwita (2009) and Shembuli (2010) [Swahili] and Zivenge (2009) [Tsonga]. This entails that during lexical borrowing, word structures of the donor languages are transferred into the morphology of words of the receiving languages.

In other words, it means, , that some languages allow their lexical items to be borrowed and used by other languages. In such a common morphological process, the donor language imposes its word structures to the receiving (target) language. In explaining this trend, Scotton and Okeju (1972:368-369) state 'the languages of numerically and culturally dominant peoples are considered the more likely donors in lexical borrowing while the less prominent peoples are more often the borrowers.'

Further, the observation by Scotton and Okeju informs us that during lexical borrowing, the traditions of the donor languages are tranfered into the cultures of the receiving languages. This adds to the aforementioned imposition of the word structures and cause both lexical and cultural influence of donor languages upon target languages.

At this juncture, it is plausible to establish that one of the productive ways to form newer words in a language is through borrowing (Bauer 2001) and it is common across world languages (Bauer 2004). Perhaps now we should offer the definition of the notion borrowing.

6.2   Conceptualising lexical borrowing

Two common terms used to describe the phenomena presented in this chapter are **borrowing** and **loanwords**, whose meanings have changed in order to cater for the usage in the study of morphology, as a branch of linguistics. **Haspelmath** (2009:36) and Chesley (2010) use the term **lexical borrowing** to refer to another term for loanwords.

It is known that choices and preferences for the technical terminologies in various works are apparent. For instance, for the sake of simplicity, words like **adoption** or **adaption** are used by many linguists in preference to these words (which are further defined in a sub-section immediately below) (see Batibo & Rottland 2001) while other linguists also use the term **lexical borrowing** (see Hock & Joseph 1996). Still, many other linguists prefer words such as **transfer(ence)** or **copying** for borrowing and **integration** and **retention** for issues associated with modification of loanwords in the target language (see **Haspelmath 2009**).

It is better to give a list of terminologies which will be frequently used in the discussion in this chapter:
(1)   *borrowing*
        lexical borrowing
        loans
        loanwords
        adoptation

adaptation
copying

It is well known that the term borrowing refers to the reproduction in one language patterns previously found in another. Hock and Joseph (1996) provide the following view:

> A very common result of linguistic contact is lexical BORROWING, the adoption of individual words or even of large sets of vocabulary items from another language or dialect. (Hock & Joseph 1996: 241). (emphasis is of the authors).

Materials which are borrowed from another language and used in the target language are called **loans**, (**borrowings**, which is redefined below) or **loan words** (also written as **loanwords** as in several linguistic resources). The elements which are borrowed, i.e. loan words range from lexical entities (words) to sounds.

The notion loanwords and borrowings differ in that borrowings are newer while loanwords have been adopted already. Ayres-Bennett and Carruthers (2001: 325) put it right as they say that words begin as borrowings then move to loanwords. They warn that, however, the question of when a word becomes a borrowing and when it ceases to be one is clearly highly problematic to decide.

Poplack *et al.* (1988: 52) provide definitions of lexical borrowing and loanwords. They say:

> Lexical borrowing involves the incorporation of individual L_2 words (or compounds functioning as single words) into discourse of L_1, the host or recipient language, usually phonologically and morphologically adapted to conform with the patterns of that language, and occupying a sentence slot dictated by its syntax. The status of 'loanword', however, is traditionally conferred only on words which, in addition, recur relatively frequently, are widely used in the speech community, and have achieved a certain level of recognition or acceptance, if not normative approvals...

Let me draw a scenario from borrowing and loan words in Kiswahili in order to help readers get a better understanding of these terms. A number of words of foreign origin exist in Kiswahili. Such lexical items borrowed into Kiswahili lexicon from languages like English and Persian could be exemplified by words like *mashine* 'machine' and *masweta* 'sweaters, pullovers' as well as *mabwana* 'men, gentlemen' and *pesa* 'money' respectively. The process of getting words from English and Persian into Kiswahili is called, in morphological terms, borrowing and the lexical entries borrowed are referred to as loan words (loans). Usually loan words co-exist with the native words in a given language. Other examples of loan words into Kiswahili will be presented in the course of presentation in this chapter. But loan words and lexical borrowings are the preferred terminologies because the word borrowing has semantic connotations like being related to theft or take and return which may hamper a clear grasp of the essence applied to the field of morphology (Hock & Joseph 1996). Also, borrowing could mean that the loan words will be returned to the donor language, which in fact is not the case because usually donor languages do not lose the borrowed words.

Furthermore, in some literature there is use of expressions like **source words** and **donor languages** as well as **recipient language** (see **Haspelmath & Tadmor 2009: 18; Chesley 2010: 233). In other works,** borrowing is not limited to getting words from an individual language (**donor language, source language**) into the receiving language (**target language, borrowed language**) rather it may transcend into a major geographical area. This is well exemplified, in African linguistics of course by the spread of the iron smelting and animal keeping words of non-Bantu languages into Bantu languages, languages scattered almost in all areas south of the Sahara (see Vansina 1995; Batibo 1996; Nurse 1997; Chami 2006 among others). This implies that 'in some cases, words spread over vast territories through a chain of borrowings' (Hock & Joseph 1996: 242).

When words come from a foreign language, such words are adopted with different status. Such distinct incorporation processes form the basis for defining the various types of borrowing. Based on French, Ayres-Bennett and Carruthers (2001: 325) provide the various kinds of borrowing. A summary of so is provided below with French and Kiswahili examples. Some ideas from Honken (2006) and Chesley (2010) are also referred to hereunder.

Straight borrowing: Here both the sense and the form of the word are copied from donor language without adaptation, as in *walkman* 'stereo, music system' from English to French and *kiosk* 'cabin shop' from English into Kiswahili. It means that both the word and its meaning are adopted by native speakers as lexical word in the recipient language (Chesley 2010). Here the morphological and graphical conventions of the donor language are not affected by the morphological and graphical conventions of the target language.

Adapted calque: Forms (words) of foreign origin are adapted. Following Chesley (2010), here the morphological and graphical conventions of the donor language might be affected by the morphological and graphical conventions of the target language. For example, usually English loanwords are adapted by taking a French suffix e.g. *conteneur* 'container, receptacle' from English into French. Another example is by using Kiswahili affixes, as in *kitabuni* 'in the book' and *ghalani* 'in the store' from Arabic into Kiswahili.

Semantic calque: A foreign sense or meaning is borrowed. This is shown by words *développer* 'develop' and *réaliser* 'accomplish, realize' from English into French and *usiku mwema* 'good night' from English into Kiswahili.

Pseudo-borrowing: This entails that words of foreign origin are borrowed but with different meanings. For instance, in French and German, there are words which look-like English words but they are not in typical English usage, e.g. *Handy* 'cell phone' (German) and *tennisman* 'tennis player' (French).

Fused loans: In African languages, a number of words seem to be nativised to the extent that even native speakers cannot decide whether they are loans or not. Honken (2006) mentions that a number of words in Khoisan languages are fused and it become very hard to decide their origins.

6.3   Approaches to borrowing

6.3.1   Introduction

In the study of linguistic morphology, **borrowing** is given some significant weight because it has, on the one hand, to a large extend, an influence on the lexicon of the languages concerned. On the other hand, phonological and syntactic impact of borrowing on native sound systems and syntactic structures cannot be ignored. This chapter offers an insight to the contribution of borrowing, as a word formation process, to the morphology of the target language.

One of the areas of theory which has been contributed to through studies on borrowing is phonological theory. Borrowing and phonological theory seem to be interwoven today. For example, while Batibo (2002) contributes to the autosegmetal and markedness theories in his analysis of Kiswahili syllable structure, Mwita (2009) employs the optimality theory on his account of the adaptation of Arabic loanwords in Kiswahili.

Borrowing is also approached from another angle of linguistics, namely historical and comparative linguistics. In African linguistics, borrowing is well described in its contribution to the history of the peoples of Africa (see Vansina 1995; Batibo 1996; Nurse 1997). In such works the use of lexical loans has been mentioned as a significant tool to decipher the relationships and contacts which Africans had had amongst themselves and their contacts with the outside world particularly people from Asian continent (e.g. Persians and Arabs) as well as people from Europe (e.g. Portuguese).

The history of Europe has partly been studied and an analysis of proto-forms of the current Indo-European languages has been done. Thus, we get Germanic languages such as German and English, Celtic languages such as French and Italian etc.

This book, however, is not intended to review these approaches rather it is typically inclined to the morphological analysis of the borrowed words. Therefore, only brief accounts of the contacts between native English and Kiswahili speakers and peoples from the outside world has been hinted in the subsequent sections below. Much attention is paid to the detailed morphological analyses.

The question of the contribution of **loanwords** to the native phonological patterns, existing lexicons as well as syntactic structures in each language remains central to the description of grammar of the language concerned. It means that a grammar of any language does not stay intact because languages grow as they are dynamic in nature because specifically speakers of such languages are dynamic (Hock & Joseph 1996). Thus, the share that borrowing brings about into the receiver language cannot be underestimated because it transports with it some morphological (as well as phonological) inputs none existent in the target language. This is the reason that studies on borrowing in contact languages have grown enormously particularly in African languages and Kiswahili in particular (see Zawawi 1979; Lodhi 2000; Batibo & Rottland 2001; Owino 2003; Mwita 2009; Zivenga 2009; Shembuli 2010 among others) as well as other languages (see Hock & Joseph 1996).

The growth of languages is studied relatively to their contacts. For example, the history of English language, which is closely related to the morphology of its words, is captured from the early invasions of the Vikings (Scandinavians) to the current Norman (French) conquest (Knowles 1997). Works on borrowing in African languages date far back, may be even before the works by Gower (1952) and Greenberg (1960). Still to date, borrowing seems to be even covered from a typological point of view (see chapters in **Haspelmath & Tadmor 2009**).

The growth of the body of literature on borrowing in African linguistics does not rule out the fact that literatures on borrowing per se have not been growing in such much as general morphological linguistics (see Booij 2005; Katamba & Stonham 2006) and in the study of individual languages such as Dutch (see Booij 2002) or Nootka (see Stonham 2004). The assumption here would be that such languages seem to have borrowed much in its earlier stages that words of foreign origin have been nativized long ago or fewer contacts happened hence loan words are only few in the lexicon.

Quite a number of linguists have raised concern on the different patterns in morphology of the present day languages which have been none existent in such languages before but have been accommodated in a course of time after the imposition from source languages. Such new forms of words in target languages emanate from in-coming forms from donor languages whose structures undergo **adaptation** or **adoptation** in the receiving languages.

The Kiswahili morphology, for instance, has been impacted enormously by the newer morphologies of donor languages to the extend that one may miss a point to draw very typical boundaries of Kiswahili morphology from, say, Arabic morphology. This is because the strong influence had been from Arabic words (see Zawawi 1979; Lodhi 2000; Mwita 2009; Shembuli 2010), English (see Gower 1952) or loan words from other languages (see Lodhi 2000). In the course of the discussion herein such influences will be revealed at a deeper length. At this point it is necessary that we provide what essence does borrowing is.

6.3.2   Adaptation and nativisation mechanisms

6.3.2.1   Adapatation mechanisms

Adaptation techniques involve phonological and morphological modifications. The best known phonological processes are epenthesis and segmental deletion (Newman 2000; Batibo 2002; Mwita 2009) and from morphological pint of view, affixation is quite productive in loanwords nativization (Shembuli 2010).

Syllable structure: each language has its own syllable structure. For example, Kiswahili permits V, CV, CCV etc. hence restricts open syllables (syllables ending in consonants), while english allows VC, CV, CCV, VCC etc. hence has both open and closed syllables. During lexical borrowing, syllable structures are adjusted.

Mwita (2009: 51) says the idea of loanword adaptation or nativization at the phonological level is governed by syllable well-formedness in the recipient language. When a word is borrowed from one language to another, in most cases it violates some constraints of syllable well-formedness. The recipient language moves fast to fix the problem. For example, many languages try to avoid complex onsets and codas.

Vowel epenthesis: Languages which do not permit open syllables and some sequences of consonants usually insert vowels between consonants or at the final position in the words. For example, Newman (2000) mentions that word final consonants are avoided in Hausa through insertion of a vowel. Newman (2000: 317) pointed out that all indigenous Hausa words end in vowels, thus, any loanword is assigned with a vowel at the end, e.g. *court > kōtù*.

Batibo (1996: 38) notes that this is by far the most common method of consonant cluster nativisation in Kiswahili. It involves the insertion of a vowel between two consonants or after a consonant in a syllable final position. Epenthesis involves a violation of faithfulness because the epenthetic segment has no counterpart in the input, as in Arabic loanword *asl > asili* 'origin' (Mwita 2009:51).

Segment deletion: Segment deletion is another way to accommodate loanwords in a target language. It means that some segments are deleted when the forein words are being localized. For example, viwed from optimality theory, segment deletion is a violation of faithfulness because an input segment has no counterpart in the output, e.g. *ammar > amiri* 'begin' and *amm > amu* 'uncle' (Mwita 2009: 55).

Consonant cluster avoidance and tolerance: In other cases, consonant clusters (sequences of consonants) are avoided particularly through vowel epenthesis. For instance, in Hausa, elimination of consonant clusters is one of the ways of incorporating words of foreign origin into the language. This is because Hausa does not have true consonant clusters (Newman 2000). This is illustrated by the words *plot > fulotì* and *cement > sìmintì*.

As opposed to consonant cluster elimination, there are a few cases where target languages tend tolerate consonant clusters. For example, Kiswahili maintained clusters that were in the borrowed Arabic word, as in *unwan > anwani* 'address' and *sultan > sultani* 'king, ruler' (Mwita 2009: 56). Other examples include *stakabadhi* receipt',*kiosk* 'cabin shop' and *posta* 'post office'.

Inflectionalisation: From morphological point of view, a number of words of foreign origin are inflected with the recipients grammatical features like the gender marker prefix in Ateso, e.g. *itabon* 'book' and the noun class prefixes in Bantu languages like Kiswahili and Setswana, e.g. *masharti* 'instructions, regulations' in Kiswahili and *mokarateng* 'in the card' in Setswana. Here we get prefixes *i-*, *ma-* and *mo-* in these languages respectively.

Derivationalisation: Also, morphologically, as a means of naturalization, some loanwords are derived into other words in a recipient language, e.g. in Kiswahili *feli* 'fail' becomes *fel-ish-an-a* 'cause to fail each other' and *mfelishaji* 'one who causes someone else to fail' [< *fail*, English].

It is established that words of foreign origin are borrowed into the target languages and then undergo nativisation. On the level of nativisation, Scotton and Okeju (1972: 370) provide a good background on the status of loanwords by pointing out two criteria used to decide whether a word of foreign origin is nativized or not in Ateso (Nilotic):

Our criteria for saying whether or not a word has been integrated into Ateso are (a) whether or not the loan conforms to Ateso phonotactics (i.e. occurrence and co-occurrence rules for Ateso sounds) and (b) whether or not the loan is inflected as if it were a native Ateso word (i.e. nouns inflected with a gender prefix and some suffixal change to mark plurality, verbs inflected with personal and other relationship prefixes for tense/aspects as well as with suffixes which also indicate various other relationships).

6.3.2.2   Related terminologies

Adaptation is central to borrowing and word-formation processes in any language. With reference to borrowing, Ayres-Bennett and Carruthers (2001: 324) record the following for French:

> Clearly many words of foreign origin borrowed into the language during the course of its history are no longer perceived as foreing by native speakers, e.g. *chiffre* 'figure' [Arabic], *violin* [Italian] and *chocolat* 'chocolate' [Spanish].

From the above citation, we learn that adoptation (sometimes referred to as adoptation) and nativisation (indigenisation) are related terms. While borrowing is differentiated from **nativisation** which entails integration of foreign words into one's native structure of a language, nativisation is synonymous to **adaptation/adaptation** (Zivenge 2009) which is preferred by other authors of loan words such as Batibo and Rottland (2001) and Mwita (2009).

These terms entail that words (with their properties) from other languages are brought into the target language, usually with a different word structure. Different works on borrowing focus on analyses of phonological and morphological changes that occur to those loan words that are being incorporated into the target language as a result of borrowing (see Batibo & Rottland 2001; Mwita 2009; Zivenge 2009; 2010 among others). In other words, Hock and Joseph (1996:243-244) asserts that:

> The first thing that comes to mind when we think of borrowing is the adoption of individual lexical items…. However, through vocabulary borrowing other linguistic elements may be acquired…. For instance, extensive vocabulary borrowing can introduce new MORPHOLOGY…… Vocabulary borrowing also can introduce new SOUNDS, or new contexts for old sounds…… In addition to individual lexical items, languages may adopt combinations or COLLOCATIONS of words …(emphasis of authors).

In one of our cases, nativisation or adaptation entails that the source languages, such as Persian, English, Portuguese, Indian, Arabic and German in the case of Kiswahili (Hurskainen 2004: 201), has phonological and morphological inventories that are different from those of the target language. Since languages are different, it is significant to account for how loan words are then incorporated into recipients so that they become recognized that language's linguistic environment.

As far as nativisation of loan words is concerned, Zivenge (2009: 9) says:

> With advanced interaction and contact amongst languages, change is inevitable. Some languages develop and others die as a result of contact and subsequent borrowing. A language that borrows and adopts phonological and morphological elements of other languages that are characteristically different dies and those that borrow and nativize, maintain their status..... Nativization is thus a way of protecting the language from death, in situations of excessive borrowing.

In the case of Kiswahili language, it may not have killed the donor languages like Persians, Arabic and English rather it just benefited from their lexicon, morphology and sound system. Likewise, donor languages have not lost words which were borrowed into Kiswahili.

As borrowing brings into the receiving languages linguistic concerns related to the grammar of the language in question, Lodhi (2000) presents the adaptation of borrowed words in Kiswahili emphasizing on aspects of grammar rather than lexicon and paying more attention to Arabic and oriental structure loans and grammatical imposition. Also, he focuses on **rephonologization** which, according to Zivenge (2009), is similar to phonological nativisation.

As it was pointed out earlier, scholars like Hock and Joseph (1996), Batibo and Tottland (2001) and Zivenge (2009) contend that the integration or nativization, of a word in a borrowing language's system, in our case Kiswahili, is not really a genuine part of the word-finding process itself, but nevertheless important with regard to the first realization(s), once the speaker has decided to use a borrowing.

6.4   Contact zones and how word borrowings occur

6.4.1   Introducing contacts and borrowing

An important point to be noted here is that borrowing does not begin elsewhere but upon contact between one language, source and target languages. It is obvious that borrowing from other languages depends much on which target language comes into contact with first as well as the duration of their contact

Let us draw an example from Tanzania using the Cushitic language, Iraqw. Mous and Qorro (2009: 106) report that Kiswahili exerts more influence on Iraqw because it is a dominant national language, used in formal situations, and is a source of loanwords for new concepts. There was also a previous and long contact between Iraqw and Datooga [Nilotic language] and datooga was a prestigious language in the area. Since most Datooga clans became Iraqw, then a number of Datooga [words] must have been integrated into Iraqw. Since there are no other languages which are in constant contact with Iraqw, then it is not easy to find loanwords other than from English which is taught is schools (Ibid: 106).

Mous and Qorro (2009: 110) report that most of the loanwords in Iraqw are additives (insertions) for modern concepts; and in most of the semantic fields, Kiswahili is the number one donor language. In the field of domestic animals, Datooga offered the most loawnwords into Iraqw.

Some of the modern concepts offered as per donor languages are noted in what follows. In fact, only major donor languages are mentioned herein, in order of the number of loanwords listed in the resource chapter, i.e. Mous and Qorro (2009: 110): (i) modern agriculture [Swahili], modern food and utensils [Swahili], modern instruments [Swahili], reading, writing and schooling [Swahili], modern medicine [Swahili], modern government [Swahili], domestic animals [Datooga], and modern dress [Datooga].

In Iraqw, a number of loanwords are assumed to have entered into Iraqw at an earlier stage. Mous and Qorro (2009: 113) report that Datooga is a donor language for catle names, e.g. *areer* 'red cow' [<*areera* 'red'] and *nawéet* 'name of a cow born on the road' [< *naweeda* 'road'].

Borrowing takes place even between neighbouring languages. For example, Mkude (2004) mentions of borrowings between Luguru, Kagulu, Kami, Nguu and Kutu. Swilla (2000: 298) mentions that historical contacts between Chindali, Nyakyusa, Chilambya, Malila and Nyiha resulted in considerable borrowing from each other.

This discussion reminds me of some of my students at the University who came to my office to challenge the way I graded their research based assignment. The problem was centred around the source language for the loan words *shati* 'shirt' and *shule* 'school' found in one of the Bantu languages spoken in northern Tanzania. Their take was that the former was borrowed direct from English and the later from German while my understanding is that these words have been borrowed from Kiswahili. My defence inclined towards the fact that the earlier the contact the first the influence and the late the contact the late the impact. Therefore, I argued that these words reached other Bantu language through Kiswahili where they occur as nativised loan words.

This leaves us to the point that most of the works which deal with loan words will always stipulate clearly the context of contact between source language and the recipient language. Take for example works by Batibo and Rottland (2001) about adaptation of Datooga loanwords in Sukuma as well as Mkude (2004) for the influence of Kiswahili on Luguru in Tanzania. These authors have spared some space to describe the nature of the contact between the languages presented in their works because such a context determines the level of impact associated with contacts.

Datooga (Nilotic language of Tanzania) speaking people came into Sukuma (Bantu language) speaking areas and settled around 1600-1700 in Tanzania. Thus, Sukuma-Datooga contacts had been established for a long period of time, about 200-300 years. The linguistic impact of Datooga into Sukuma is well signalled by the Datooga names of villages settled by Sukuma people, e.g. *Selelya, Sayu Sayu, Gabu* etc. and adaptation of Datooga names by some Sukuma people, e.g. *Sita, Magina, Shigilu, Masuka* etc. (Batibo & Rottland (2001: 13). This informs us that contacts between people speaking two languages need to take place for a reasonably longer period of time so that languages influence each other.

Mkude (2004: 181-184) reports that early contacts between Kiswahili speaking people and Luguru speakers (as well as other Bantu languages) revolved around Islamisation,

Christianisation and trade. Also, Kiswahili (and English) being the official language in Tanzania has impacts on these languages. For example, in Luguru, Kiswahili words are used even in places where Luguru words existed. For example, words like *liyai* and *linanda* are used in modern Luguru instead of *lifinga* 'egg' and *ulili* 'bed' respectively.

6.4.2 Lexical borrowings in English

English has experienced various major changes in its history. Knowles (1997: 3) says 'the English language has not existed in isolation and has been in close contact with other Europena languages'. The result of these prolonged contacts is the existence of lexical items of foreign origin in the language. Minkova and Stockwell (2009: 2) states one thing is certain: well over 80 percent of the total vocabulary of English is borrowed.' Of these total foreign words, it is suggested that the percentages of modern English words derived from several languages as follows: French 29 percent, Latin 29 percent, Germanic words 26 percent, and words of other foreign origins 16 percent.

On classical grounds, English language had experienced influence, in terms of vocabulary, from three major historical contacts. On contemporary experiences, due to its spread all over the globe, English language encountered language contacts with several world's languages. In what follows I present each of these influences in detail.

The influence of Norse languages: The history of English language begins with its contacts with Norsemen who spoke languages of Danmark and Norway (Danish and Norwegian). According to Knowles (1997: 34-35), Norsemen attached Anglo-Saxons in 787 and 793 and their settlements led into larger invasions as from 860s.

In contemporary English, it is estimated that there are 400 Norwegian and Danish words. Several of Norse loanwords refer to objects and concepts, while others involve the Danish culture. Following Knowles (1997: 40-41), illustrative examples are offered in (2):

(2)   *law, fellow, husband, husting, call, knife, sky, skin, take, sky*

English-French contacts: The Normans (French people) conquered England around 1066 and their rule stayed longer. Knowles (1997: 47) says 'the length and nature of the contact between English and French resulted into the large-scale borrowing into English of French words and expressions'.

Even in other literatures, it is reported that most of the French vocabulary appearing now in English was imported over a long period of time since the Norman Conquest in 1066 (Monkova & Stockwell 2009). During this time, hundreds of French words had been introduced in English. A few are given here:

(3)   *crown, beef, veal, mutton, liberty, justice, eagle, falcon, rabbit, collage*

English-Latin contacts: After the Normans, Latin (the language of the Bible and civilisation) dominated English language. It was only in 14th century that English was started to be used in the Bible (Knowles 1997: 63). Even after Latin had ceased to function, it remained as a language of the Church and it was taught (perhaps it even taught today) as a subject in universities (Ibid: 75).

A number of words of Latin origin appear in the lexicon of English today. A few examples include:

(4) *vulgar*   vulgus 'crowd'
     advocacy   vox 'voice'
     dental   dens 'tooth'
     condense   densus 'thick'

Contacts between English and African langauges: English has a number of lexical items which are suggested to have come from the contacts between English speakers and with West African peoples.

(5) *voodoo* (Ewe and Fon 'spirit')
     banana (Wolof)
     bogus (Hausa – book-boko) 'meaning fake or fraudulent'
     chimpanzee (Chiluba - DRC)
     kola (Temme, Mandinka)
     kwashiorkor (Ga language of Ghana)

Also, some words in English lexicon are of Bantu origin.

(6) *shamba*   'farm'   [Swahili]
     safari   'journey, travel' [Swahili]
     impala   [Zulu]
     mamba   [Zulu, Swahili]
     tsetse   [Tswana *tsetse*, Luhya *tsiisi*)
     ubuntu   'African ideology' [Bantu languages]
     vuvuzela   'musical instrument; [Zulu or Nguni]
     zebra
     zombie   [Kikongo *zumbi*, Kimbundu *nzambi*]

English-Arabic contacts: A mountain of English words are Arabic loanwords. A few examples are provided below.

(7) alcohol   *al-kohl*
     algebra   *al-jabr*
     cotton   *qutn, qutun*
     lime (fruit)   *lim*
     mattress   *matrah*

6.4.3 Lexical borrowings in Kiswahili

Swahili-Persians contacts (about 800-1920): Historically, it is difficult to stipulate with precision the actual time Persians came to the coast of east Africa; however, Persians (also known as Shirazi in East Africa) are famously known for the involvement in trading activities and not colonization of the East African coast and most of them had settled permanently along the coast of East Africa particularly in Zanzibar even today; as a result their language's impact on Kiswahili through borrowing is noticed.

Nurse and Hinnebusch (1993) pointed out that based on archaeological and linguistic data, the earliest Kiswahili settlements along the coast are usually assigned to 800 C.E. or slightly earlier. Lexical reconstructions for Proto-Sabaki (Proto-Swahili) show that few were derived from Persian (or Arabic) during most of the first millennium C.E. these items are also attested in Arabic and/or Indic languages in an identical or similar form, which means these languages could also be the source. Also, these items are not cognate across the Kiswahili dialect spectrum, which means that, although reconstructed from the early proto-stage, they more likely entered Kiswahili later. Schadeberg (2009: 80) mentions the period of 800-1920 as the period of the contact of the east African coast (Swahili coast) to Asia via the Indian ocean. The few items of general reference at this stage include the following (Nurse & Hinnebusch 1993).

(8) pula   'steel'
     bwana   'man, gentleman'
     chai   'tea'
     achari   'pickle'
     serikali 'government'
     pamba   'cotton'
     kasa   'turtle'

By about 1700, when the first recorded documents in Kiswahili appeared, Kiswahili vocabulary was much as it is today, containing several hundred items from Persian (Nurse & Hinnebusch 1993). Thus, most of these entered Kiswahili between 800 and 1700. Nurse and Hinnebusch (1993) gain say the recentness of their arrival is corroborated by their having undergone only recent and local sound shifts affecting Kiswahili.

Moreover, they cluster in certain categories, namely tools, ornaments, spices, plants, household items, and maritime and kinship terms, which are said to have been introduced by Persian traders in East Africa. Also, they involve social organizations like governments and administrations.

Swahili-Arabic spheres of contacts: Historians and archaeologists have not established enough historical or archaeological evidence to allow them to state exactly when and where either the Kiswahili language or the Kiswahili culture emerged (Whiteley 1969) but data point towards the fact that the Kiswahili speaking people have occupied their present territories since well before 1000 AD (Chami 2006; Massamba 2007). Arab traders are known to have had extensive contact with the coastal peoples from at least the 6th century AD, and Islam began to spread along the East African Coast from at least the 9th century.

People from Arab and the Persian Gulf settled in Zanzibar and helped to spread both Islam and the Kiswahili language and culture along the coats into the interior. They reached to the major trading and cultural centers such as Sofala (Mozambique), Kilwa (Tanzania) in the south, Mombasa and Lamu in Kenya and Mogadishu (Somalia) in the north, as well as the Comoros Islands and northern Madagascar in the Indian Ocean (Massamba 2007).

Schadeberg (2009:82) points out that between 1000 and 2000, Arabs dominated the Kiswahili coast and, according to him, they had with them the Islamic culture and civilisation partuclarly between 12th and 13th centuries.

Starting from about 1800, the rulers of Zanzibar organized trading expeditions into the interior of the mainland. They established permanent trade routes, and Swahili-speaking merchants settled in stops along the new trade routes. After Germany seized the region known as Tanganyika (present-day mainland Tanzania) for a colony in 1886, it took notice of the wide (but shallow) dissemination of Kiswahili, and soon designated Kiswahili as a colony-wide official administrative language (Whiteley 1969).

The major area of contribution that Arabs brought into Kiswahili civilization is Islamic religion. It becomes important to notice the impact of vocabulary related to religion to Kiswahili lexicon. Thus, Arabic loan words for this domain of cultural contact area include the examples in (9). A number of Islamic oriented loans have entered into Kiswahili through Islamisation of the East African people by Arab people.

(9)   *shehe*   'sheikh'
        Kurani   'Quran'
        hiji   'make a pilgrimage'
        ibada   'worship, religion'
        chuo   'Islamic school'
        sali   'pray'
        nabi   'prophet'

The second area where Arabs contacted Kiswahili speakers much is on trade and caravan routes, spreading all along the coast into the interior. Here one would succinctly assume that several loan words of Arabic origin were entered into Kiswahili. A few examples appear in (10). These are some of the words which are typically used in trade.

(10)   *bidhaa*   'merchandise trade goods'
        safu   'row'
        safari   'travel, trip'
        hamsini   'fifty'
        thamani   'value'
        hesabu   'rewards count'

Arabs were good at travelling and oceanic environments. This means they have introduced a number of loans into the lexicon of Kiswahili. Such loan words such as the following must have entered into Kiswahili vocabulary due to environmental experiences of Arabs.

(11)   *tufani*   'hurricane'
        kusi   'southerly wind'
        kaskazi   'northerly wind'
        bahari   'ocean, sea'
        mashariki 'East'

Swahili-English contact zones: In Tanzania, English-Swahili contacts strengthened during the British colonial rule between 1918 and 1961. This is because English was introduced in Tanzania as a colonial language when the British took over from the Germans in 1918. English was used as a language of the government business and those who could use it were able to get employed by the British government. Also, the British rule used most of the resources to promote English through the school system. Furthermore, since English was so valued during this time, those few Tanzanians who went to school were eager to learn it for their personal gains.

Swahili, on the other hand grew steadily as a lingua franca. Even the governors of Tanzania and Zanzibar and other East African countries during colonialism were convinced that Kiswahili was a viable lingua franca for the Tanzania and across East Africa and therefore saw the need to standardise (Rubagumya 1991). Even members in the Legislative Council were allowed to use Kiswahili when the speaker satisfied himself that the concerned members could not express themselves well if they used English. Kiswahili, an indigenous language, gained widespread use as the language of basic education in the first four years of primary schooling throughout the colonial period (Roy-Campbell & Qorro 1997). However, it seems some British officials did not like the use of Kiswahili in the education system.

The contact between English and Kiswahili had never been in all domains of language use rather it had only been in specific contexts of language use. Gower (1952: 155) had longer observed that, we quote:

> Anyone seeking to record words that have been introduced into Swahili by borrowing from English, must search in those spheres where contact with European culture impinges most widely and affects large numbers of Africans.

Therefore, the impact of English loan words is felt much in areas where Kiswahili speakers had contacts with Europeans who used English in their day-to-day executions of various responsibilities in Eastern Africa in general and Tanzania in particular.

Firstly, introduction of Western education and administration structures brought with them manners through which such projects were implemented. A number of words entered into Kiswahili through formal schooling whereby words such as atlasi 'atlas', kufeli 'to fail', skuli 'school' and kupasi 'to pass' entered into everyday Kiswahili. Administration had introduced words of English origin into Kiswahili words like mesenja 'messenger' and meneja 'manager, director'.

The second area involved western medical care and health facilities which were provided mostly by missionaries and colonisers. Here we find words like daktari 'doctor', nesi 'nurse', malaria 'malaria', aspirini 'aspirin' and hospitali 'hospital' (see Gower 1952). These words were introduced through medical and health facilities which are adopted and are at use today in Tanzanian and Kenyan Kiswahili speaking environments.

The area of infrastructure and transportation also contributed greatly in contact between Europeans and Africans who speak Kiswahili. Such environments as the harbours in Dar es Salaam, Zanzibar, Kilwa and Mombasa experience longer communications between English speakers and Kiswahili speakers as co-workers or passengers. Other transport areas like urban centres and points along railways and highways were affected most. Thus, words in (12) represent the influence of English on Kiswahili under this sphere because they entered into Kiswahili from English through transport arenas.

(12)   *lori* 'lorry'
       stesheni 'station'
       treni 'train'
       reli 'railway'
       baiskeli 'bicycle'
       motokaa 'motor car'
       buldoza 'bulldozer'

Another area was entertainment during Western colonisation of East Africa which witnessed the introduction of new ways of amusements and leisure whose names and actions were well expressed in English words rather than African words hence Kiswahili speakers had to copy some words into Kiswahili. The contact period had left behind some words like those listed in (13).

(13)   *penalti* 'penalty' and *kona* 'corner kick' in football
       sigara 'cigarette', *kilabu* 'club' and *bia* 'beer' in drinking points
       sinema 'cinema' and *dansi* 'dance' in areas of leisure

Lastly, Gower (1952) reports that in those days when Kiswahili people contacted Europeans, people speaking English had a different life style in terms of food and eating manners, dressing style, dancing ways and many other ways. Such a contact area brought into Kiswahili many words. Also, other English loan words in Kiswahili are included in the following.

(14)   *fasheni* 'fashion'
       shati   'shirt'
       gauni   'gown'
       keki 'cake'
       advansi 'advance' [military, education]
       asbestosi 'asbestos' [building]

6.4.4 Lexical borrowings in French

Two major sources of information for French loanwords are followed herein, namely Poplack et al. (1988) and Chesley (2010). The study by Poplack *et al.* (1988: 50) examined 'the integration or assimilation of the English-origin words in our data base, both in terms of French linguistic (phonological, morphological, and syntactic) categories, and in terms of their historical persistence (versus recency), their level of usage within the community, as measured by overall frequency, and their dispersion across semantic fields'. It should be noted that their focus is Canadian French with existing corpuses therein. Chesley (2010: 231) 'examines the occurrences of new lexical borrowings in a French newspaper corpus to determine whether the phenomenon of English lexical borrowings (Anglicisms) is different than the phenomenon of non-English borrowings'. Her focus, on the other hand, is on newspapers in Metropolitan French.

Findings show that the average amount of loanwords in French is low perhaps because the use of loanwords is regulated. Poplack *et al.* (1988: 57) found that only 1 percent loanwords are of English origin, while Chesley (2010: 233) found that only 1.7 percent is of English origin. On average loanwords, Poplack *et al.* (Idib) found under 3.3 percent of loanwords in French, while Chesley (Ibid) found that only 2.6 percent loanwords in spoken usage in the language.

Poplack *et al.* (1988) found that there are four layers of lexical borrowings into French, namely:

i. Loanwords without linguistic needs: *business, chum, gang, building, appointment, okay* etc.

ii. Loanwords (newer items) from English which may not have a current French equivalent: *tennis, hockey, hamburger, fun* etc.

iii. Well-established loanwords which are very old and well-established loanwords which may no longer be perceived as borrowed by the speakers themselves: *tougher, deplugger, sandwich, club, steak* etc.

iv. Equally integrated words:*coper, firer* etc.

Chesley (2010: 231) reports that in France, the 1975 Bas-Lauriol Law and 1994 Toubon Law tend to regulate use of foreign words in French. This makes France an exceptional in having such legislations which are widely thought that these measures are to protect French against English.

Nonetheless, the fact is that the number of lexical borrowings from one language to another is a quantifiable statistic that can gauge the interaction of two cultures. She examines how interaction between French and other languages by examining the patterns of lexical borrowings in French. She concludes that English dwarfs all other languages (Ibid: 239). Some donor languages into French (Chesley 2010: 239)

Language	Some examples
English	*lobbying, bond, week-end, parking* 'parking lot', *dérégulation, joint venture*
Russian	*perestroika, glasnost,*
German	*Land* 'country', *deutschmark* 'German currency',
Latin	*res nullius* 'unowned property', *manu militari* 'with the help of the military'

6.5   Loanwords and word-structures

The analysis and discussions of the adoption processes that speakers of African languages undertake are offered in this section. These are ways of accommodating loan words from the donor languages to the different target languages in Africa.

6.5.1 Structure of loanwords in Kiswahili

We have seen that a number of languages have contributed to the lexicon of Kiswahili. In this line, Schadeberg (2009: 86) mentions the following percentages of the loanwords in Kiswahili (caution: I informatively mention only five major donor languages with only high estimates and percentages given by the original author in order to give a rough picture):

(i)   **Arabic** and Indian Ocean Arabic (321 loanwords) – **20** percent,

(ii)   **English** (74 loanwords) – about **5** percent,

(iii)   **Hindi** (74 loanwords) about **4** percent,

(iv)   **Persian** (about 54 loanwords) – **3** percent, and

(v)   **Portuguese** (16 loanwords) – about **1** percent.

Phonology: On nativisation, syllable structures are involved and on this question, Mwita (2009: 51) says "[T]he idea of loanword adaptation or nativization at the phonological level is governed by syllable well-formedness in the recipient language. When a word is borrowed from one language to another, in most cases it violates some constraints of syllable well-formedness. The recipient language moves fast to fix the problem. For example, many languages try to avoid complex onsets and codas."

Vowel epenthesis (vowel insertion): Epenthesis is indicated by Batibo (2002: 5) as a process that involves the insertion of a full or epenthetic vowel between two consonant segments. In Kiswahili, it is illustrious that Batibo (1996: 38) notes that this is by far the most common method of consonant cluster nativization in Kiswahili. It involves the insertion of a vowel between two consonants or after a consonant in a syllable final position. Epenthesis involves a violation of faithfulness because the epenthetic segment has no counterpart in the input, as in Arabic loanword *asl* > *asili* 'origin' (Mwita 2009: 51).

Another scholar, Batibo (2002: 6), presents the nativisation strategies of loanwords into Kiswahili. He mentions the sound patterns modified through epenthesis in such words as *serikali* 'government', *elufu* 'a thousand', and *masurufu* 'allowance' [< Arabic].

Segment deletion: Segment deletion is another way to accommodate loanwords in Kiswahili. Viewed from Optimality Theory, segment deletion is a violation of faithfulness because an input segment has no counterpart in the output, e.g. *ammar* > *amiri* 'begin' and *amm* > *amu* 'uncle' (Mwita 2009: 55).

Batibo (2002: 5) mentions the nativisation strategies of consonant clusters of the loanwords into Kiswahili through consonant deletion. He mentions the consonant sounds modified through deletion in words like *batiza* 'baptize', *picha* 'picture', and *penati* 'penalty' [< English].

Cluster tolerance: Batibo (1996, 2002) acknowledges the existence of consonant clusters at the onset of borrowed words and give examples like *speaker* 'in parliament', *hosteli* 'hostel', *fikra* 'idea', *stempu* 'stamp', *aprili* 'April', and *stovu* stove'. Thus, Batibo (1996: 39; 2002: 2) notes that the language has become unique among Bantu languages due to its insensitivity to consonant clusters.

Mwita (2009: 56) also reports that there are a few cases where Kiswahili maintained clusters that were in the borrowed Arabic word, as in *unwan > anwani* 'address' and *sultan > sultani* 'king, ruler'.

However, Mwita (2009: 52) argue that there are rare cases on which word initial onset consonant cluster in Arabic loanwords in Kiswahili. Also, he argued that procedurally, an epenthetic vowel breaks up clusters of two consonants at the beginning of a word, as well as clusters of three consonants in medial position. But a medial cluster of two consonants is not broken up by epenthesis, as this can be split between two syllables without the need for a complex margin: where the first consonant syllabifies as a simple coda, and the second as a simple onset, for example, between /l/ and /t/ to get <sul-tani> in *sultani* 'king, ruler'.

Morphology: Kiswahili, generally as a Bantu language, has a typical agglutinative word structure with a fairly elaborative though reduced noun classifications and a complex but modified verbal morphology. In order to offer only a basic morphological structure of the language, this section describes three major word-classes, nouns, adjectives and verbs. Apart from that, some fundamental agreement patterns are provided too.

Furthermore, on morphological integration, Schadeberg (2009: 94) found that each major word category, i.e. noun, adjective, and verb has its own morphological characteristics which loanwords have to be adjusted to. For example, noun tend to be grouped into the different noun classes, e.g. noun classes 9/10 as in *samaki* 'fish' [<*samak*, Arabic] and noun classes 5/6 as in *kaburi/makaburi* 'grave/graves' [<*qabr*, Arabic].

The main morphological way of adopting Arabic loan verbs is through assigning derivation processes which are commonplace in Kiswahili. For example, this process is attested in several Arabic loan verbs which are nominalised through suffixation process (Shembuli 2010: 52) and a few examples are provided in (16).

(16) **Verbs**   **Nouns**

Verbs		Nouns	
dai	'to claim, to demand'	*ma-dai*	'the claims'
tahini	'examine'	*m-tahini-wa*	'candidate'
adhini	'call Moslems to pray'	*mw-adhini*	'a caller of Moslems'
badili	'change'	*ma-badili-ko*	'changes'
badhiri	'embezzle'	*wa-badhiri-fu*	'embezzle'
tabiri	'to forecast'	*wa-tabiri*	'the forecasters'
tafiti	'investigate'	*u-tafiti*	'investigations'
laghai	'cheat, trick'	*m-laghai*	'liar'

The verbs of Arabic origin in the first row are in Kiswahili morphology which permits them to undergo prefixation by the noun class prefixes like m- and ma-, which is a common behaviour of Kiswahili, as well as other Bantu languages, as shown in the second row. Also, such verbs of this kind allow suffixation of the nominalising morphemes like -wa and -ko, a common derivation process in bantu languages.

English loan verbs in Kiswahili undergo the same morphological processes which in turn re nativized by making them more like Kiswahili words. Perhaps the following examples from TUKI (2001) will help to substantiate this point.

(17)

Verbs		**Nouns**	
feli	'fail'	'm-feliji	'failure' [*feli* 'failure']
faulu	'pass'	u-faulu	'pass level'

A number of Arabic loan words, particularly nouns and adverbs in Kiswahili have been made verbs through suffixation process (Shembuli 2010: 52). Such derived verbs are exemplified in (18) whereby the suffixes -u, verbal extensions -ish- and -an- are applied to nouns and such suffixes change the verbs to nouns.

(18)

Nouns		**Verbs**	
baki	'remainder'	*bakisha*	'keep'
taarifa	'information'	*taarifu*	'inform'
taifa	'nation'	*taifisha*	'nationalise'
bahati	'fortune, luck'	*bahatisha*	'take changes'
hatari	'danger'	*hatarisha*	'endanger'
hesabu	'arithmetic'	*hesabiana*	'count for each other'
shuruti	'(by) force'	*shurutisha*	'to force'

Suffixation is a very common derivation process applied to English loan nouns in Kiswahili. i am not very much sure that suffixation works well with English loan words due to its great applicability in English language, as Katamba (1993) and Booij (2005) report. English nouns which become verbs after suffixation are exemplified in (19). Also, some verbs of Arabic origin become adjectives after affixation (20).

(19)

Nouns		**Verbs**	
feli	'fail'	*felishana*	'cause to fail each other'
faulu	'pass'	*faulishana*	'make pass one another'

(20)

Verbs		**Adjectives**	
baini	'realise'	*bainifu*	'evident'
haribu	'destroy'	*haribifu*	'destructive'
zini	'fornicate'	*zinifu*	'adulterous'

6.5.2 Structure of loanwords in French

First of all, some word categories are prone to borrowing. It is shown in Ottawa-Hull corpus that the majority of loanwords falls into the category of nouns (64 percent), followed by verbs (14 percent, interjections and frozen expressions (12 percent), adjectives (8 percent), and conjunctions (1.5 percent) (Poplack 1988: 63).

Second, the masculine-feminine gender assignment is the main linguistic adjustment acted upon loanwords. (Poplack 1988: 66-67), based on some 550 borrowed types, show indications of feminine or masculine gender assignment to loanwords which they claim is achieved earlier in the assimilation process. Some examples include:

(21)   *traite* 'treat' (87 percent Feminine)
        business (85 percent Feminine)
        football (79 percent Masculine)
        bar (75 percent Masculine)
        building (60 percent Masculine)
        baseball (58 percent Masculine).

In the same spirit, Ayres-Bennett and Carruthers (2001) also find that English loanwords are adapted by taking a French nominal suffix e.g. *conteneur* 'container, receptacle'.

Third, Poplack (1988: 68) finds that 'all verbs in the corpus are placed in the first conjugation (the *-er* class) and conjugated according to French patterns... Widespread verbs include words given in (22):

(22)   *afforder, brainwasher, checker* 'check out, undergo a medical examination'
        delivrer, deplugger 'unplug',
        figurer 'conclude',
        feeler, mover 'change residence, change place of'
        runner 'direct, drive (vehicle)', *shopper, skipper* 'cut class, skip'
        tougher to tough it out', *user* 'to utilize' etc.

Also, integration of French verbal-morphology as shown by words *développer* 'develop' and *réaliser* 'accomplish, realize' from English into French (Ayres-Bennett & Carruthers 2001).

Moreover, the majority of plural nouns in the corpus, follow French rules for plural marking, i.e. they show [Ø] affixation, e.g. *hockey, plant, pride* etc. This pattern excludes the lexicalized plurals *jeans, shorts, comics* 'cartoons', *mumps* etc.

6.5.3 Adaptation in other languages

Adaptation processes discussed in detail for Kiswahili and English above tend to happen in other languages as well. For example, loanwords are integrated into Iraqw morphology through gender and number assignments. Mous and Qorro (2009: 116) found that there is a difference in the final vowel endings for gender in this language: masculinity is marked by vowels [o, u], e.g. *kalaamu* (masc) 'pen', *kalaabu* (masc) 'book' and *mudoogo* (masc) 'cassava' while feminine nouns endi in [i, e, a], e.g. *shuule* (fem) 'school', *mikeete* (fem) 'bread', *gaseeti* (fem) 'newspaper', and *chupa* (fem) 'bottle'.

Number is a derivational process in Iraqw; for some loanwords, it is the singular which is derived while for others, it is the plural which is derived, depending on the feature number of the source language (Mous & Qorro 2009: 117). A good example is the Kiswahili loanword *kiti-angw* 'chair' vs. *kiti-eer* 'chairs'. This is the norm even with loanwords with invariant numbers in the donor language, they receive derivation suffix in Iraqw, e.g. Kiswahili loanword *askáari* (fem) 'solders' vs. *askáar-mo* (masc) 'solder'. But some loanwords maintain the number of the source language, e.g. *matofaali* 'bricks' [*matofali* 'bricks' Swahili].

Another point worth noticing here is that in Iraqw, verbs that are borrowed must be verbalized by the causative derivational suffix *-s* or the durative derivational suffix *-m*.

Marten and Qorro (2009: 118) gives examples like *shitak-uus* 'accuse' [<*shitaki* Swahili] and *paasii-ɲ* 'iron' [<*pasi* Swahili].

6.6   The context of usages of loanwords in Kiswahili

Borrowing words from another language is not something native speakers of a particular language should be ashamed of. In fact, ancient languages such as Persians, English, French and Arabic borrowed tremendously from other languages and will continue to do so over a course of time because languages contacts can not be eliminated so long as mankind remains as such mobile as have been for centuries.

Schadeberg (2009: 87) points out that the English loanwords into Kiswahili are for modern world (modern clothing and modern legal system), Arabic has influence on several areas as per history of Kiswahili, and Portuguese has influence on ship building.

The question of use of loan words is not of less significance here. Kiswahili loan words from all languages are used in day-to-day communications amongst the speakers of the language. Hurskainen (2004) reports of the use of loan words of English and Arabic origin in different domains of language use in Kiswahili. He used a corpora approach to the studying of the loan words in Islamic based contexts like Quran-oriented institutions, Kiswahili literature particularly creative works by Kiswahili speakers, the media especially Kiswahili newspapers and radio stations, Christian-oriented writings like the Bible, as well as health related Kiswahili writings. His findings focused on Tanzanian Kiswahili are quite interesting to the study of utilisation of loan words in everyday conversations.

Let us draw a comparison of usage of loan words of Arabic and English origin in Kiswahili. In his work it is indicated that in normal contemporary news texts the proportion of Arabic loan words is about 16 percent while that of English is only 6 percent. Second, the overall percent of Arabic loan words used in Quran amounts 16 while English has almost nothing to offer in this domain. However, English contributes to other domains related to the Quran because the overall amount of English loan words in Kiswahili in other domains of Islamic religion is 2 percent while that of Arabic is as higher as 19 percent. This does not guarantee the presence of English loan words in Christian-oriented documents like the Bible because Arabic loans here are as low as 12 but this is higher than English loans which are fewer in number. Kiswahili literature is another area where Arabic loans are highly used. Euphrase Kezilahabi in his novels uses 14 percent of Arabic loans and only 1 percent of English borrowed words. Shaaban Robert has Arabic words in Kiswahili amounting to 21 percent while English words are almost absent. Lastly, documents related to healthcare has a total of 19 percent Arabic oriented Kiswahili words and only 5 percent of English oriented words.

The summary above serves to inform us that loan words are used frequently in various domains of language use in Kiswahili contexts. The data pointed out that the percentage of Arabic loan words used in these domains is higher than the amount of English words used (Hurskainen: 216). If one would wish to record the amount of Arabic and English loan words in important domains of language use such as media (news), literary works (novels), religion (Quran and Bible) and education (healthcare), then should understand that about 16 percent of the overall percentage is Arabic and only 1 percent is English in Tanzanian Kiswahili. Also, the amount of nouns of Arabic origin used is about 28 percent and verbs is 21 percent. Nouns of English origin amounted to only 3 percent by average and verbs are in insignificant number.

Recent studies show that another environment where English words are used in Kiswahili texts in Tanzania is the area of commerce in not only formal communications but also advertisements in media. Lusekelo (2010) reports that apparent feature in commercial advertisements in Kiswahili newspapers is the use of code-mixing between Kiswahili and English words. Thus, in a country like Tanzania where English and Kiswahili enjoy the prestigious positions in education, courts, and bureaucracy (Batibo 1995), the presence of the two languages in the commercials becomes inevitable. Words such as *kampuni* 'company', *droo* 'draw' and *sementi~simenti* 'cement' are a commonplace in such advertisements.

New ways of introducing loanwords into Kiswahili is via media. Lusekelo (2010) observes that usages of terms in the language of sports as revealed by the Kiswahili newspapers covering the 2010 FIFA World Cup Tournaments in South Africa. We conclude that words of foreign origin are borrowed into Kiswahili and become localized. For instance, the words *vuvuzela* and *sauzi* 'South Africa' had found their way into the language of sports and politics in Tanzania due to the FIFA World Cup competitions in 2010. Also, several other words are employed by sports journalists in Kiswahili newspapers which are typical soccer words. Some of these words, like *fiti* 'fit' and *mastaa* 'stars' are of English origin but are localized into Kiswahili. At last one notices that the language of sports uses a unique style.

Resources cited:

Awagana, Ari, Ekkehard Wolff & Doris Löhr. 2009. Loanwords in Hausa, a Chadic language in West Africa. In: Haspelmath, Martin & Tadmor, Uri (eds). *Loanwords in the World's Languages: A Comparative Handbook.* Berlin: Mouton de Gruyter. pp. 142-165.

Ayres-Bennett, Wendy & Carruthers, Janice. 2001. *Problems and Perspectives: Studies in the Mordern French Language.* Essex: Pearson Education Limited.

Baldi, Sergio. 1989. On the semantics of Arabic loanwords in Hausa. In: frajzyngier, Zygmunt (ed). *Current Progress in Chadic Linguistics.* Amsterdam: John Benjamins. pp. 285-301.

Batibo, Herman M. 1995. The growth of Swahili as language of education and administration in Tanzania. In: Putz, Marten (ed). *Discrimination through Language in Africa: Perspectives on the Namibian Experience.* Berlin: Mouton de Gruyter. pp. 57-80.

Batibo, Herman M. 1996. Loanword clusters nativization rules in Tswana and Swahili: A comparative study. *South African Journal of African Languages,* 16 (2): 33-41.

Batibo, Herman M. 2002. The evolution of the Swahili syllable structure. *South African Journal of African languages*, 22(1): 1-10.

Batibo, Herman M. & Rottland, Franz. 2001. The adoption of Datooga loanwords in Sukuma and its historical implications. *Sprache und Geschichte in Afrika*, vol. 16/17. pp. 9-50.

Booij, Geert. 2002. *The Morphology of Dutch*. Oxford: Oxford University Press.

Crowley, Roger, Marvin L. Bender, Charles A. Ferguson, Hailu Fulass, & Getatchew Haile. 1976. The Amharic language. In: Bender, Marvin L., J. Donald Bowen, Robert L. Cooper & Charles A. Ferguson (eds.). *Language in Ethiopia*. London: Oxford University Press. pp. 77-98.

Chami, Felix. 2006. *The Unity of African Ancient History 3000 BC to AD 500*. Dar es Salaam: E & D Ltd.

Chesley, Paula. 2010. Lexical borrowings in French: Angilicisms as a separate phenomenon. *French language studies*, vo. 29: 231-251.

Gower, R.H. 1952. Swahili borrowings from English. *Journal of the International African Institute*, vol. 22(2): 154-157.

Greenberg, Joseph H. 1960. Linguistic evidence for the influence of the Kanuri on the Hausa. *The Journal of African History*, 1(2): 205-212.

Haspelmath, Martin. 2009. Lexical borrowing: Concepts and issues. In: Haspelmath, Martin & Tadmor, Uri (eds). *Loanwords in the World's Languages: A Comparative Handbook*. Berlin: Mouton de Gruyter. pp. 35-54.

Haspelmath, Martin & Tadmor, Uri (eds). 2009. *Loanwords in the World's Languages: A Comparative Handbook*. Berlin: Mouton de Gruyter.

Hock, Hans H. & Joseph, Brian D. 1996. *Language History, Language Change, and Language Relationship: An Introduction to Historical and Comparative Linguistics*. Berlin: Mouton de Gruyter.

Honken, H. 2006. Fused loans in Khoesan. *Pula*, vol. 20(1): 75–85.

Jaggar, Phili J. 2010. The role of comparative/historical linguistics in reconstructing the past: What borrowed and inherited words tell us about the early history of Hausa. In: Haour, Anne & Rossi, Benedetta (eds.). *Being and Becoming Hausa: Interdisciplinary Perspectives*. Leiden & Boston: Brill. pp. 35-58.

Katamba, Francis. 2003. Bantu nominal morphology. In: Nurse, Derek & Philippson, Gérard (eds.) *The Bantu languages*. London: Routledge. pp. 103-120.

Knowles, Gerry. 1997. *A cultural history of the English language*. London: Arnold.

Lusekelo, Amani. 2010. Morphology-pragmatics interface: The case of the Tanzanian commercials in Swahili newspapers. *Afrikanistik Online*. [http://www.afrikanistik-online.de/archiv/2010/2711/].

Lusekelo, Amani. 2013. Swahili loanwords nativisations in the languages of Tanzania. *HURIA Journal of the Open University of Tanzania*, vol. 14, pp. 151-162.

Mkude, Daniel J. 2004. The impact of Swahili on Kiluguru. In: Bromber, Katrin & Smieja, Birgit (eds.). *Globalisation and African Languages: Risks and Benefits.* Berlin: Mouton de Gruyter. pp. 181-197.

Mous, Maarten & Martha Qorro. 2009. Loan words in Iraqw, a Cushitic language of Tanzania. In: Haspelmath, M. & Tadmor, U. (Eds.). *Loanwords in the World's Languages: A Comparative Handbook*. Berlijn: De Gruyter Mouton. pp. 103-123

Mwita, Leonard C. 2009. The adaptation of Swahili loanwords from Arabic: A constraint-based analysis. *The Journal of Pan African Studies,* 2(8). pp. 46-61.

Nurse, Derek. 1997. The contribution of linguistics to the study of history in Africa. *Journal of African History*, 38: 359-391.

Owino, Daniel. 2003. *Phonological Nativisation of Dholuo Loanwords.* Doctoral thesis. University of Pretoria

Poplack, Shana, David Sankoff, & Christopher Miller. 1988. The social correlates and linguistic processes of lexical borrowing and assimilation. *Linguistics,* vol. 26: 47-104.

Schadeberg, Thilo C. 2009. Loanwords in Swahili. In: Haspelmath, Martin & Tadmor, Uri (eds). *Loanwords in the World's Languages: A Comparative Handbook.* Berlin: Mouton de Gruyter. pp. 78-102.

Scotton, Carol Myers & Okeju, John. 1972. Loan word integration in Ateso. *Anthropological Linguistics*, 14 (9): 368-382.

Shembuli, Musa M.S. 2010. Mabadiliko ya kifonolojia na kimofolojia wakati wa utohoaji maneno ya Kiarabu katika Swahili: Mifano kutoka Kamusi ya Kiswahili Sanifu (TUKI 2004). *SWAHILI: Journal of the Institute of Kiswahili Studies,* vol. 73. pp. 45-57.

Swilla, Imani N. 2000. Borrowing in Chindali. In: Kahigi, Kulikoyela, Yared Kihore & Maarten Mous (eds) *Languages of Tanzania.* Leiden: Research for Asian, African and Amerindian studies. pp. 297-307.

TUKI (Taasisi ya Uchunguzi wa Swahili). 2001. *Kamusi ya Swahili-Kiingereza.* Dar es Salaam: Institute of Kiswahili Research.

Vansina, Jan. 1995. New linguistic evidence and the Bantu expansion. *Journal of African history,* 35. pp 173-195.

Zawawi, Sharifa.1979. *Loan Words and their Effect on the Classification of Swahili Nominals.* Leiden: Brill Archive.

Zivenge, William. 2009. *Phonological and Morphological Nativisation of English Loans in Tonga.* Doctoral thesis, University of South Africa.

Exercise Six

6.1   Study carefully the following loanwords in Kinyakyusa, Kindali, Kinyamwanga and Kinyiha Bantu languages of Tanzania (Swilla 2000; Lusekelo 2013).

> *isopo* 'soap'
> *isupuni* 'spoon'
> *ifulupi* 'envelope'
> *ibatani* 'button'
> *mande* 'Monday'
> *sisala* 'scissors'
> *ukoloti, ikoloti* 'court'
> *ibokoshi, obokosi* 'box',
> *hendeli* 'handle'
> *ichaalichi, ikyaliki* 'church'
> *ikanisa* 'church'
> *itempeli, tembile* 'church'
> *isukuulu, insukulu* 'school'
> *ikipatala, ichipatala* 'hospital'

1.   In the list of the loanwords provided, how many of them are nouns and verbs?
2.   What are the morphological changes associated with those words?
3.   What are the phonological changes associated with those words?

6.2   Select one language spoken in Tanzania. Study carefully loanwords in that language. Then attempt to answer these questions:

1.   In the list of the loanwords provided, how many of them are nouns and verbs?
2.   How are such words adopted into the morphology of the language in question?
3.   In what manners are such words adapted into the phonology of that language?

7 Compounding

7.1 Introducing compounding

The fascinating linguistic phenomenon covered in this chapter emanates from joining mainly two (in other cases more) words in order to create new words which cater for given lexical senses. As the title of this chapter reads, this kind of word-formation process is technically known as **compounding**.

It seems that basic way to form compounds (resulting words in compounding process) is through two-word combinations. Perhaps a few examples from the three focal languages offered in (1) will substantiate this claim (some of these tokens appear in Katamba 1993; Gast 2008; Mohamed 2001; Rowlett 2007; Desmetes & Voilling 2009):

(1) a. *classroom*   [English]
         guideline
         user-friendly
         book-keeping
         polling station

     b. *bata mzinga* 'turkey'   [Swahili]
         bata bukini 'goose'
         garimoshi 'a train'
         mshikadau 'shareholder'
         mlalahoi 'proletariat'

     c. *autoradio* 'car radio'   [French]
         casse-pied 'coastguard'
         lèche-vitrine 'windscreen-wiper'
         gratte-papier 'pen pusher'
         centre-ville 'town centre'
         solution-miracle 'miracle cure'

As examples in (1) show, compounding is attested in several languages and compound words are a common place in at least all languages. At a global level, this is even shown in the literature whereby works, e.g. Bauer (1983) and Katamba (1993) particularly for English and Booij (2002) for Dutch, set independent chapters that cover compounds in various word-categories. African languages such as Hausa [Nigeria/Niger] (Newman 2000) and Amharic [Leslau 1995] have been analysed following compounding word-formation process.

Furthermore, specific to English language, several articles appear to have paid attention to the analysis of the phenomenon described in this chapter (cf. Benecez 2004a, b; Gast

2008). French compounds are studied in works such as Desmetes and Voilling (2009). The search for articles on compounding in Kiswahili could not yield the best results[18]. But literature for compounding in other African languages exists. For instance, specific to Bantu languages, a detailed work of compound nouns in Northern Sotho is offered by Mphasha (2006). Also, other works such as Musehane (2007a) and Kula (2009) offer the description of nominal compounds in Bantu languages.

Another important piece of information to consider is about the word categories which are compounded. It seems that significant word categories, namely nouns and verbs, (perhaps even adjectives and adverbs) tend to undergo compounding more regularly than other word-categories across world languages. The analysis of such words, therefore, will help us to have a better understanding of what kinds of words we are dealing with in this chapter.

It is noted that **content words** are more prone to being compounded than grammatical words. However, grammatical words can also show compounding. To shape the introduction I offer some examples of the compounded content words in (2).

(2)	**Compounds**	**English**	**Categories**	**Resulting Categories**
	bata mzinga	'turkey'	Noun+Noun	Noun
	mwananchi	'citizen'	Noun+Noun	Noun
	mjamzito	'pregnant'	Adjective+Adjective	Noun
	mshikadau	'shareholder'	Verb+Noun	Noun
	vivyo hivyo	'exactly'	Noun+Adverb	Adverb
	chezashere	'to mock'	Verb+Noun	Verb

Using these examples, we may conclude, therefore, that word-formation processes involve compounding and **compound words** (also called **compounds**) contain at least two bases which are both words (Katamba & Stonham 2006: 55). The idea that compounded words become one word is supported by Spencer (1991: 14) who says 'some languages exhibit the compounding of two nouns to produce a single compound noun'.

With regard to major word categories, nouns seem to have more compounds than verbs. This is obtained in the literatures which point towards the picture that nouns are more compounded than adjectives and verbs at least across African languages. For instance, Leslau (1995: 247) reports that there are a considerable number of compounded nouns in Amharic, while Newman (2000: 110) reports that approximately 70 percent of compound words (regardless of their internal structure) in Hausa are nouns.

The same picture seems to be obtained in European languages, i.e. nominal compounds outnumber other compound words. This is confirmed by Bauer (1983: 202) who says 'the vast majority of compounds in English are nouns'. This is also concluded for Dutch as Booij (1992: 37) says 'the most productive type of compounding in Dutch is nominal compounding'.

---

18 The efforts done to search for published works for compounds in Kiswahili probably could not benefit from papers in Kiswahili journal (Institute of Kiswahili Studies). Perhaps any mention of sources from readers will help to improve a future version of this book.

However, the foregoing claim does not rule out the possibility of having languages across the globe which do not employ compounding as a means of word-formation. Referring to Nootka, for instance, Stonham (2004: 234) says 'regular compounding has been ruled out as a process in the language'. Perhaps several other languages do also not support compounding.

The different kinds of word-categories which undergo compounding in Kiswahili, French and English are presented in the subsequent sections of the chapter. In what follows, the notions compounding and compounds are further defined.

7.2 Defining the notions compounding and compounds

7.2.1 Compounding

These two words are essential towards a good grasp of the morphological matter covered in this chapter, i.e. **compounding** and **compounds**. We saw briefly in section 8.1 above that the term compounding is preferred terminology for this word-formation process.

This process received attention in the description and analysis of languages of the world, though with other labels as well. For example, Mohamed (2001: 35) says 'the process of compounding words that function independently in other circumstances is called **composition**.' This is also supported by Bauer (2004: 32) who says 'composition is the process of forming compounds'.

There is also another term in the literature which also refers to compounding. It is said that **incorporation** also refers to a special kind of compounding which involves two lexical items (Bauer 2004: 54). Thus, the list of compounding terminologies is:

(3)   *compounding*

        incorporation

        composition

Having seen the alternative names, now we can define this notion. By definition, the term **compounding** is a special form of derivation in which instead of adding affixes to a stem, two or more words are put together to make a new lexical unit. In the focal languages (English, Kiswahili and French), new words can be formed from the already existing words by this process, i.e. at least two individual words being coupled together to form a compound word.

Some tokens of examples given in (1) above can be used to substantiate the amalgamation of two separate words to form a compound (which is defined immediately below). We see the combinations: *book-keeping* [$<_N book+_V keeping$] for English, *batamzinga* [$<_N bata$ 'duck'$+_N mzinga$ 'cannon'] 'turkey' for Kiswahili and *ouvre-boîte* [$<_V ouvre$ 'open'$+ _N boîte$ 'tin'] 'can-opener'. (Notice the different word-classes which combine to form compounds). The combined words work as individual words, separate from the source terms.

The resulting words (compounds) become independent words, readily available for the next morphological operations. This is mentioned in the definition of this notion by Musehane (2007b: 181) who says:

Compounding, as a productive word formation process, involves the combination of at least two roots or stems. Additional morphemes are attached to form grammatically classifiable lexical entities that have the status of a single word.

In other literature, it is also indicated that compounding is the joining of two or more words belonging to the same or different categories to form new nouns (Bauer 1983; Booij 2002). That is, when a language needs a new noun, it can make use of existing words. For example, with the growth of scientific knowledge, new technical and scientific terms are commonly invented in this way. As it is briefly mentioned above, the compounds across languages may consist of, for instance, a noun and a noun, a verb and a noun, and an adjective stem or a noun and an adverb.

7.2.2 Compounds (compound words)

Newman (2000: 109), using Hausa language, offers the best background information on the notion **compounds** as he says 'compounds are sequences of two or more words that are bound together in such a way as to constitute a single word, e.g. *fahar-hula* [<white+cap] 'civilian'. It means that the word *fahar* which means 'white' combines with another word, *hula* which means 'cap' to create a third word *fahar-hula* which means 'civilian'.

This word is also defined in other works such as Hurford (1994: 43) that defines a compound as a word or short sequence of words, composed of shorter words, but acting more or less as a single word. It means that individual words such as *book* and *keeping* and *bata* 'duck' and *mzinga* 'cannon' are shorter (in morphological shapes) than the resulting words, i.e. *book-keeping* and *batamzinga* 'turkey'.

It is said even in important volumes on morphology that compound words are longer than simple words but do not usually form whole phrases on their own. For example, Katamba (1993: 54) states 'a compound word contains at least two bases which are both words, or at any rate, root morphemes'. Hence a compound is a unit consisting of two or more bases. Although two word compounds are the most common ones in Kiswahili and English, it would be difficult to limit the number of words per compound.

Another feature of a compound is, it is invariably lacking derivational features when it is formed. This is succinctly observed by Bauer (2004: 32) who says 'a compound contains two or more stems but has no derivational affixes attached to it'.

Here perhaps the English example *book-keeping* offers the best illustration. The *-ing* is inflectional in nature (Bauer 1983). This word functions altogether as one element. The other word, *book-keeper* probably gives bad impression that the derivational suffix *-er* is available in English compounds. Readers should understand that this nominalising suffix is attached as a second tier of the derivational process. In line with cyclist condition (Katamba 1993), thus, compounding began and the resulting word is exposed to the second derivation process.

7.2.3 Compounds vs. Phrases

Since compounds result from joined lexical words, then the question of how we manage to draw a boundary between a compound and a phrasal expression remains significant at this point. In trying to draw a boundary between a phrase and a compound, Newman (2000) mentions three criteria to be observed.

He has succinctly pointed out that the essential feature that distinguishes compounds from similar phrases is their **lexical integrity**, i.e. components of the compounds appear necessarily as so (united together as one), without permitting permutations (variations), insertions, substitutions, or deletions, at least in Hausa (Newman 2000: 109). He mentions the substitution of positions is not allowed for compounds like *fahar-hula* 'civilian', but it is permitted a phrases like *fahar hula* 'white cap' or *hula fara* 'white cap'. This means that the expression *fahar-hula* is a compound while the last two expressions, *fahar hula* and *hula fara*, are noun phrases.

Lexical integrity is also attested in French. Jones (1996: 206) says compound nouns differ from noun phrases because compounds are inseparable, e.g. in a phrase made of noun and adjective in which an adjective is a modifier, it follows the head-noun immediately as in *absence totale de preuves*. However, in compound nouns the adjective must follow the entire expression: *une voiture de sport rouge*.

The same is true for Kiswahili because compound nouns function as independent words as in *garimoshi moja chakavu* 'one wrecked train' and *wajasiliamali wawili walemavu* 'two lame entrepreneurs'. Even English compounds are modified with the canonical syntactic pattern: DETERMINER+PRE-MODIFIERS+HEAD+POST-MODIFIERS, as in *the small bedroom in the house* and *the actual boiling point*.

Another essential feature surrounds the order of noun and its dependents (**DP internal agreement**). The pattern in each noun is strictly observed for each language. Perhaps we should use Hausa data. It is established that the order of noun-adjective [nominal+modifier] is strict, at least in Hausa, whereby all modifiers come after the head word in nominal phrases, e.g. *gidan-sauro* [house-mosquito] *bàbba* [net] 'big mosquito net' which cannot change to **gidan- bàbba -sauro* (Newman 2000: 109).

This pattern is also true for Kiswahili, as said above, NPs with compound-heads observe Noun-Determiner-Modifier order: *garimoshi hili chakavu* 'this wrecked train' and *batamzinga wetu wawili* 'our two turkeys'. This is true even for English compounds whih follow the canonical syntactic pattern, e.g. *the small <u>bedroom</u> in the house*.

The third distinguishing criterion is tone patterns. For instance, compounds in Hausa have tone patterns different from individual words. This is shown in (4) below whereby the compound has distinct tone patterns from isolated words which compose it.

(4)   *gaáshin-baki* 'mustache'

   gáshi [H-L tone] 'hair'

   bakii [long final vowel] 'mouth'

In the discussion in the following sections, attention is paid, among other things, on the patterns that help to distinguish compounds from phrases. In what follows, the discussion of different manifestations of compounds in the sample languages is offered.

7.3   The structure of compound words

In this section the details about internal structure of the compounds in target languages is offered, focusing on word-categories and resulting structures. We begin to discuss the orthographic representation of compounds.

7.3.1 Orthographic representation

Several ways exist in the way resulting compounds manifest as far as the writing system is involved: single-word style, conjoined compounds, hyphenation style and separate words style. Since we are dealing with the writing system here, we better survey some of the existing works and see what styles are employed therein.

In existing literary novels for Kiswahili, more patterns of representations of compound words are used. For example, the compounds like *walalahoi* 'proletariats', *mwananchi* 'citizen' and *mjasiliamali* 'enterpreneur' are typical fused elements which occur singly (see e.g. Mbogo 2003; Babu 2007). In existing technical books for Kiswahili (e.g. Mwita & Mwansoko 2003; Massamba 2004), a number of compounds are hyphenated, e.g. *isimu-jamii* 'sociolinguistics' and *elimu–mimea* 'botany'. Other compounds appear with a linking element as for *jeshi la maji* 'marine army' and *mpaka wa mji* 'town border'.

In Kiswahili newspapers in Tanzania, compound words are written as single words, e.g. *mlalahoi* 'proletariat'; in other cases they appear as separated words, as in *wafanya kazi* 'workers'; hyphenation is also a fashion of writing these compounds, as illustrated by *kitega-uchumi* 'investment'; and the use of particles to join them is also attested, as in *jeshi la mgambo* 'militia people'.

In French writing system, Ayres-Bennett and Carruthers (2001: 345) say, 'there are several orthographic possibilities for compounds: (i) hyphenated words, e.g. *press-bouton* 'press-button', (ii) fusion, e.g. *télécarte* 'call-card', (iii) juxtaposition, e.g. *chaise longue* 'beach chair', and (iv) compounds joined by elements *de* and *à*, e.g. *robe à fleurs* 'flowers dress'' [translations mine[19]].

In underscoring the functions of the different orthographic representation in the written words in French, Rowlett (2007: 17) says:

> The varying degrees of closeness between the component parts of complex nouns can be reflected in the orthographic representation. The least close relationship is reflected by writing the compound as unhyphenated separate words: *haut fourneau* 'blast furnace'. A closer relationship is represented with hyphenation: *centre-ville* 'town centre'. A particularly close relationship can be reflected by writing the compound as a single word: *autoradio* 'car radio'.

---

19 Thanks to Nelius Neckemia, French Unit, Dar es Salaam University College of Education.

In the vast amount of English literature, compounds are sometimes hyphenated, e.g. *book-keeping* and *short-lived*. Some tokens of compounds appear as free separate words, e.g. *drift ice*, *call girl* and *thinker tank*. Several compounds in the language appear as fused words, e.g. *checklist, guideline, playboy* and *bedroom* (see Bauer 1983; Katamba 1993; Gast 2008).

Following the above mentioned orthographic choices, Newman (2000: 109) cautions that there are inconsistent styles because some compounds can be written as a single word, others are separated, while the rest are hyphenated. His option is to use hyphens throughout his volume so as to make a distinction between common phrases and compounds. One general point worth underlining here is that these patterns are attested across the world languages.

7.3.2 The structure of Kiswahili compounds

The scrutiny of Kiswahili compounds formed by the combination of lexical categories seems to yield only three patterns: noun-noun, noun-adjective and verb-noun. In what follows we describe each pattern.

Noun-noun compounds: As for the internal structure of compound nouns in Kiswahili, it is shown that this language is having a good deal of compound nouns which are formed by the combination of one noun and another noun, as exemplified in (5) below.

(5) *magarimoshi*   'trains'   [<*magari* 'cars' + *moshi* 'smoke']
     batamzinga   'turkey' [<*bata* 'duck' + *mzinga* 'cannon']
     mbwa mwitu 'wild dog'   [<*mbwa* 'dog' + *mwitu* 'forest']
     elimu-mimea 'botany' [<*elimu* 'education' + *mimea* 'plants']

A number of plant names in Kiswahili are made of compound nouns formed by the joining of two lexical nouns. Some examples are given below (see TUKI 2001; Legère 2003).

(6)   mbuyukuku   *Dombeya cincinnala*
        mtundamabwe   *Euclea natalensis*
        mchungwakayaye *Sonchus oleranceus*
        njugumawe   'bambara nuts'
        mkundebara   *Vigna frutescens*
        mbangiwazimu   *Conyza pyrrhopappa*
        mkungumanga   'nutmeg tree'

Noun-adjective compounds: It seems that Kiswahili has other compound nouns which are formed by the combination of a noun followed by an adjective, as demonstrated by (7)

(7) $[[siasa]_N[kali]_{Adj}]^{20}{}_N$ 'leftist'
     $[[mwelekeo]_N[hasi]_{Adj}]_N$ 'negative attitude'
     $[[mwelekeo]_N[chanya]_{Adj}]_N$ 'positive attitude'

---

20 Some students suggest that all these elements are not compound words rather noun phrases. In an example like: *Siasa zao kali zimewaponza* 'their leftist politics have affected them', the possessive seem to intervene the two elements. Perhaps this is possible because with these words the *lexical integrity principle* could not be satisfied.

In Kiswahili, a couple of compounds seem to be formed by an expression which we see that it gives a kind of adjectival reading in the language. We will call such compounds as **adjective (mwana)-noun compounds**. Such expressions give the interpretation similar to "X of". This is common with the word *mwana* 'child, off spring' which is categorized as a noun (see TUKI 2001). We offer examples in (8) below.

(8)
mwanaisimu	'linguist'
mwanampotevu	'prodigal son'
mwanaharakati	'activist'
mwanamaji	'sailor'
mwanamapinduzi	'revolutionist'
mwanajeshi 'soldier'	
mwanadamu	'human being'
mwanachuo	'student (college, university)'
mwanaharamu	'bastard'
mwanamkiwa	'orphan'

Another bunch of Kiswahili compounds of the structure noun-adjective compounds seem to be formed through compounding procedures and derivational processes. The second part of the compound undergoes morphological alterations while the first part of the word remains unmodified. Perhaps we should follow these examples which will help to make us have a better understanding of this word-formation process attested in the language.

(9)
mwanafunzi	'pupil, student'
mwanagenzi	'apprentice'
mwanambee	'first born'
mwanapwa 'sailor, fisherman'	
mkurugenzi	'director'
mkurufunzi 'tutor'	

The second words of these compounds undergo some morphological changes. For example, in *mwanafunzi* 'pupil, student', the word *kujifunza* 'to learn' is modified to *-funzi*. Likewise, the word *mbele* 'front' is changed to *mbee*. In this chapter, such kinds of compounds are referred to as modified compound nouns.

The word *mkurugenzi* 'director' above, for instance, is made of the word *mkuru* 'chief, head' and another verbal element. The resulting meaning here is a nominal thus we may assume correctly that the compounds in (14) above are left-headed and though the new meaning comes from the combination of the two elements.

Verb-noun compounds: The primary observation is that some compounds in this language are formed by the combination of verbs and nouns. However, (10) shows that all these compounds receive the nominal prefixes, e.g. *m-/wa-* [1/2].

(10)
m-vuja-jasho	'proletariat'	[<*m-vuja* 'leak' + *jasho* 'sweat']
wa-vuja-jasho	'proletariats'	[<*wa-vuja* 'leak' + *jasho* 'sweat']

| *m-chimba madini* | 'miner' [<*m-chimba* 'dig' + *madini* 'minerals'] |
| *wa-chimba madini* | 'miners' [<*wa-chimba* 'dig' + *madini* 'minerals'] |

Examples in (10) show the way verbs combine with nouns to create nominal compounds. The main morphological point to be observed here is the usage of the noun classes before each initial verbal-element. Such compounds are several in the language, e.g. (11) for classes 1/2 and (12) for classes 7/8 in Kiswahili.

(11)
mfanyabiashara	'business man/woman'
wafanyakazi	'workers'
mtunzahazina	'storekeeper'
mtunzafedha	'bursar'
washikadau	'stakeholders'
kipamkono	'the wedding fee'
wavujajasho	'proletariats'
vitega uchumi	'investments'

(12)
kifunguamimba	'the first born'
kifungamimba	'the last born'
mwendawazimu	'madman'

Also, Kiswahili language contains a lexicon which reveals a good number of plant names which are made of compound nouns formed by the incorporation of one verb and another noun, as illustrated in (13) (see TUKI 2001; Legère 2003).

(13)
mchinjadamu	'banana plant with red stem, roots and fruit'
kifauongo	*Memosa pudica*
mzalianyuma	*Phyllanthus sp.*
mdakakomba	*Sonchus oleranceus*
mvunjakondo	*Cleone spinosa*
mtemachui	*Canthhium pallidum*
mvunjashoka	*Haplocoelum inopleum*
mvumasimba	*Psidium guajava*

7.3.3 The structure of English compounds

English compounds are described in detail in Bauer (1983: chp. 7, section 7.2). Other works offering detailed analyses of English compounds include Benczes (2004a, b), Gast (2008) and Minkova and Stockwell (2009). In what follows, we present the combinations that yield compound words in the language: noun-noun, noun-verb, verb-noun, and adjective-noun.

Noun-noun compounds: The majority of compounds in English are created through a combination of a noun and another noun. It is reported by Bauer (1983: 203) that 'the majority of compounds of this class are endocentric'. A few examples (with three orthographic representations) are provided below.

(14) a. *ice cream*
          woman doctor

      b. *girl-friend*
          house-wife

      c. *hatchback*
          bedroom
          doghouse
          armchair
          ashtray

Noun-verb compounds: A number of compounds in the language are created by combining nouns and verbs, as illustrated in (15) below.

(15) *birth control*
      nosedive
      sunshine
      moonlight
      sunlight

Verb-noun compounds: Some compounds in English are made of verbs combined with nouns, in that order. A number of these compound words are formed by the combination of the gerund and noun (16a), while others are formed by verbs and nouns (16b). However, Bauer (1983: 203) suggests that gerund-noun compounds do not offer a wide range of semantics than the verb-noun compounds.

(16) a. *breaking news*
          shooting match
          fishing rod
          sleeping sickness
          washing machine

      b. *breakfast*
          cut-throat
          pickpocket

Noun-gerund compounds: English makes use of typical nouns combining with gerund (verbs) to create compound words (17).

(17) *book-keeping*
      window shopping
      bee-keeping
      ground breaking

Adjective-noun compounds: English makes use of typical adjectives combining with nouns to form words (19).

(19)   *software*
       hard-stuff
       fast-food

7.3.4 The structure of French compound words

French has compounds which are created by compounding process as the morphological formation of lexemes from lexemes, not functional words such as determiners, prepositions, and pronouns (Desmets & Villoing 2009).

Verb-noun compounds: These compound words in French are numerous. They are created by combination of verbs and nouns. Some examples are offered in (20) (Rowlett 2007; Desmets & Villoing 2009):

(20)   *grille-pain* [<grill+bread] 'toaster'
       perce-oreille [<pierce+ear] 'earwig'
       tournevis [<turn+screw] 'screwdriver'
       lèche-vitrine [<lick+window] 'window-shopping'
       ouvre-boîte [<open+tin], 'tin opener'
       traîne-buisson [<hang around on+bush] 'animal'
       reveille-matin [<wake up+morning] 'alarm clock'
       grippe-sou [<grab+penny] 'penny pincher'
       taille-crayon [trim+pencil]'pencil sharpener'

Desmets and Villoing (2009) say the semantic relation between the verb and noun is not absolutely uniform, nor as predictable as it would be in a syntactic structure. The nouns perform agentive, patient and locative roles.

Unlike English and Kiswahili, verb-noun compounding is characteristic of Romance languages such as French. Desmets and Villoing (2009) claim that the verb-noun compounding process is much less productive in languages such as English which employs another compounding process synthetic compounding, i.e. combining two nouns, e.g. *truck-driver*, *dish-washer* and *whale-hunting*.

Noun-noun compounds: compound nouns of this kind are firmly established in the language. Rowlett (2007: 14) says the complex nouns in French are head initial and can be composed of noun-noun. Some examples of compound nouns are provided in (21).

(21)   *autoradio* [<car+radio] 'car radio'
       centre-ville [<centre+town]'town centre'
       porte-fenêtre [<door+window] 'French window'
       poste-clé [<post+key] 'key position'
       solution-miracle [<solution+miracle] 'miracle cure'

Some noun-noun compounds are coordinated by the particle *de* 'of' hence their structures are noun-*de*-noun compounds (Rowlett 2007: 14). A few examples are given in (22)

(22)   *chemin de fer*   [<path of iron] 'railway'
        voiture de sport [<car of sports] 'sports car'
        vin d'honneur [<wine+honour] 'wine-reception'
        chateau d'eau [<castle of water] 'water-tower'

Jones (1996: 206) claims that these nominal expressions may be plausibly analysed as compound nouns. Also, he says that this N + *de* + N pattern is extremely common in the language.

Other noun-noun compounds are coordinated by the particle *à* to, at' (Rowlett 2007: 14) hence they have the internal structure noun-*à*-noun as shown in (23).

(23)   *verre à vin* [<glass to wine] 'wineglass'

7.4   Semantic manifestations of compounds (Senses of compounds)

This section is envisaged to offer semantic analysis of the compounds in the representative languages. The classification of compounds is also done by the semantic classes under which the resulting compounds make. In order to offer the best explanation under this category, it is of vital to distinguish between **endocentric** and **exocentric** compounds in the formation of English and Swahili[21] compound words.

Generally two criteria are employed to demarcate endocentric compounds from exocentric compounds (Benczes 2004a):
- headness in relation to each other (syntactic criterion)

- semantic relationship between the compounded words (semantic criterion)

7.4.1 Endocentric compounds

Headedness criterion: The majority of compounds in several world languages are endocentric (Benczes 2004a). This kind of compounds has a head and the meaning of the head controls the resulting meaning and the word-category of the compound. Here we need to underscore the functions of the heads in compounds which seems to draw a boundary between English compounds and Kiswahili compounds.

In Bantu morphology, based on **headedness** principle, in some compounds, the **left-most** word in a compound is likely to control the syntactic patterns for the compounds. This is true for *batamzinga* 'turkey' and *garimoshi* 'a train' in Kiswahili. The same is mentioned for Bantu in Mphasha (2006) that endocentric compounds are compounds that have a head which possesses identical features with the head of a phrase.

It is shown in the literature for English that 'a compound can be classified as endocentric if the compound has the same grammatical function as the head member' (Benczes 2004a: 11). Therefore, in *blackbird* and *drawbridge* the compounds have the function of

---

21 Readers should understand that my command of Kiswahili and English is at least reasonable enough to decide on grammaticality of the examples, while I rely on examples from sources for French. This warrants me to exclude classification of the French compounds from this section.

the nouns, similar to the heads *bird* and *bridge*. In another source, it is said 'endocentric compounds are those compounds that denote a special case of their **righthand** member (their head)' (Gast 2008: 273).

The following are examples of endocentric compounds in English (24a) (Gast 2008) and Kiswahili endocentric compounds (24b):

(24)   a.   *armchair*
                 whetstone
                 blackbird
                 scatterbrain
                 dressing room
                 boiling point

        b.   *batamzinga* 'turkey'
                 mjasiliamali 'entrepreneur'
                 njugumawe 'bambara nuts'
                 garimoshi 'a train'

Word-class criterion: Following Bauer (2003) who states that endocentric compounds denote a sub-class of the items denoted by one of their elements, and Gast (2008) who says the right-most element is the head, here the semantics of the compound nouns, for instance, *bata mzinga* 'turkey' is a result of the meaning of the word *bata* 'duck' hence the former is the head and the source of the semantic property of the resulting compound.

This is stipulated in other sources for English. For example, Benczes (2004a: 11) says 'a compound is semantically endocentric if the head element specifies the class of entities to which the compound belongs'. Therefore, the compound *armchair* is endocentric because it is a kind of chair (Ibid). Another scholar, Gast (2008: 273), says 'accordingly, *whetstone* is endocentric because every *whetstone* is a stone'.

7.4.2 Exocentric compounds

Headedness principle: A few exocentric compounds are attested across languages. In a simple definition, exocentric compounds do not have heads (Gast 2008: 273). Therefore, *pickpocket* and *breakbones* are not types of *pocket* and *bone*. Perhaps the Kiswahili examples *mvuja-jasho* 'proletariat' is the best illustration of exocentric compounds in the language.

Word-category criterion: Bauer (2003) indicates that exocentric compounds denote something which is not a sub-class of either of the elements in the compound, that is, they are not hyponyms of either of their elements. What Bauer means is that it is possible to have the most extreme cases where the compound's category is not identical to the category of either of the component members, and it is also possible to find a compound whose sense is not mainly determined by either of the component elements.

The following are examples of exocentric compounds in English (25a) (Benczes 2004a; Gast 2008) and Kiswahili exocentric compounds (25b):

(25) a.   *turnkey*
             pickpocket
             bluestocking
             fireman
             firelog

      b.   *mvuja jasho* 'day worker'
             mjasiliamali 'entrepreneur'
             mwanamichezo 'sports man'
             mwana-anga 'astronomist'

One of the interesting aspects of exocentric compounding is that one cannot always tell by the words it contains what the compound means. Put in other words, the meaning of a compound is not always the sum total of the meanings of its parts. Literature point out that these kinds of compounds do not have meanings derived from the two source words. In Kiswahili, may be the word *mjamzito* 'pregnant woman' would work as the best example because the meaning is derived from an adjective *mja* 'of X type' and another adjective *mzito* 'heavy'.

7.4.3 Syntactic interpretations of compounds

Syntax plays a vital role in describing the linguistic morphology of compounds across languages. Several syntactic parameters are put in place to classify the compound in the world languages including the **headiness** (Booij 2002; Benczes 2004a) and **definiteness** (Musehane 2007a; Kula 2009). Thus, in this section we discuss the syntax of compounded words because several compounds mentioned in Bantu languages are nouns (Mphasha 2006; Musehane 2007a; Kula 2009). The same is true for English (Benczes 2004a; Gast 2008) and French (Rowlett 2007).

Headedness: If we begin with nouns in Bantu languages, these are sometimes characterized semantically thus nouns belonging to the same noun class may share certain semantic features. Therefore, the noun classes show a semantic relationship of the member nouns. The good case is Kiswahili noun class 1/2 which denotes human beings. Compound nouns behave the same in Bantu languages because they show a variety of noun classes. Legère (2009) found that in Vidunda, plant names have noun classes in 3/4, 5/6, 7/8, 9/10 and 11/10 or 4. Furthermore, Legère (2009: 220) articulates that 'the overwhelming majority of the plant names are allocated to class 5 (NCP *i-*). It is fascinating to observe that, as indicated above, the plural NCP is that of class 4'.

In what Legère (2009: 224) calls "complex plant names", he found that in the Bantu language Vidunda [G38], compound plant names consisting mainly of a verb + noun combination. He goes on to say the two compound members are separated by a hyphen. The initial vowel *i* is the NCP, as all examples belong to class 5. No other noun classes contained compounds as plant names.

One of the reasons that we use data from other Bantu languages herein is that such facts seem to apply to Kiswahili compounds. See the following words:

(26) **Compounds**   **English**

    ma-garimoshi   'trains'
    wa-chimba madini   'miners'
    m-vujajasho   'proletariat'
    m-lalahoi   'day worker, proletariat'
    mw-anamichezo   'sportsman'
    ø-garimoshi   'train'
    mw-ananchi   'citizen'
    wa-namichezo   'sportsmen'
    wa-nanchi   'citizens'

The feature headedness could be captured easily using the attachment of the grammatical elements to the head word. In fact, plural markers, gender elements, case affixes, as well as noun class markers would always attach to the head-noun in the compounded nouns. This is attested in African languages.

Musehane (2007a: 33) mentions that the right most word looks like a head, as he says, 'the head is defined in terms of the position of a constituent, not in terms of the relation between categories that are based on their respective types. In terms of this definition, the rightmost category in X^n with feature complex X will be the head. The definition thus accounts for all the cases of right-headed compounds'. Later, he contends 'when a compound is right headed, it means that the second (i.e. right hand) element supplies the main meaning of the compound, while the preceding element is the modifier's (Musehane 2007b: 181).

This is not the end as he also pointed out that a pre-prefix could be the head as he says, the pre-prefix of the first noun becomes the head of the structure (Musehane 2007a: 34). It appears that the last option is attested across Bantu languages as Mphasha (2006: 603-604) says, 'in the morphological structure of these compound nouns, the noun class prefix of the first noun is the head of the compound, as in *motho-sebata* 'person who looks like a carnivore', *mo-* is the head which take other elements.

This kind of pattern is also attested in other languages. For example, 'Dutch compounds are right-headed: the right constituent is the head, and hence determines the semantic class, the syntactic category, and – in the case of nouns – the gender of the compound' (Booij 2002: 141). This is exemplified by the Dutch words like those in (27) below (Booij 2002: 142, 153).

(27) $[[bureau]_N[lade_N]_N$ 'desk drawer'
     $[[groot]_A[vader_N]_N$ 'grandfather'
     $[[kook]_V[pot_N]_N$ 'cooking pot'
     $[[auto]_N[vrij_A]_A$ 'car free'
     $[[licht]_A[grijs_A]_A$ 'light grey'

Definiteness is another parameter used to characterise compound nouns, at least in Bantu family. It is suggested that the augment functions to designate definiteness in Bantu nouns. For instance, Visser (2010: 299-301) claims that in the Bantu language Xhosa (South

Africa) the presence of the noun pre-prefix signals definiteness and its absence indicates indefiniteness. This is well exemplified by uncompounded nouns like *i-siselo* 'the cold drink' and *u-titshala* 'the teacher', whereby the pre-prefixes *i-* and *u-* mark definiteness.

A number of compounds in the Bantu family seem to carry the pre-prefixes. The Nyakyusa (Tanzania/Malawi) examples in (28) are apparently carrying the pre-prefix *a-*:

(28)   *amakomakipiki* [a-ma-koma-ki-piki] 'lizard'
        akapelafumbi   [a-ka-pela-fumbi] 'whirl wind'
        aßatulanondwa [a-ßa-tula-nongwa] 'sinners'

However, there is a debate of the highest position available in Bantu NPs and the category that occupies that position. For example, on the one hand, Carstens (1993, 2008: 152) claims that since Bantu languages lack articles, the noun raises to the determiner position. Therefore, it is the noun which is heading the NPs in Bantu languages particularly Sample Bantu languages.

On the other hand, Carstens (2008: 152) claims that in Bantu, modifiers can be adjoined to the left or to the right of noun's base position, yielding variability in post-nominal modifier orders. In such kind of analysis we find that this claim is plausible to the Eastern Bantu languages like Kiswahili (Rugemalira 2007; Lusekelo 2009b).

7.6   Further analysis of compounds

Several morphological issues could be raised and discussed in syntactic paradigm following compounds presented in the preceding sections. In this section, attention is paid to a number of these issues that surface in Kiswahili, mainly: possession in compound nouns, semantic interpretations of compounds, and concordial agreements.

7.6.1 Resulting word categories in Kiswahili

The adjectival-like and modified compound nouns in Kiswahili seem to demonstrate some kind of possessive. To such compounds, Musehane (2007a: 38-39) derived another way of describing such compounds in Tshivenda. He labels them as **compound nouns as descriptive possessives** because the morphological structure of these compound nouns may show some resemblance to other syntactic structures as there is a resemblance between the descriptive possession and the compound noun. Furthermore, the compound nouns of this kind can potentially take the possessive concord between them. Therefore, the 'possessive' describes the first noun in a compound in terms of a quality and not necessarily in terms of possession.

The same is applicable to Kiswahili compounds of such kind. In fact we may use the possessive particle or element (say it be preposition even if Kiswahili lack truer prepositions thought it has a number of borrowed preposition (Mohamed 2001)) *wa* 'of' to draw a link between the first word and the second word in the compounds. The following examples will help us have a better understanding of this process.

(29)   *mwana wa isimu*   'child of linguistics, linguist'
       mwana wa hewa   'child of air, pilot'
       mwana wa kijiji   'son of village, villager'
       mwana wa michezo   'son of sports, sports man'

In the above examples the element *wa* 'of' is used to indicate some kind of possession of the second element to the former. Moreover, we may argue that this is a good indicator that the words with *mwana* 'child' seem to give possession. Mohamed (2001: 35) put it rightly as follows: "These contain the particle -*ana* (son, daughter) as the first immediate constituent of the compounds. The second element does not take a class-prefix if it is a noun but shows an adjectival concord if it is an adjective".

Some Kiswahili compounds are nouns which appear with the particle *wa* 'of' but they are not extensions of the compounds which appear with *mwana* 'child', as discussed above. This is exemplified by these compounds. Put in other words, some Kiswahili compounds are nouns which appear with the particle *wa* 'of' but they are not extensions of the compounds which appear with or without it.

(30)   *askari wa mgambo*   'militia people'
       askari wa kukodi   'militia, mercenaries'
       mpaka wa mji   'town border'
       mpaka wa nchi   'country border'

This is further supported by Mohamed (2001: 34) who suggests that some compounds in Kiswahili are formed when they take the deverbative suffix -a, as in *kifungua mimba* 'the first born'. They are followed by qualifier nouns used to particularize the meaning of the compound in question.

A number of compounds in Kiswahili do get formed through other particles. This also helps us to derive the possession readings from these tokens.

(31)   *jeshi la maji*   'marine army'
       jeshi la mgambo   'militia army; auxiliary police'
       nyama ya nguruwe   'pork'
       elimu ya mimea 'botany'
       elimu ya wanyama   'zoology'
       kila pembe ya nchi   'every corner of the country'

Another interesting area of discussion about nominal compounds revolves around the presence of a number of compounds which seem to be made of a possessive and a noun. Such compounds are exemplified in (32) below.

(32)   *mwenyekiti*   'chairperson'
       wenyenacho   'rich persons, bourgeoisies'
       mwenyenzi   'Almighty'
       mwenyezi   'Almighty God'
       mwenyekichaa   'madman'
       mwinyimkuu   'paramount chief'

On the one hand, the word mwenye 'possessing, with, having' is treated as a **complementary adjectival** in Kamusi *(http://africanlanguages.com/Swahili/)* (But does not appear in TUKI 2001). Thus, in all elements in the first group above the element mwenye is used to indicate some form of possessiveness though the resulting compounds remain nouns.

On the other hand, the express mwinyi 'possessor, owner, landlord' is treated as a **nominal** in Kamusi *(http://africanlanguages.com/Swahili/)* and mwinyi 'lord; feudal lord; landlord; bourgeois; somebody who likes to enjoy life without working' appears also as a noun in TUKI (2001). Consequently, in all elements in the second group above the element mwinyi is used to point out possessiveness though the results are compound nouns.

We note that the majority of the Kiswahili compounds are nouns which fall under endocentric and exocentric clusters. We said earlier that **endocentric compounds** have a head and the meaning of the head controls the resulting meaning of the compound. Kiswahili reveals that some compound nouns are left-headed, like *bata nzinga* 'turkey' and *njugumawe* 'bambara nuts' result from the meanings of the first words in the compounds, i.e. *bata* 'duck' and *njugu* 'nuts'. Therefore, the former is the head and the source of the semantic property of the resulting compound.

Some compound nouns in Kiswahili are right-headed in the sense that the meaning of the second word in the compound brings about the meaning of the entire compound. This is exemplified by the word *mwanaisimu* 'linguist' and *mwanajeshi* 'soldier' which have the words *isimu* 'linguistics' and *jeshi* 'army, military' as the source of meanings of the compounds.

A good number of Kiswahili compound nouns are exocentric because their interpretation or meaning is something which is not a sub-class of either of the elements in the compound. These kinds of compounds have meanings derived from the two source words in Kiswahili. The word *mjamzito* 'pregnant woman' would work as the best example because the meaning is derived from an adjective *mja* 'of X type' and another adjective *mzito* 'heavy'.

7.6.2 Synthetic compounds or verbal compounds in English?

There are at least two perspectives up on the status of the verb+noun compounds. In this section we will present these perspectives using English, Dutch and Tshivenda examples.

The first perspective sees verb-to-noun or noun-to-verb compounds as a type of compounding which is resulting into verbs. Lieber (1983: 265-266) calls them **synthetic compounds** or **verbal compounds** in which the second stem is derived from a verb. Synthetic compounds are right-headed and typically the first stem is interpreted as an internal argument of the deverbal second stem. This is typically the case in English whereby the compound as a whole bears the category of the second stem, as shown below in which adjectival compounds are formed from the combination of a noun and a verb. According to Lieber (1983), the structure of the synthetic compound in the preceding examples assumes a verb, i.e. an argument structure which is a kind of a feature, subject to percolation (see Musehane 2007b).

(33)
strange-sound	Adj.	>	strange-sounding	Adj.
hand-weave	V	>	hand-woven	Adj.
hand-make	V	>	hand-made	Adj.
home-make	V	>	home-made	Adj.

Another perspective is that the resulting element might correctly be a verb compound. Booij (1992) uses the term verbal compound differently as he refers to a combination of the left constituent which is a verb and the right constituent a noun and the resulting word becomes a verb. Booij (1992) describes the verbal element as the first element, while the second element is a noun and the resultant word is a verb as shown below (see Musehane 2007b).

(34)
copy-cat	V	'Don't you dare copy-cat me!'
pick-pocket	V	'Be careful of people pick pocketing in the market place!'

As mentioned above, it seems compounding is a kind of word-formation which is characterized for nominal formation in many languages. Booij (2002: 161) mentions that, even though it has compounding as one of the word-formation process dominant in the language, and though compounding is unproductive in Dutch, there a fewer verbal compounds in the language. Musehane (2007b: 205) concludes that "Tshivenda does not have compounds which belong to the lexical category of the verb, even if one of the elements of the compound is a verb."

Resources cited:

Ayres-Bennett, Wendy & Carruthers, Janice. 2001. *Problems and Perspectives: Studies in the Modern French Language.* Essex: Pearson Education Limited.

Babu, Omar. 2007. *Kala Tufaha.* Nairobi. Phoenix Publishers.

Benczes, Réka. 2004a. Analysing exocentric compounds in English: A case for creativity. *The even yearbook,* vol. 6. pp. 11-18.

Benczes, Réka. 2004b. On analysability of English exocentric compounds. *Jezikoslovije,* vol. 5(1-2): 1-21.

Booij, Geert. 1992. Compounding in Dutch. *Rivista di Linguistica,* 4(1). pp. 37-59.

Booij, Geert. 2002. *The Morphology of Dutch.* Oxford: Oxford University Press.

Carstens, Vicki. 1993. On nominal morphology and DP structure. In: Mchombo, Sam (ed.) *Theoretical Aspects of Bantu Grammar 1.* California: CSLI Publications. pp. 151-180.

Carstens, Vicki. 2008. DP in Bantu and Romance. In: De Cat, Cécile & Demuth, Katherine (eds.). *The Bantu-Romance Connection: A comparative investigation of Verbal Agreement, DPs, and Information Structure*. Amsterdam: John Benjamins. pp. 131-165.

Desmets, Marianne & Villoing, Florence. 2009. French VN lexemes: morphological compounding in HPSG. *Proceedings of the HPSG09 Conference*. CSLI Publications.

Gast, Volker. 2008. Verb-noun compounds in English and German. *ZAA*, vol. 56(3): 269-282.

Hurford, James R. 1994. *Grammar: A Student's Guide*. Cambridge: Cambridge University Press.

Hurskainen, Arvi. 2004. Loan words in Kiswahili. In: Bromber, Katrin & Smieja, Birgit (eds.). *Globalisation and African Languages: Risks and Benefits*. Berlin: Mouton de Gruyter. pp. 199-217.

Jones, Michael A. 1996. *Foundations of French syntax*. Cambirdge: Cambridge Univeristy Press.

Kula, Nancy. 2009. Nominal compounding in Bemba. *A Talk at World Conference on African Languages (WOCAL 6)*, University of Cologne, 17-21 August 2009.

Legère, Karsten. 2003. Plant names from North Zanzibar. *Africa & Asia*, no. 3. pp. 123-146.

Legère, Karsten. 2009. Plant names in the Tanzanian Bantu language Vidunda: Structure and (some) etymology. In: Matondo, Masangu, Fiona Mc Laughlin and Eric Potsdam (eds). *Selected Proceedings of the 38th Annual Conference on African Linguistics*. Somerville, MA: Cascadilla Proceedings Project. pp. 217-228.

Leslau, Wolf. 1995. *Reference Grammar of Amharic*. Wiesbaden: Harrassowitz.

Lieber, Rochelle. 1983. Argument linking and compounds in English. *Linguistic Inquiry*, vol. 14: 251-285.

Lusekelo, Amani. 2009b. The structure of the Swahili noun phrase: Evidence from fictional narratives. In: Burger, Willie & Pienaar, Marné (eds.) *Die Tand van die Tyd: Opstelle Opgedra aan Jac Conradie*. Bloemfontein: Sun Press. pp. 45-60.

Massamba, David P.B. 2004. *Kamusi ya Isimu na Falsafa ya Lugha*. Dar es Salaam: Institute of Kiswahili Research, University of Dar es Salaam.

Mbogo, Emanuel. 2002. *Watoto wa mama ntilie*. Dar es Salaam: Heko.

Mohamed, A. Mohamed. 2001. *Modern Swahili Grammar*. Nairobi: East African Educational Publishers.

Mphasha, Lekau E. 2006. *The Compound Noun in Northern Sotho*. Doctoral thesis, University of Stellenbosch.

Musehane, Nelson M. 2007a. Morphological structure and semantic classification of noun+noun compounds. *South African Journal of African Languages*, vol.1. pp. 29-42.

Musehane, Nelson M. 2007b. The structure and semantic classification of compounds with a verbal component. *South African Journal of African Languages*, vol.4. pp. 181-205.

Mwita, A.M.A & Mwansoko, H.J.M. 2003. *Kamusi ya Tiba*. Dar es Salaam: Institute of Kiswahili Research.

Rowlett, Paul. 2007. *The syntax of French*. Cambridge: Cambridge University Press.

Rugemalira, M. Josephat. 2007. The structure of Bantu noun phrase. *SOAS Working Papers in Linguistics*, vol. 15: 135-148.

Visser, Mariana. 2010. Definiteness and specificity in Xhosa determiner phrase. In: Legère, Karsten & Thornell, Christina (eds). *Bantu Languages: Analysis,* Description and Theory. Köln: Rüdiger Köppe Verlag. pp. 295-314.

Exercise Seven

7.1   Examine the following data from Kiswahili:

> *magarimoshi* 'trains'
> *vitega uchumi*   'investments'
> *mwanamichezo* 'son of sports, sports man'
> *wachimba madini* 'miners'
> *askari wa mgambo* 'militia people'
> *mwanaharakati* 'activist'
> *batamzinga* 'turkey'
> *askari wa kukodi* 'militia, mercenaries'
> *elimu ya mimea* 'botany'
> *mwanamaji* 'sailor'
> *elimu ya wanyama* 'zoology'

1. Data show various kinds of compounds. Based on this data, how many types of compounds in this language?

2. Describe the kinds of compounding obtained in (7.1.1) above.

7.2   Offering vivid examples, differentiate between endocentric and exocentric compounds in English and Dutch languages.

8 Introduction to Theories of Morphological Analyses

8.1 Introduction

In the preceding chapters, a number of morphological issues have been mentioned and discussed. Also, data from English, Kiswahili and French (our focal languages) and some other languages (e.g. Hausa, Chinese, Herero, Subiya etc.) have been offered and described. This chapter of the book offers introduction to three theoretical orientations which are employed in the analysis of morphological data. The intention is to enable students of linguistics to attempt to provide both descriptive and theory-based analyses of morphological data, at least at a basic level.

The main provision offered in this book will enable students of linguistics to receive the primary theoretical tools which may help them to analyse data. Any reader who wishes to study these theories in detail may consult recommended sources, mainly Spencer (1991), Katamba and stonham (2006) and Plag (2002).

After this introduction, therefore, the chapter is divided into three sections. Section 8.2 is envisaged to present the gist of lexical morphological theory, particularly in the analysis of English affixes. Section 8.3 discusses the templatic (autosegmental) theory of morphology for the analysis of infixation in Arabic. Lastly, the contemporary theory of optimality (McCarthy 2002, 2008) is offered in section 8.4, capturing reduplication in tonal Bantu languages.

8.2 Lexical morphology theory in affixation

8.2.1 Introductory remarks

Generally, the lexical morphology theory examines the link between morphology and phonology of the structure of words. It is established that there is a relationship between word formation and the manner of pronunciation of those words. Such an interface between phonology and morphology intrigued scholars to study actual patterns of the relationships (Spencer 1991; Katamba 1993).

The fascinating relationship between phonology and morphology was first noticed by phonologistsPaul Kiparsky and John Goldsmith, among others, in the late 1970s and in the first half of 1980s. It is their involvements in phonological theories which pushed them to name this phenomenon **lexical phonology theory** (Katamba 1993). Specifically, it is reported that the phonologist Paul Kiparsky analysed data and proposed *Lexical*

Phonology Theory in a series of his works in the 1980s. Some of the well-known and influential works include: (i) From Cyclic Phonology to Lexical Phonology (1982), (ii) Lexical Phonology and Morphology (1982), (iii) On the Lexical Phonology of Icelandic (1984), and (iv) Lexical Phonology of Sanskrit Word Accent (1984) (see Spencer 1991; Katamba 1993).

Later on this theory was taken up by morphologists as well. In the late 1980s and early 1990s, the works of morphologists such as Andrew Spencer and Francis Katamba influenced the nomenclature for this theory to change to **lexical morphology theory**, a term which is highly preferred in linguistic morphology (see Katamba 1993), though other morphologists maintain the traditional nomenclature, theory of lexical phonology (see Plag 2002).

8.2.2 Two central themes in lexical morphology theory

Although a number of ideas has been proposed under lexical morphology theory, two major ideas need be underscored herein so as to make readers understand the notions in the expression theory of lexical morphology.

The first central theme is that there are hierarchical orderings of the morphemes in words. It means that affixes in word structures occur in **lexical strata**. This entails that the morphology of words is **layered** – i.e. normally affixes attach to stems which, in turn, form new stems where new affixes can be further attached to, on and on, in a strict fashion.

In the following examples (1), three English words (*move, power, happy*) show concatenation of some affixes, namely *-ment, -ful, -ness, -er, -ly* and *-s*, as shown in (1a). We observe in these words that when two or more affixes are added, as in (1b), the kind of order given therein must be observed. Otherwise, any irregularity causes ungrammaticality of the constructions, as illustrated in (1c).

(1)   a.   Basic word order as per strata of one affixes:

move	*move-ment*
move	*move-r*
serious	*serious-ness*
power	*power-ful*

        b.   Basic word order as per strata of two or three affixes:

move	*move-r-s*
power	*power-ful-ness*
happy	*happi-ness-less-ly*

        c.   Non-Basic word order as per strata of two or three affixes

move	**move-s-r*
power	**power-ness-ful*
happy	**happi-ly-ness-less*

This can be explained in other words as the normal word structure possesses affixes and stems which have affixes which are arranged in a strict order that observe hierarchy.

Thus, the affixes are not arranged haphazardly/randomly rather the affixation follows a strict order of the morphemes within a word. This is what is known as lexical strata (Katamba 1993).

The second central theme surrounds the way affixes trigger changes to the roots they are attached. Generally to each morpheme/affix attachment to a root/stem, there is a **phonological implication(s)**. Put in other words, each affix attached to a root/stem has some phonological implication(s). In other words, morphological affixes do trigger phonological changes to words they attach to.

These implications suggest that there are affixes which **do not trigger phonological** changes once attached to a stem to produce a new word in languages like English. Likewise, there are affixes which **trigger phonological** changes once attached to a stem to produce a new word in languages.

It is established that some affixes fall into Level I because they trigger segmental changes in the roots while others are Level II because they do not trigger any phonological changes in the roots. Perhaps some examples from Katamba (1993) will suffice to illustrate this point:

(2)   Origin: *wide*   /waɪd/   (Adj)
       Level 1:   *wide-ly*   /waɪdlɪ/   (Adv)
       Level 2:   *wid-th*   /wɪdθ/   (N)

       Origin: *broad*   /brɔ:d/   (Adj)
       Level 1:   *broad-ly*   /brɔ:dlɪ/   (Adv)
       Level 2:   *bread-th*   /bredθ/   (N)

       Origin: *long*   /lɒŋ/   (Adj)
       Level 1:   ---   ---   ---
       Level 2:   *length*   /leŋθ/   (N)

The claim above is substantiated with a number of data from English. As we saw in examples, these words show only **segmental changes** in English words. Some more examples we wish to share:

(3)   Origin: *view*   /vju:/
       Level ?²²: *vision*   /vɪʒn/
       Level ?:   *visible*   /vɪsəbl/

       Origin: *move*   /mu:v/
       Level ?:   *mover*   /mu:və/
       Level ?:   *movers*   /mu:vəz/

The word *view* has been attached with suffixes -*ion* and -*able*. We see the resulting words reveal segmental changes. Unlike *view*, the next lexical entry, i.e. *move* has been attached with suffixes -*er* and -*s* but does not manifest any phonological changes. In this

---

22 A question mark placed infront of the label wants to instruct the reader to reflect a little bit further on the layer to which suffix morphological change operates.

case, Level 1 is made of affixes *-ion* and *-able* which do trigger phonological changes once attached to a stem to produce a new word, while Level 2 affixes are *-er* and *-s* which do not trigger phonological changes once attached to a stem to produce a new word in the language.

The story of the phonological changes of the affixation does not end there. There are affixes which trigger **auto-segmental** changes once attached to stems. The Auto-segmental features affected include **stress** patterns in English. (In other languages, tone patterns are included in auto-segmental features). Thus, some affixes in some words trigger changes in stress patterns in English words.

In (4) below, we would like to offer some examples from Katamba (1993) and a couple of others we would like to share with you:

(4) a. *televise*   / ˈtelɪvaɪz/
         televisual   / ˌteliˈvɪʒuəl/

     b. *photograph*   / ˈfəʊtəgra:f/
         photographic   / ˌfəʊtəˈgræfɪk/

     c. *mass*   / ˌmæs/
         media   / ˌmi:diə/
         mass-media   / ˌmæsˈmi:diə/

     d. *book*   / bʊk/
         keeping   / ˈki:pə/
         book-keeper   / ˈbʊkki:pə/

We see that there are differences in the auto-segmental features (i.e. stress patterns) of the English words in (4) above. This is exposed by the introduction of the English suffixes *-ual* and *-ic* in (4a) and (4b) respectively. Also, data in (4c) and (4d) show that the **compounds** trigger the change of stress patterns. This is revealed because we find that the position of the primary stress (herein marked as ‘) changes from the initial position to the word medial. Also, there is the introduction of the secondary stress at the initial positions (herein marked as ˌ). Furthermore, we learn that stress is introduced even to the word *book* which initially had no primary stress.

At this juncture, we can argue that there are three processes, i.e. **meaning alterations**, **segmental change** as well as **auto-segmental change** that may occur at the same time. The affixation and compounding processes which are derivational in nature have phonological implications because words change their segmental and auto-segmental features once some affixes are attached to the words or compounds amalgamated. Thus far, we may conclude that in the Lexical Morphology Theory, morphological alterations have phonological implications.

8.2.3 Lexical strata in English

Since we have established the divisions, now it would be informative enough if we analyse the order of the affixes in English words. We will manage to order them properly if we observe the pattern suggested (see Katmba 1993; Plag 2002; Booij 2005):

(5)   Inflections-Derivations = Root = Derivations-Inflections

Thus, derivation is one of the word-formation or word-building processes highly employed in English. As we discussed in previous chapters, Katamba (1993) says derivation process involves morphemes which alter the meaning or grammatical category of the base, while inflection do not change word mean rather offer grammatical functions.

The organisation of the architecture of affixes in (5) seems to be true to several English words. Perhaps further examples will help us have a much deeper understanding of the patterns suggested in the theory of lexical phonology.

(6)	a.	*-ion*	*erect*	/ɪˈrekt/	V
			erection	/ɪˈrekʃn/	N
			erections	/ɪˈrekʃnz/	N
	b.	*-er*	*modify*	/ˈmɔdifaɪ/	V
			modifier	/ˈmɔdifaɪə/	N
			modifiers	/ˈmɔdifaɪəz/	N (pl)
	c.	*-ism*	*modern*	/ˈmɔdən/	N
			modernism	/ˈmɔdənɪzəm/	V
	d.	*-ist*	*capital*	/ˈkæpɪtəl/	N
			capitalist	/ˈkæpɪtəlɪst/	Adj/N
			capitalist	/ˈkæpɪtəlɪsts/	N (pl)

Basically, we find that English has a number of derivational affixes which don't trigger segmental and auto-segmental properties of some roots. They change/alter the word-classes and meanings of the roots. Also, the derivational affixes are placed closer to the roots.

The story does not end there rather it moves to the ordering of the derivation affixes as well. Currently, it is established by Katamba and Stonham (2006: 92) that technically, affixes which **don't trigger** phonological features of the root are labeled **neutral** affixes. Affixes which **trigger** phonological changes are called **non-neutral**. In the order of affixes in (5) above, usually the non-neutral forms occur close to the root while neutral ones are placed afar. Any change of these strict positions leads to ungrammaticality.

The order of these affixes could be examined by the use of the root establish which can be extended further as in (7). We see that new English words are a result of several affixations to the root and/or stem.

(7) *establish*   V
    establish-ment   N (non-human)
    establish-ment-arian   N (human)
    establish-ment-arian-ism   N (process/movement)
    di-establish-ment   N (negative, non-human)
    dis-establish-ment-arian   N (negative, human)
    dis-establish-ment-arian-ism   N (negative, movement)
    anti-dis-establish-ment   N (positive, non-human)
    anti-dis-establish-ment-arian   N (positive, human)
    anti-dis-establish-ment-arian-ism   N (positive, movement)
    anti-dis-establish-ment-arian-ism-s   N (positive, movement, plural)

In the word *establish*, the non-neutral derivational affixes, *-ian, -ment,* and *dis-* occur close to the root while neutral derivational affixes, namely *-ism* and *anti-* are placed afar. The former affixes are Level I and the latter are Level II. Following Spencer (1991), Plag (2002: 214) has listed affixes as follows (Since we discussed their functions in chapter 3, then here we offer only the list):

(8)   a.   Level I suffixes: *-al,-ate, -ic, +ion, -ity, -ive, -ous*
                Level I prefixes: *be-, con-, de-, en-, in-, pre-, re-, sub-*

        b.   Level II suffixes: *-able, -er, -ful, -hood, -ist, -ize, -less, -ly, -ness, -wise*
                Level II prefixes: *anti-, de-, non-, re-, sub-, un-, semi-*

Affixes belonging to one stratum can further be distinguished from the affixes of the other stratum two other properties. Plag (2002: 214-215) mentions that Level I affixes tend to be of foreign origin, mostly Latinate, while Level II affixes are mostly Germanic so English affixes perhaps. Also, Level I affixes can attach to bound roots and to words, while Level II affixes attach to words (bases), e.g. *electric* the suffix attaches to the root *electr-* and adjective-forming of Level II suffix *-ly* only attaches to words such as *widely* and *earthly* (Ibid).

8.3 Autosegmental theory in morphology

In the preceding section, the theory that deals with affixation is discussed. In that theory, the affixes have implications during their attachments to roots, as a means of word-building process. In this section, we deal with sound patterns and their way of forming new words mainly in the tonal languages, namely Herero [Namibia/Botswana], Runyambo (Tanzania) and Mandarin Chinese, as well as in a Semitic language Arabic.

8.3.1 Introductory remarks

Autosegmental theory of phonology was developed from the late 1970s and in 1980s to account for various phonological issues which were not accounted for in the previous phonological means. It is shown that autosegmental theory of phonology was a counter-argument to the linear phonology theory propounded by Chomsky and Halle (1968) in

Sound Patterns of English (SPE) which underscored that phonology was a property of segments (consonants and vowels). The main formulations of autosegmental theory were advanced by Goldsmith (1976).

Later it was taken into the study of word-creation in non-concatinative languages of Semitic nature, e.g. Hebrew (Modern Hebrew), Arabic, Tigrinya [Ethiopia/Eritrea] and Amharic [Ethiopia] (Besnier 1987: 201). In this kind of analysis, it is posited that segments, vowels and consonants, are on separate tiers from other supra-segmental features in these languages. Thus, autosegmental phonology accounts succinctly these phenomena by posting that such C(ononant)-V(owel) segments are in CV-tiers.

Hayward (1988: 132) pointed out succinctly that there are three morphemic elements at the level of phonological representation for stems in non-concatenative morphology. These levels are as follows:

- **Consonantal melody** which consists of two, three, or four consonants which make the basic lexical identity of the root in Semitic languages such as Hebrew, Arabic and Amharic. For example, in Arabic words *ktb* 'write' and *gdl* 'kill' while in Amharic *sbr* 'break' and *tlf* 'rob' are illustrative of consonant melody tier. As you see that these words carry three consonantal layers. This tier is commonly called **skeletal tier** in most contemporary works (Katamba 1993; Katamba & Stonham 2006).

- **Vocalic melody** consists of one or more vowels which, together with the prosodic template, bear grammatical roles and sometimes lexical information. The vocalic melody tier is exemplified by Arabic *katib* 'writer, secretary' and *gadl* 'he kills' as well as Amharic *sabra* 'I am breaking'. Here vowels have been inserted (infixed) so as to mark grammatical functions, *sabra* 'I am breaking' [progressive aspect] and derivational goals, e.g. *katib* 'writer, secretary'. Following Katamba (1993), in this book this is referred to as **vocalic melody tier**.

- **Prosodic template** which defines the canonical shape of a given stem form in terms of C and V elements.

These tiers do not occur in isolation rather there is a kind of linking of elements of the two melodic tiers to the C and V elements of prosodic templates. This is accomplished by means of conventions of association that is within the theory of Autosegmental Phonology (Hayward 1988: 133).

Goldsmith (1990) argued that autosegmental phonology is a theory of phonological representation. It developed a formal account of ideas that phonological representations consist of more than one linear sequence of segments. (Formerly in SPE, Chomsky and Halle (1968) established that sound patterns occurred in some linear order). Also, each linear sequence constitutes a separate tier. However, the co-registration of elements on one tier with those on another is represented by association lines. There is a close relationship between analysis of segments into distinctive features and in autosegmental analysis; each feature in a language appears on exactly one tier.

8.3.2 Templatic morphological theory in infixation and tonology

The templatic morphological theory is a result of **Autosegment**al **Theory** which we said it was propounded by scholars such as John Goldsmith and Paul Kiparsky (Katamba 1993). It is suggested that some lexical features occur above the **consonant** and **vowel** layers. These features are associated with both **grammatical** and **lexical** differences. These features include tone, segmental [CV] **insertion** and vowel length.

For example, **tone**, occurring above the skeletal layer, is captured using the Templatic Theory. Herero [Bantu language of Namibia/Botswana] offers the best example of tone change which is lexical derivational in nature (Möhlig & Kavari 2008: 41).

(9) *hora*   'be stiff'   [CV+L-CV+L^{23}]
     hóra   'to remove hair'   [CV+H-CV+L]
     hórá   'to ripen'   [CV+H-CV+H]

The theory of lexical phonology could not capture the derivational processes which do not involve segments (consonants and vowels only). However, under templatic theory of morphology, the data in (9) above could be captured in a template as those in Figure 1 (a-c). The actual word-building process manifests on vocalic melody tier, i.e. tone patterns bring about meaning changes.

Figure 1:   *Tone patterns and word-formation in Herero*

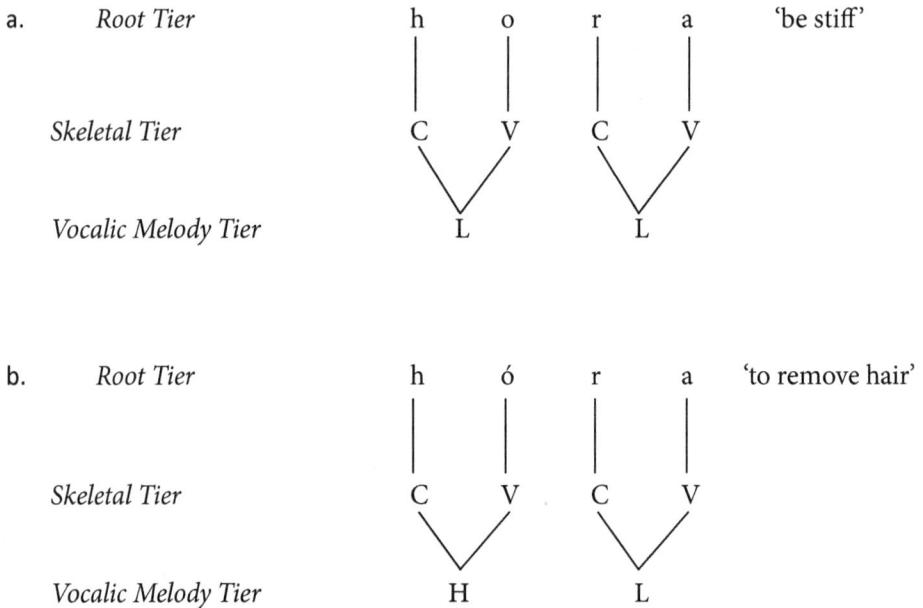

a.   Root Tier   h   o   r   a   'be stiff'

       Skeletal Tier   C   V   C   V

       Vocalic Melody Tier   L   L

b.   Root Tier   h   ó   r   a   'to remove hair'

       Skeletal Tier   C   V   C   V

       Vocalic Melody Tier   H   L

---

23 While CV represent segments (consonants and vowels), H-L represents the autosegmental features associated with tone, i.e. H: high tone and L: low tone.

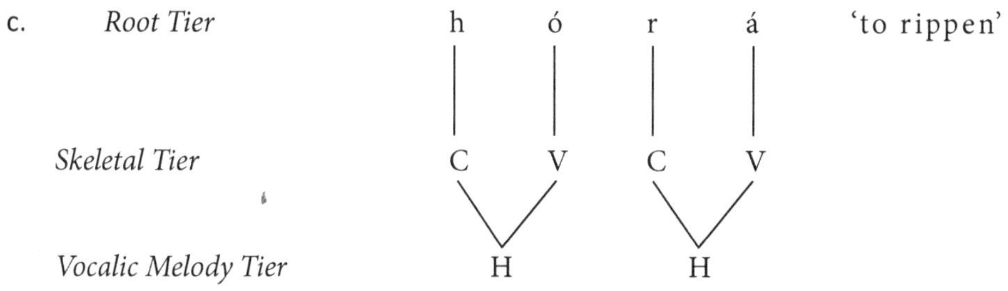

c.   *Root Tier*   h   ó   r   á   'to rippen'

      Skeletal Tier   C   V   C   V

      Vocalic Melody Tier   H   H

Here we observe that three meanings associated with segments *h-o-r-a* are generated: be stiff, to remove hair, and ripen. Such meaning changes are a result of derivations wich are well captured in templatic theory of morphology. Thus, it is assumed that the derivation processes take place in the vocalic melody tier because the changes in sound patterns (vocal patterns) by using tone do trigger changes in meaning. Thus, templatic theory captures this pattern easily.

This kind of derivation is not a property of Herero alone rather other Bantu languages reveal the same patterns. For instance, Rugemalira (2005: 16) gives these data:

(10)   *enda*   'stomach'   [V+L-NCV+L]

       énda   'louse'   [V+H-NCV+L]

       enju   'house'   [V+L-NCV+L]

       énju   'grey hair'   [V+H-NCV+L]

Figures 2 and 3 below represent the above data once analysed using templatic morphological theory:

Figure 2:   Tone differences and word-creation in Runyambo

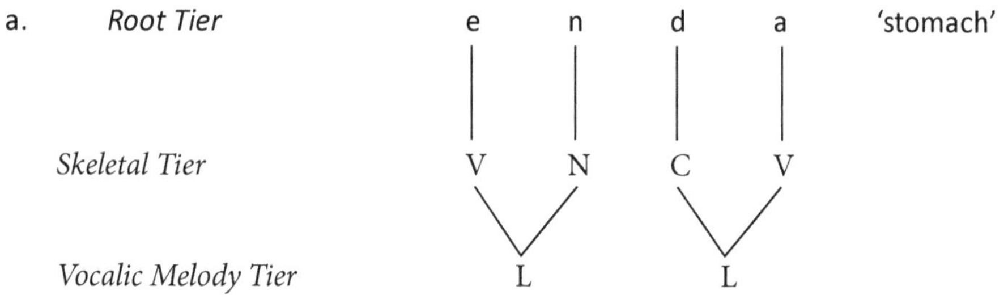

a.   *Root Tier*   e   n   d   a   'stomach'

      Skeletal Tier   V   N   C   V

      Vocalic Melody Tier   L   L

b. *Root Tier*   e   n   d   a   'louse'

Skeletal Tier   V   N   C   V

Vocalic Melody Tier   H   L

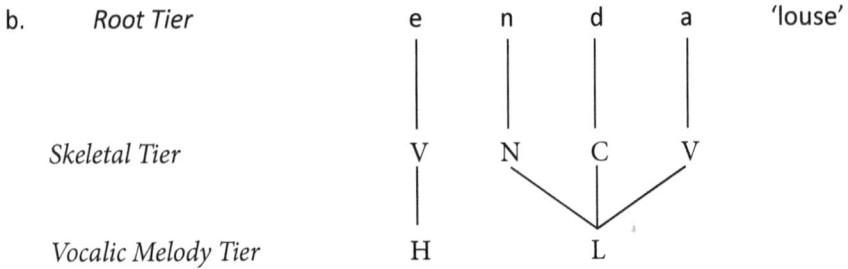

Figure 3:   *Tone differences and word-creation in Runyambo*

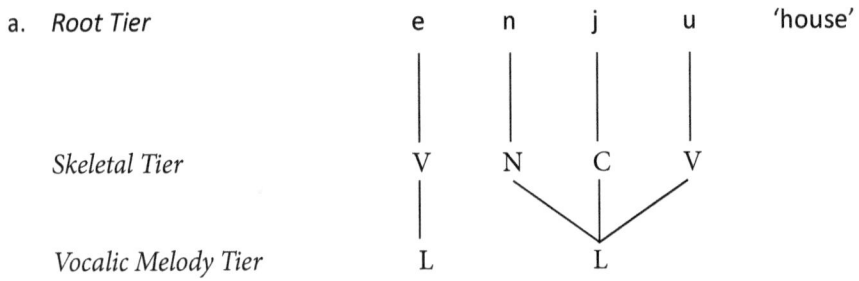

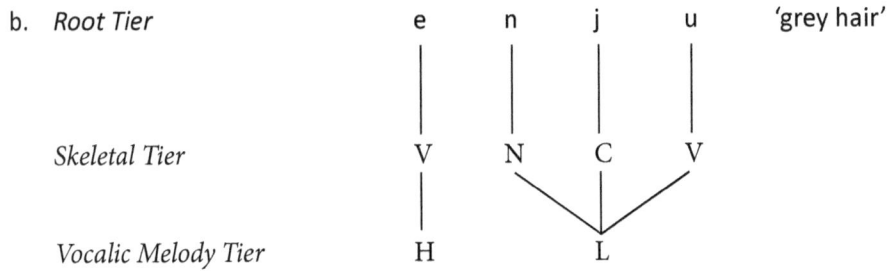

a. *Root Tier*   e   n   j   u   'house'

Skeletal Tier   V   N   C   V

Vocalic Melody Tier   L   L

b. *Root Tier*   e   n   j   u   'grey hair'

Skeletal Tier   V   N   C   V

Vocalic Melody Tier   H   L

The analyses in Bantu languages are applicable in other languages as well. Mandarin Chinese, for instance, offers the most complex tone patterns which, though, could be easily captured in templatic morphological theory. Lin (2001: 45) has these examples:

(11)   bā   'eight'   [C-V+HH]
       bá   'pull out'   [C-V+H]
       bǎ   'target'   [C-V+HH]
       bà   'father'   [C-V+HH]

We see that the C-V patterns receive different meanings depening on how the tone is assigned to them. Such data could be captured in a templatic analysis as follows:

Figure 4:   *Tone differences and word-creation in Mandarine Chinese*

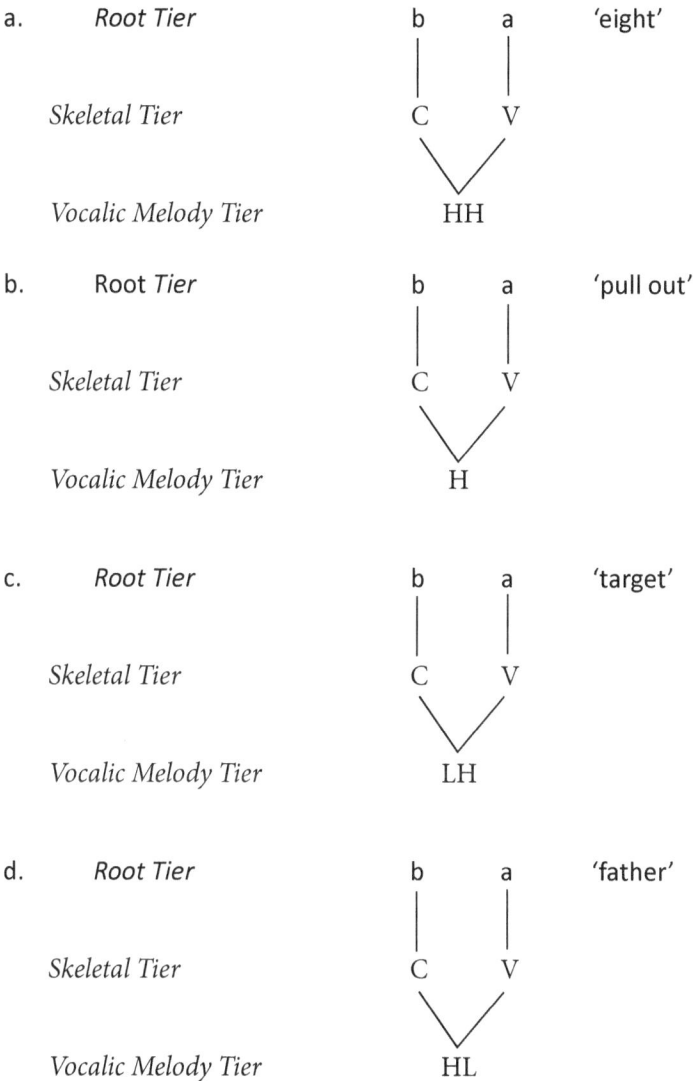

a.   *Root Tier*   b   a   'eight'

       Skeletal Tier   C   V

       Vocalic Melody Tier   HH

b.   Root *Tier*   b   a   'pull out'

       Skeletal Tier   C   V

       Vocalic Melody Tier   H

c.   *Root Tier*   b   a   'target'

       Skeletal Tier   C   V

       Vocalic Melody Tier   LH

d.   *Root Tier*   b   a   'father'

       Skeletal Tier   C   V

       Vocalic Melody Tier   HL

Another case which is analysed nicely under templatic theory of morphology is
vowel-insertion (which can also be analysed in Templatic Morphological Theory as given
in Figure 5). In fact, Arabic employs infixation as a means of word-building. Katamba
and Stonham (2006: 163) provide this example:

(12)   *ktb*   'write'   [C-C-C]
       kataba   'he wrote'   [CV-CV-CV]
       kitaab   'book'   [CV-CCV-CV]
       katib   'secretary'   [CV-CCV-CV]

Likewise, the theory of lexical morphology, which could not capture the derivational processes which do not involve segments, is helped by templatic morphological theory in analysing infixation in Arabic. Under templatic theory of morphology, the data in (10) above could be captured in a template as those in Figure 5 (a&b). The actual word-building process manifests on vocalic melody tier, i.e. insertion of vowels brings about meaning changes.

Figure 5:   Vowel insertion and word-formation in Arabic

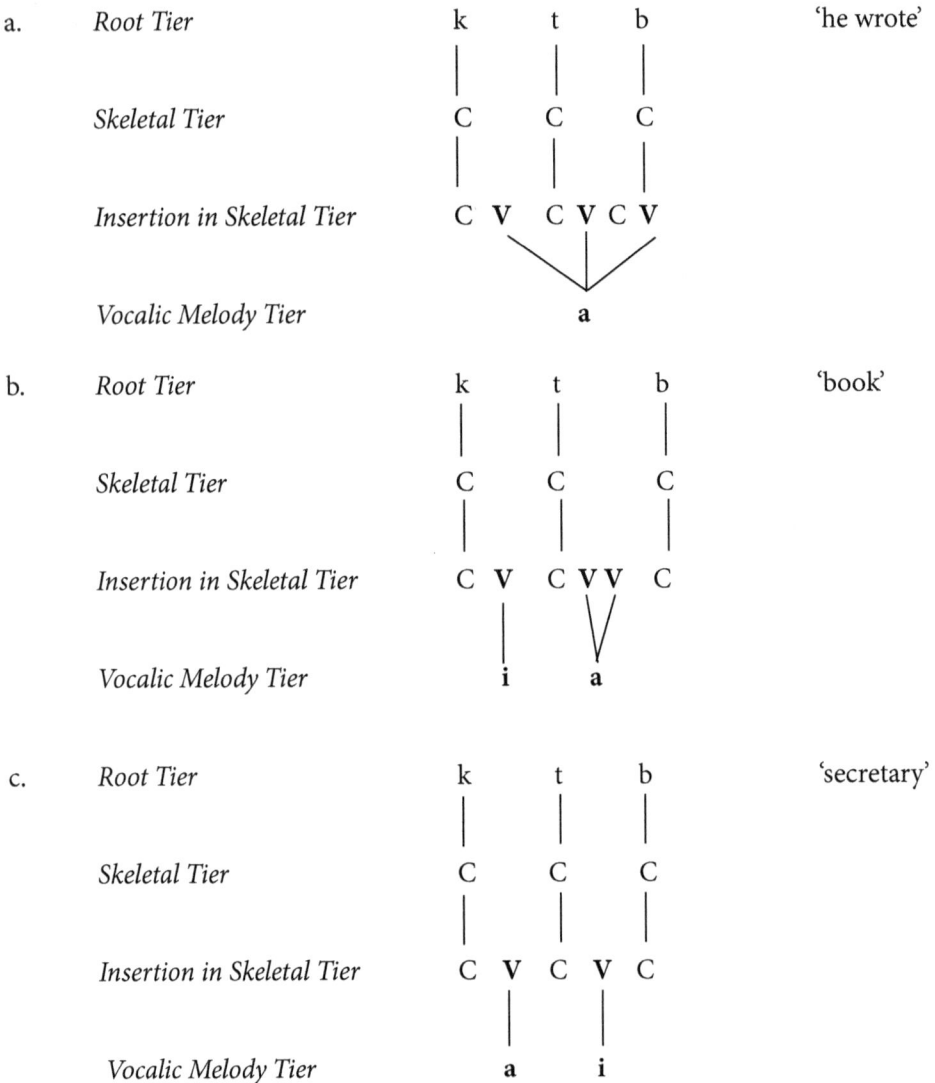

a.   Root Tier   k   t   b   'he wrote'

      Skeletal Tier   C   C   C

      Insertion in Skeletal Tier   C V C V C V

      Vocalic Melody Tier   a

b.   Root Tier   k   t   b   'book'

      Skeletal Tier   C   C   C

      Insertion in Skeletal Tier   C V C V V C

      Vocalic Melody Tier   i   a

c.   Root Tier   k   t   b   'secretary'

      Skeletal Tier   C   C   C

      Insertion in Skeletal Tier   C V C V C

      Vocalic Melody Tier   a   i

It should be understood that, for both tone changes and vowel insertion (infixation), the derivation processes take place in the vocalic melody tier because the changes in vowel patterns (vocal patterns) by using vowel insertion changes and tone patterns do trigger change in meanings as well. Thus, effortlessly, templatic morphological theory captures these patterns.

8.4   Optimality theory in morphology of reduplication

8.4.1   Introductory remarks

Optimality theory (regularly abbreviated as OT) is all about putting the linguistic candidates into comparisons and then choosing the best set which violates the least constraints (McCarthy 2002: 3). The universal grammar (UG) provides constraints (CON) which are universally present in all grammars but each constraint operates at the level of language-particular. Violations of the constraints are acceptable but are tolerated at the minimal point. The outputs that violate the least ranked constraints are more optimal.

In a summary form, we can capture the basic architecture of the OT below (Legendre 2001: 4; McCarthy 2002: 10).

(13)   Input → [GEN] → Candidates Set → [EVAL] → Optimal Candidate (Output)

In OT, two very essential end points: Input and Output. To identify the best outputs from the inputs, we must observe the following principles:

- *Input* must resemble the features of the *Output*:
- *Faithfulness* constraints to maintain the information that occurs in the input hence - no occurrence of information in the output that does not exist in the input, [no insertion of a segment(s)], and every segment in the input to appear in the output, [no deletion].
- *Markedness* constraints lie in the heart of OT which deals with the relation of meaning to form.

A large body of work in OT is on phonology rather than on morphology and syntax (Russell 1997; Legendre 2001; Katamba & Stonham 2006). But OT is a linguistic theory for all branches - phonology, syntax etc. (McCarthy 2002: 193). There is much literature for OT on Bantu reduplication (cf. Downing 2009; Hyman 2009). Bantu syntax is also analyzed using OT (cf. Woolford 2001).

8.4.2   Reduplication in Bantu languages

In chapter 5 we established that it is a common agreement that reduplicated elements copy the materials of the base with their phonological features. OT can be used to analyse reduplication in Bantu languages. It means that the selections of the well-formed and ill-formed tokens in Kiswahili given in (14) below observe the principles of OT.

(14)   Reduplication in Swahili

a.   *piga*   hit
      pigapiga   hit repeatedly

b.   *kupiga*   to hit
      kupigapiga   to heat repeatedly
      kupigakupiga   ???

c.   *pigana*   hit each other
      piganapigana   hit each other repeatedly
      pigapigana   ???
      piganapiga   ???

d.   *la*   eat
      kulakula   to eat frequently
      ʔlala   eat frequently
      liwa   be eaten [edible]
      liwaliwa   be eaten frequently
      kuliwaliwa   be eaten frequently ???
      liwakuliwa   be eaten frequently ???

We also established that other languages demonstrate both segmental and autosegmental doubling. This means that the copying takes segements (CV), as well as the presence of the high tones in the base will also be realised in the reduplicated ones. Following Mathangwane and Mtenje (2010), in Wandya, only segments are copied, as in (15). In Subiya, the whole features of the word are copied, including tone, as in (16).

(15)   *lúma* 'bite'   >   *lumalúma* 'bite repeatedly'
        físa 'hide'   >   *fisafísa* 'hide continuously'

(16)   *zíma* 'walk' > *zímazíma* 'loiter'
        lyá 'eat' >   *lyályá* 'eat continously'

Some languages like Wandya leaves behind tones during reduplication. Take for instance the verb *lúma* 'bite' which has segmental features CVCV and supra-segmental features H-L. Its reduplicated counterpart, *lumalúma* 'bite repeatedly' has the segmental features similar to the base, i.e. CVCVCVCV but distinct tone patterns as it has L-L-H-L. This entails that the tone pattern of the base is not realised in the reduplicant.

In other bantu languages, e.g. Subiya, tones are also copied. Thus, the verb *zíma* 'walk' has the tone pattern high and low (H-L) which are repeated in the reduplicated verb *zímazíma* 'walk about aimlessly' to form the sequence of tones labelled H-L-H-L. The other verb, *lyá* 'eat' has the tone pattern H which is copied in the reduplicated verb, *lyályá* 'eat continuously' to result in the pattern H-H. This applies to the last word too. One important point to be accentuated here is that copying of the base involves all the phonological materials in Subiya.

To be precise, we can capture a few constraints in OT using a Reduplicant (RED) which is said to be characterized as follows:

(17) 1. BASE   the RED must resemble the base, i.e. Faithfulness constraint

      2. MIN   minimally it is two syllables only, no more, no less hence Markedness constraint.

      3. SEG   copy only segments in languages like Wandya; or copy both segments and autosegments in languages like Subiya.

It is shown in Tableaux 1 that only segmental features are copied in Wandya, while Tableaux 2 shows that both segments and tones are doubled in Subiya.

Tableaux 1: Reduplication in Wandya

lúma	BASE	MIN	SEG
lumialumia	*!		
kulúmakulúma		*!	
lumalúma			*!
☞ *lúmalúma*			

Tableaux 2: Reduplication in Subiya

zíma	BASE	MIN	SEG
kuzímakuzímo	*!		
kuzímakuzíma		*!	
zimazíma			*!
☞ *zímazíma*			

It means that the first candidate in Tableaux 1 has violated the most significant constraint which requires the base to be similar to the reduplicant. The following candidate violated the second constraint which requires the minimum reduplicant to be two syllables. The next candidate is out because it copied even auto-segments (tone) so it violated segmental requirements.

Likewise, in Tableaux 2, the first candidate has violated the most significant constraint which requires the base to be similar to the reduplicant. The following candidate violated the second constraint which requires at least the minimum reduplicant to be two syllables. The next candidate is out because it has not copied auto-segments (tone) so it violated tonal requirement.

At this juncture, we can say that optimality theory (OT), therefore, helps to understand the patterns of reduplication in several Bantu languages which have different segmental and autosegmental patterns (for further details, see Downing 2009; Mathangwane & Mtenje 2010).

Resources cited:

Besnier, Niko. 1987. An autosegmental approach to metathesis in Rotuman. *Lingua*, vol. 73: 201-223.

Chomsky, Noam & Halle, Morris. 1968. *Sound Pattern of English*. New York: Harper and Row Publishers.

Downing, Laura J. 2009. Linear disorder in Bantu reduplication. *A Talk at the Workshop on the Division of Labor between Morphology and Phonology & Fourth Network Meeting*. Amsterdam: Meertens Instituut.

Goldsmith, John. 1976. *Autosegmental Phonology*. PhD dissertation, MIT.

Goldsmith, John. 1990. *Autosegmental and metrical phonology*. Oxford: Basil Blackwell.

Hayward, R.J. 1988. In defence of the skeletal tier. *Studies in African Linguistics,* vol. 19(2): 131-172.

Hyman, Larry M. 2009. The natural history of verb-stem reduplication in Bantu. *Springer* vol. 19: 177–206.

Kiparsky, Paul. 1982. Lexical morphology and phonology. In *The Linguistic Society of Korea*. pp. 1-91.

Legendre, Géraldine. 2000. Morphological and prosodic alignment of Bulgarian clitics. In: Dekkers, Joost, Frank van der Leeuw & Jeroen van de Weijer (eds.). *Optimality Theory: Phonology, Syntax and Acquisition*. Oxford: Oxford University Press: 423-462.

Marlo, Michael R. 2002. Reduplication in Lusaamia. *Indiana University Working Papers in Linguistics Online* (Accessed: 15.10.2008).

Mathangwane, Joyce & Mtenje, Al. 2010. Tone and reduplication in Wandya and Subiya. In: Legère, K. & Thornell, C. Eds. *Bantu languages: Analysis, Description and Theory*. Köln: Rüdiger Köppe Verlag. pp. 175-189.

McPherson, Laura & Mary Paster. 2009. Evidence for the Mirror Principle and Morphological Templates in Luganda Affix Ordering. In: Ojo, Akinloye & Lioba Moshi (Eds.). *Selected Proceedings of the 39th Annual Conference on African Linguistics*. pp. 56-66. Somerville, MA: Cascadilla Proceedings Project.

Mohanan, Karuvannur P. 1986. *The Theory of Lexical Phonology*. Dordrecht: Reidel.

Möhlig, Wilhelm J.G. & Kavari, Jekura U.   2008.   *Reference Grammar of Herero (Otjiherero)*. Köln: Rüdiger Köppe Verlag.

Prince, Alan & Smolensky, Paul. 1993. Optimality Theory: Constraint Interaction in Generative Grammar. *MS*. Rutgers University and University of Colorado at Boulder. (Accessed 21.03.2010).

Rugemalira, Josephat M. 2005. *A Grammar of Runyambo*. Dar es Salaam: LOT Publications, University of Dar es Salaam.

Russell, Kevin (1997). Optimality theory and morphology. In: Archangeli, Diana & D. Terence Langendoen (eds). *Optimality Theory: An Overview.* Oxford: Blackwell Publishers: 102-133.

Woolford, Ellen. 2001. Conditions on object agreement in Ruwund (Bantu). In: Benedicto, Elena (ed). *The Umass Volume on Indigenous Languages.* Amherst, MA: GLSA.

Yu, Alan C. L. 2007. *A Natural History of Infixation.* Oxford: Oxford University Press.

Exercise Eight

8.1   Provide an optimality theoretic account of the following Lusaamia data from Marlo (2002):

bakakonakona	'They sleep all the time'
*bakakonabakona	
mwiimbiraimbira	'I'm singing to him continuously
*mwiimbiramwiimbira	
mutatematema	'Don't chop up that tree'
*mutatematatema	
anatematema	'He will chop'
*anatemaanatema	
akalakasyalakasya	'He is dropping them'
*akalakasyakalakasya	
yeekesyakesya	'He is roaming around'
*yeekesyaeekesya	

8.2   Describe the following Arabic data from Yu (2007: 9, 77) using autosegmental phonology theory:

ktb 'write'
kita:b 'book'
katab 'to write'
iktatab 'he copied'
katab 'he wrote'
yektub 'he is writing'

www.ingramcontent.com/pod-product-compliance
Lightning Source LLC
Chambersburg PA
CBHW072141090426
42739CB00013B/3243